Toward a Translation Criticism: John Donne

TRANSLATION STUDIES
BRIAN J. BAER, EDITOR
Albrecht Neubert, Gert Jäger, and Gregory M. Shreve, Founding Editors

1 *Translation as Text*
   Albrecht Neubert and Gregory M. Shreve
2 *Pathways to Translation: Pedagogy and Process*
   by Donald C. Kiraly
3 *What Is Translation? Centrifugal Theories, Critical Interventions*
   by Douglas Robinson
4 *Repairing Texts: Empirical Investigations of Machine Translation Post Editing Processes*
   by Hans P. Krings
   Edited by Geoffrey S. Koby
5 *Translating Slavery, Volume I: Gender and Race in French Abolitionist Writing, 1780–1830*
   Edited by Doris Y. Kadish and Françoise Massardier-Kenney
6 *Toward a Translation Criticism: John Donne*
   by Antoine Berman
   Translated and edited by Françoise Massardier-Kenney

Toward a Translation Criticism:
John Donne

Pour Une Critique des Traductions: John Donne

By Antoine Berman

Translated and Edited by Françoise Massardier-Kenney

The Kent State University Press

KENT, OHIO

© Editions GALLIMARD, Paris, 1995
Translation © 2009 by The Kent State University Press, Kent, Ohio 44242
All rights reserved
Library of Congress Catalog Card Number 2009016876
ISBN 978-1-60635-009-6
Manufactured in the United States of America

Library of Congress Cataloging-in-Publication Data
Berman, Antoine.
   [Pour une critique des traductions. English]
   Toward a translation criticism : John Donne / Antoine Berman ; translated and edited by Francoise Massardier-Kenney.
       p.   cm.
   Includes index.
   ISBN 978-1-60635-009-6 (pbk. : alk. paper) ∞
   1. Donne, John, 1572–1631—Translations into French—History and criticism. 2. English language—Translating into French—History. 3. Translating and interpreting—France—History. 4. Donne, John, 1572–1631—Appreciation—France. I. Massardier-Kenney, Françoise. II. Title.
PR2248.B4713 2009
821'.3—dc22   2009016876

British Library Cataloging-in-Publication data are available.

13   12   11   10   09   5   4   3   2   1

Contents

Translator's Introduction — vii
French Editor's Note — xix
Introduction — 1

PART I: THE PROJECT OF A "PRODUCTIVE" CRITICISM — 23
The Concept of Translation Criticism
The Different Kinds of Translation Analysis
   Henri Meschonnic's Engagé Analyses
   Descriptive Socio-critical Analyses (Toury, Brisset)
Toward a Method
   Translation Reading and Rereading
   The Readings of the Original
   In Search of the Translator
   The Translating Position
   The Translation Project
   The Horizon of the Translator
The Analysis of the Translation
   Forms of the Analysis
   The Confrontation
   The Style of the Confrontation
   The Foundation of the Evaluation
The Reception of the Translation
Productive Criticism

PART II: JOHN DONNE, TRANSLATIONS, AND RETRANSLATIONS — 81
The Translators
   The Book and Its Translation Horizon
The Translation Project
   A Very Selective Anthology
   A Poetic Anthology

    A "French Donne"
    An Archaizing Version
Critical Examination of the Project
    The Poetic Version
    The "French Donne"
    Donne and the English Poetic Domain
"Sapho to Philaenis"
"Going to Bed"
Octavio Paz: "Antes de acostarse"
August Morel: "De sa maistresse allant au lict"
A New Translation of Donne in French
Toward Retranslations of Donne
Prose Is the Other of Poetry

PART III: ABOUT THE RECEPTION OF THE DENIS AND FUZIER
TRANSLATION OF 1962   201
A Globally Positive Reception with "Some Reservations"
    Jean Grosjean's Approval
    The Illusion of Ignorance
    The Illusion of Archaism
    The Illusion of Pure Poetry
    The Absence of Criticism of the Project
The Translation Horizon of the 1960s
Mallarmé, Valéry, and the Poetic Horizon of the 1960s

Works Cited   227
Index   239

Translator's Introduction

Toward a Translation Criticism is Antoine Berman's last work, and his most ambitious one. In it, Berman develops the theoretical principles and the practical application of a method hinted at in his previous works such as *L'épreuve de l'étranger* (1984),[1] in which he studies the formative role of translation in romantic Germany, and "La traduction et la lettre ou L'auberge du lointain" (1985),[2] in which he analyzes the translations of authors ranging from Chateaubriand to Hölderlin and proposes the notion of an ethics of translation. The notion of ethics developed in "La traduction et la lettre," which calls for a translation that is non-ethnocentric and which stipulates that the creativity required by translation must be focused on the re-creation of the original in the other language without being overdetermined by the personal poetics of the writer-translator (40), informs Berman's conception of *Toward a Translation Criticism* and the form in which he presents this conception.

The premise of *Toward a Translation Criticism* is that translation has reached a stage at which it aspires to be more than a practice. It is ready to reflect on the translation experience itself, to think about translation in a way that combines theoretical considerations with the experience of translation. Berman's notion of theory, of thinking about a practice, is that of a thinking that states *general* truths, rather than *universal* truths (such as those of science and mathematics).[3] It is no surprise that Berman's book is divided

---

1. Published in English as *The Experience of the Foreign: Culture and Translation in Romantic Germany*.

2. This edition based on Berman's seminar at the Collège International de Philosophie was reedited by the publisher Seuil in 1999 but is not yet available in English. Literally the title means "Translation and the Letter, or The Inn of the Distant" but is generally translated as "Translation and the Letter, or The Inn of the Faraway."

3. This conception of theory goes back to the Aristotelian definition developed in *The Nicomachean Ethics*.

into two separate but interlinked parts, each focused on one element of this ethics of translation: theory (reflection) and practice (experience). In the first part, he presents what he calls a general "productive" criticism, while in the second part he applies the general theoretical principles of this criticism to the analysis of the translations of John Donne's work into French and Spanish. Before presenting his conception of criticism, Berman describes the existing methods developed by "traductologie."[4] These range from the study of target-oriented norms (the study of translated literature as a genre that submits to the expectations of the target language) to analysis focusing on the differences between the original and the translation to catalog the "defects" of the translations without analyzing the causes of these defects.

In contrast, Berman's purpose is to develop a method that is specific to translation and that can bring to light translation's capacity for self-reflection. To do so, he deliberately places the translation at the center of his inquiry and claims for the translation itself the status of an oeuvre, of a work marked by its literariness. Secondly, he avoids the naive and mostly fruitless discussions of "fidelity" and "faithfulness" that mar many discussions of translation by refocusing our attention on the translator's project and the conditions that ensure the success or failure of the translation in carrying out this project.

While Berman's view of translation criticism as a way to open up the "potential qualities" of a work is influenced by the German romantics' conception of criticism, especially as understood in Walter Benjamin's dissertation, "The Concept of Criticism in German Romanticism" (1919), his abandonment of the rhetoric of fidelity is influenced by his adoption of hermeneutics, in particular, that of the philosopher Gadamer. In *Truth and Method*, Gadamer unequivocally states that "The translator must translate the meaning to be understood into the context in which the other speaker lives. . . . The meaning must be preserved, but since it must be understood within a new language world, it must establish its validity within it in a new way. *Thus every translation is at the same time an interpretation*" (384; emphasis mine). Similarly, Berman's method recognizes that the so-called original (let us remember that the trope of "the original" is a recent concept developed within a specific historical and cultural context in the nineteenth century) is a literary text whose meanings

---

4. Coined by French theorist Jean-René Ladmiral, this term was used to describe the branch of translation studies that focuses on the scientific description of translation processes or phenomena.

are activated through a reading, be it a critical reading or a translation reading. Although few literary critics today would argue that the literary text has a stable, unified, and unequivocal meaning waiting to be perceived, most reviews of translations, which focus on the accuracy of individual word choices, still seem to assume this is the case. In this regard, we must welcome Berman's move away from the notion of a subservient "fidelity" in favor of one focusing on translation as an "especially laborious process of understanding," in Gadamer's words (386), and as respect for the integrity of a literary work where the translator seeks to attend to what is expressed *in* the means of expression of a foreign text (rather than *by* the means of expression) while preserving the character of his or her[5] own language.

In support of the "dignification" of the work of translation, Berman's method privileges the translation itself, since the first step in criticism is reading the translation as an autonomous text. This initial reading frees the translation critic from making unconscious comparisons with the source text and from failing to consider the translation as a literary text in its own right. In the second step, the translation critic must turn to the source text and analyze it in terms of its stylistic "regularities," which may involve an analysis of its rhythm and semantic and metaphoric networks. This work of analysis retraces a step in the work of the translator, since this study of the source text's means of expression should serve as the basis for the translation. A third step requires the critic to become familiar with secondary material written by the author and the translator (ranging from prefaces and afterwords to glossaries and even interviews) in order to prepare for the comparison between original and translation. Then, based on his or her interpretation of the literary work, the critic selects specific passages in the text where the singularity of the work is concentrated, what Berman calls "signifying zones."

This phase is followed by research on the translator in order to determine his or her "translating position," "translation project," and "translating horizon." Berman defines the notion of horizon, which he borrows from the work of Gadamer, Jauss, and Ricœur, as the whole "of the linguistic, literary, cultural, and historical parameters that "determine" the ways of feeling,

---

5. Writing in French, Antoine Berman uses the masculine form throughout, since the masculine form in French stands for "human beings" in general. However, since English usage is now much more aware of gender issues in language, the use of the feminine pronoun here can remind us that a significant amount of work in translation and on translation has been done and is being done by women.

acting, and thinking of the translator," as well as the horizon of expectations of readers from a particular time and place. The goal of this contextualization is not to prescribe what the translator should do or should have done, but to understand why she translated the way she did and to determine how the project is realized. This preliminary work is followed by the actual analysis, in which the critic compares the original and the translation. By anchoring the work of the translator within a specific horizon, by showing its historical and geographical situatedness,[6] Berman points to the necessity of retranslations and of course indirectly suggests that the practice of translation criticism itself is temporally situated, and that it must be replaced in a historicity that it usually claims to escape.[7]

In the second part of his book, Berman then proceeds with the criticism of several translations of John Donne's work, following the principles he has previously established. This "practice" demonstrates how difficult the task of the translation critic is, how much erudition and research are required to achieve the kind of translation criticism advocated by Berman, and how intertwined theory and practice are. In this case, the work of the critic involves knowing much about John Donne's entire corpus and his place in the world of English letters. It also requires the critic to be aware of the possibilities available in specific languages (French, English, Spanish) at a specific time (late twentieth century) in order to assess whether a translator's project can succeed or could have succeeded. In the case of Donne, Berman shows that certain translations do not have a project or fail to take into account the horizon in which they are written, in particular, the crisis in late nineteenth-century French poetry that rendered problematic the use of traditional versification forms. It is in the context of this horizon that he is quite severe with the archaizing translation of Donne in French (a severity that did not affect the economics of publishing, since this translation was recently reedited, and more importantly, since no retranslation of Donne has been written to effect the transfer of Donne into French that Berman was hoping for).

He follows this criticism with an analysis of Donne's poem "Going to

---

6. In this regard, he prefigures the essential work of Pascale Casanova in *La république mondiale des lettres* (1999), translated as *The World Republic of Letters* (2004).

7. In his essay "Antoine Berman, penseur de la traduction," poet Robert Davreu points out the non-prescriptive character of Berman's criticism and rightly links it to Berman's awareness of its historicity (22).

Bed" before reflecting on the kind of retranslation of Donne called for by this analysis. Berman's interpretation of Donne invokes the more general concept of prosaicity and demonstrates once more the interlinking of practice and theory. His powerful analyses of translations done by Yves Bonnefoy and Octavio Paz reveal his understanding of the complex interrelations between language, culture, and thought and succeed in achieving a rare combination of hermeneutic and stylistic analysis, of commentary on the original and analysis of its translations. Here Berman achieves the tasks he describes in his 1985 seminar on Benjamin's essay "The Task of the Translator" (1985). In this earlier essay, Berman called for a new form of commentary that would give access both "to the *language* of the original—to the way in which poetry and thought are deployed—and to the actual *work* of translation.... that becomes commentary of the original (of its letter) and analysis of its translation (of the way in which the letter of the original was transmitted)" ("L'âge de la traduction" 14). Finally, he analyzes the reception of the various translations of Donne and shows how their reception was (over)determined by the specific literary horizon in which the translations were produced (France in the 1960s).

. . .

The principles I used to translate Berman's text were those proposed by Berman in the text itself and reflected my desire that Berman's contribution to translation studies be made accessible to the English-speaking world. His importance in the field is not disputed: his work has been influential in France (most of Paul Ricœur's essays in his *Sur la traduction* [2004][8] could not have been written without Berman's work) and in the United States; as Paul Bandia has shown, Berman's impact is felt in the works of translation scholars ranging from Lawrence Venuti to Tejaswini Niranjana. Berman has been the subject of a number of studies, in particular those in Broda's *La traduction-poésie. À Antoine Berman* (1999) and the 2001 special issue of the Canadian journal *TTR* edited by Nouss, but the unavailability of his last major work in English has led to a simplification of his ideas, especially his insistence on the possibilities for self-reflection in translation and on the need to bring closer together the discourse on translation and the work of translation itself. My "project," to use Berman's terminology, was to make accessible to a wide number of readers the entirety of a text that is crucial to

---

8. The English edition is *On Translation: Thinking in Action*.

our understanding of what translation is, and what translation criticism can do, and thus participate in the dignification of translation advocated by the author. Because the translation of Berman's text is not limited to translation studies or French language specialists, I have opted for clarity and directness and have explained terms when needed. In this I followed Berman's own avoidance of jargon and technical terms.

The erudition of Berman's works required the addition and completion of footnotes. In his introduction, he states that one translates with books; he makes clear both that translating is a literary activity that relies on intense reading and that thinking about translation within a specific horizon necessarily evokes a tradition. In his case, as we have seen, this tradition is heavily influenced by the German romantics, the critic Friedrich Schleiermacher in particular;[9] Walter Benjamin; hermeneutic philosophers and critics; and writer-translators ranging from Hölderlin, Paz, Pasternak, and Larbaud to Bonnefoy. The footnotes in the English version now include information about available translations in English, and additional material is provided in brackets to avoid confusion. In cases where the texts cited by Berman are not available in English, I used Berman's rendering as the source text and added a note if the French translation or any published translation differed significantly from the source text. When necessary, documentation was completed or corrected. It was also sometimes necessary to provide English back-translations of the French translations of Donne in order to maintain the clarity of the specific examples Berman provides. Since the back-translations were needed essentially for pedagogical reasons (i.e., to show why Berman criticizes certain word choices or syntactic patterns), I stayed very close to the French versions to make visible the work of the French translators. In a couple of instances, Berman quotes lines by poets who wrote in French (Bonnefoy and Rilke), and these required a polished rendering. I was lucky enough to obtain the assistance of poet-translator Marilyn Hacker, who was able to do justice to these lines.

Berman's erudition, which signals his desire to embed his reflections in a tradition and to establish a dialogue among writers, translators, and thinkers of different times and places, is expressed in a tone that avoids academic dryness,

---

9. Antoine Berman produced the first French translation of Schleiermacher's seminal essay "On the Different Methods of Translation" (see Berman, *Des différentes méthodes du traduire*). It is astonishing that this seminal text had not been translated before.

opacity, or pedantry. His departure from the norms of scholarly discourse can be seen in his use of idioms, hyphens, italics, exclamation points, and sentence fragments, which emphasize the orality of his text and the movement of his thoughts. Similarly, he uses footnotes not merely to provide bibliographic information but to expand or reflect on what he is saying in the body of the text. The dialogic function of these notes makes it imperative that they be kept as footnotes so that readers can easily access them as they read the text. The essay-like form of Berman's text thus reflects his project, and I have attempted to retain its mix of formal and informal registers, as well as its extremely direct statements and judgments about critics and translators.

Berman's style is also characterized by an unusually high reliance on verbal rather than nominal forms, a trait that is more typical of English than French. This strong presence of verbal forms embedded in noun phrases (for example, *le traduire* rather than the expected *la traduction*) has the effect of reinforcing Berman's argument that translation is a creative *act,* and of emphasizing the urgency of his tone. Although this effect is less visible in English, where verbal forms tend to predominate, I have attempted to create a similar effect by using phrases with "act" such as "the translating act" or "the act of translation," rather than relying on the standard gerund "translating."

At the lexical level, Berman carefully avoids words like *le but* (goal) and *l'objectif,* which are typical of discourses seeking the status of scientific discourse (implied by terms like "traductology") in favor of words like *finalité* or *visée* (purpose), which are more abstract, more philosophical, so to speak.

Within the context of Berman's purpose of showing the work constituted by translation, the term *œuvre* is significant. It sometimes means a work, a text, or a body of work, in which case, I translated it. But it also refers to creation, to the work on language of a writer or a translator, and in those cases, I have kept the French term to indicate the difference in meaning when it was not clear in the context.

Berman opposes the use of pseudo-scientific jargon (what he calls "scientistic") but his language does include technical terms that may strike the general reader as sterile or archaic in English and that certainly are not part of standard French vocabulary. I acknowledge the presence of this tension between his lucid prose and some terms that may seem jargony. I have striven to preserve his fluid, direct, clear style but have kept some specialized terms when they evoke a specific tradition or when their precision of expression seemed integral to Berman's thought. For instance, when Berman uses the word *architectonique* (as alien in French as the English equivalent, *architectonics*), he is referring to Aristotle's concept of the systematic arrangement of knowledge developed in *The Nicomachean Ethics*, a work whose translation into French by Oresme Berman studied closely and alludes to on several occasions. Similarly, the words *systematicité* (systematicity), *organicité* (organicity), and *doxa* (common belief) bring to mind the writings of Roland Barthes, whom Berman acknowledges as a key figure of modern criticism.

Berman also uses a number of terms that require "thick translation," that is, explanations for the way and the context in which they are used. The first example of this can be found in the title *Pour une critique*, which I translated as "criticism" as opposed to "critique." In French as in German, there is only one term to cover both the general meaning and the more specialized one expressed respectively in English as "criticism" and "critique." Here "criticism" is the translation for the general meaning. Moreover, Berman uses the term *la critique* (criticism) as it was used by the German romantic writers, who established the genre of criticism, and in Benjamin's "The Concept of Criticism in German Romanticism." There the standard translation for the term is "criticism," and Berman clearly places himself within this intellectual tradition.

Other terms with a specific history include *espacer* (to space), which has to be understood within the specific history of the French tradition started by the Pléiade poet Joachim du Bellay, and which I discuss in the notes to bring attention to its particular use, especially since extant translations of the term do not adequately render its meaning.

The term "analyst," which refers to the critic (who analyzes the text and is thus an "analyst") is not usually employed in English texts, but I have kept it because it belongs to the semantic network of the German romantics who inspired Berman. Not surprisingly, it also appears in a quote from Goethe that heads Benjamin's introduction to "The Concept of Criticism." Of course, the term also evokes psychoanalysis and as such is crucial to Berman's project of proposing an "analysis of the translating subject" through interpretation (a psychoanalyst would say "through translation") of the translation. Other key terms also come from the vocabulary of psychoanalysis (e.g., drive, unconscious), and I have kept them, with the exception of the word *étayage*, which is both a general language term ("support," "shoring up") and a psychoanalytic term. The Strachey standard edition of Freud, which emphasized psychoanalysis's claim to be a science, translated the German

Anlehnung—a common term whose literal translation is "a leaning-on"—as "anaclisis," a highly technical term that is inaccessible to non-specialists and that would be inappropriate in Berman's text.

Other essential expressions include "l'épreuve de l'étranger," which is also the title of a previous work by Berman translated into English as *The Experience of the Foreign*. It is sometimes also referred to as "the trial of the foreign,"[10] following the standard modern bilingual dictionary entry, which gives "trial, test" as the translation for *épreuve*. However, Berman's expression comes directly from Heidegger's discussion of Hölderlin's poem "Remembrance" in his book *Elucidations of Hölderlin's Poetry*. In Heidegger's expression "Die Erfahrung des Fremden" (a key expression that Heidegger uses several times in the essay), *Erfahrung* is indeed "experience," something that teaches us something (about ourselves). In turn, Berman uses *épreuve* and its verbal form, *éprouver*, in the classical sense of "learning by experience," which captures Heidegger's meaning. This seemed to me an important distinction because Berman clearly conceives of translation as that which teaches us about ourselves by transforming us through an encounter with otherness.

In explaining one of Hölderlin's lines, Heidegger uses an extended metaphor that can be applied as well to Berman's project: "When its openness [i.e., the openness of the sea in the case of Hölderlin's poem, or translation in the case of Berman] is passed through, it leads to the foreign shore, which induces a reflection on what is foreign, what is to be learned, so that, with the return home, the appropriation of what is one's own can be accomplished, and the foreign that has been transformed and brought back can be presented" (*Elucidations* 163–64). Thus moves the criticism of translation, according to Berman.

. . .

Antoine Berman was born June 24, 1942, in the small town of Argenton sur Creuse, in the center of France, near Limoges. His father was a Jew from Poland, his mother French, and his grandmother Yugoslavian. The family spent most of World War II hidden in the Berry region after a police officer warned his father that they were going to be arrested. After the war, the family returned to the Oise region, near Paris, where his father managed

---

10. For instance, see Venuti, "Translation and the Trials of the Foreign." Here "trial" fits with Venuti's own project.

a shoe factory. Antoine went to the Lycée Montmorency, a high school in a bourgeois Catholic suburb. He then started to study philosophy at the Sorbonne and began writing a dissertation on the poetics of the German romantics. When 1968 arrived, he got involved in theater with his future wife, Isabelle; abandoned his dissertation; and left for Argentina, his wife's country of origin, to produce a play. The Bermans stayed there five years, during which time they lived the lives of students: they gave private lessons, directed plays, became acquainted with Latin American literature, and witnessed the end of the Perón era.

Back in Paris, Antoine Berman wanted to make known the Latin American authors he had discovered during his stay in Argentina and so began to translate for the publisher Belfond the novel *Yo el supremo* by Augusto Roa Bastos. He resumed his dissertation on the German romantics and published it with Gallimard in 1984 as *L'épreuve de l'étranger*. He then became the first director of the independent Collège International de Philosophie, founded by François Chatelet and Jacques Derrida. The Collège, totally independent of the French university system, offered a series of seminars open to a variety of scholars, students, and intellectuals who were interested in language. Berman led several of these seminars, among them one on Walter Benjamin. Under the Mitterand government, Berman was asked to found the Centre Jean Amyot, a translation center, but the center was never properly funded and Berman operated alone, on a shoestring, in an office out of Coforma, a training center for copy editors in Paris. His interest in various aspects of translation led him to organize workshops for businesses, build relations with AFNOR (the French national organization for standardization), and publish booklets on terminology and specialized translation in an effort to educate companies about translation while writing what remain major works in translation studies. He died in 1991, at the age of only forty-nine.

. . .

The translation of this book would not have been possible without the help of my fellow translators Brian Baer, Geoff Koby, Isabel Lacruz, and Sue Ellen Wright at the Institute of Applied Linguistics, who helped me verify citations from German, Russian, and Spanish, and of the librarians and editors who assisted me in my research: Marie-Claude Corriveau, Jane Faulkner, Jeff Fulk, Joan Giglierano, Jessica Hagman, Claire Joubert, Catherine Massardier, Marie-Hélène Massardier, Sarah G. Wenzel, and Raik Zaghloul.

My thanks also go to writers who kindly assisted me in finding complete citations to their work or information related to this project. In particular I wish to thank Jean-Yves Masson, Annie Brisset, Claude Duneton, Marilyn Hacker, Claire Malroux, and Ronald Christ. I am also grateful to Carol Maier for her advice, and to Bill Kenney and Doris Kadish for their close reading of the manuscript and for their useful editorial comments. I am indebted to Will Underwood, the head of the Kent State University Press, and series editor Brian Baer for their support throughout this project; to the anonymous readers whose comments made the translation better; and to the copy editor, who gave her meticulous attention to the manuscript. Finally, I am greatly indebted to Isabelle Berman, who patiently answered my questions regarding various citations and who graciously provided me with biographical information regarding her husband.

FRANÇOISE MASSARDIER-KENNEY

French Editor's Note

I took the responsibility of editing this manuscript because "This book was born under the following circumstances."[1]

Antoine Berman died November 22, 1991, at the age of forty-nine. During the three months of his brutal illness, he wrote this book, day and night, without respite. He wrote in school notebooks, with a fine and precise handwriting, at a corner of the dining room table, surrounded by his children, in extreme concentration. At the hospital, he would not sleep; instead he covered his bed with books and papers. As he made progress on his work, he would revise the text in new notebooks and ask me to throw away the old notebooks. This book was born in the form of seven spiral notebooks with blue and red plaid covers. Glued on the cover of notebook 7 was a color photocopy of a portrait of John Donne, his face extremely thin and, according to Michel Deguy—and I thought so too—bearing a certain resemblance to Antoine. Sometimes Antoine would read me passages he had just written. He would also read to friends who visited him in the hospital or at home. These passages were read aloud, but I did not yet know how much this voice would resonate in the book. There were repeated readings of the introduction, and readings of Peguy, Pasternak, Benjamin. . . . We would listen, captivated by the voice of the writing and its permanence. The words that we heard demolished the medical fortress. The poet is never sick.

"My body, this paper, this fire" (Foucault, *Histoire* 583); this body, transmuted into writing. The poem is perhaps the only form of writing that has a voice, not in the sense that the poem is written to be recited, but in the way in which the words of the poem can be heard. Is it because of this, through the unique

---

1. See introduction. Also published as "Critique des traductions: John Donne" in *Po&sie* 59 (1992): 3–20.

presence of the voice of the poem, the pure resonance of essential writing, that the poem acts as a consolation? Beyond the oppositions between what is oral and written, there is the voice of writing. This book, into which the happy and calm, decisive and open thoughts of its author lead us, also has a voice because the author's whole person is caught in the radiance of Donne's poem.

Because this book is an act of writing, it must be read as a finished book: a singular, irreversible act that gives us food for thought. Blanchot writes, "Literature . . . has for its ideal the moment . . . when life carries death and is maintained in death itself to obtain from it the possibility and the truth of speech" (35). "Death . . . is the extreme. . . . He who can dispose of it disposes of himself extremely" (133).

Respecting the integrity of the text, the editing process has only consisted of completing what was still unfinished: a few missing quotes and notes left blank. Two footnotes were added by the editor. The author was planning to add a chapter, perhaps an epilogue (as a typed outline indicates), and in notebook 5, six blank pages may indicate a missing part. Only one section, the section about the translation of Donne by Auguste Morel, which was written on separate pages, was incomplete. In the introduction, the author gave it a place between the analysis of the translation by Philippe de Rothschild and that by Octavio Paz. In order to maintain the continuity of the rest of the text, the chapter on Morel was placed after the analysis of the Paz translation; however, the introduction was not changed.

It was also necessary to modify the table of contents, which included some repetitions and imprecisions. Did the author want to divide the book into two or three parts? I chose the second possibility, for it places the analyses of Donne's translations at the heart of the book.

I would like to thank Pierre Leyris and Evanghélos Bitsoris for their help. I owe our friend Pierre Leyris thanks for his several insightful and close readings of the manuscript and his constant availability. Evanghélos Bitsoris found most of the missing references, and his invariably good advice guided the editing of the manuscript. I also wish to thank Claire Miquel for her careful typing and numerous observations about the manuscript.

Finally, my thanks also go to Georges-Olivier Châteaureynaud and the Société des Gens de Lettres, Marie-Claude Bernage, Cécile Gaudin, Nathalie Savary, Michel Camain, Jean-Pierre Berman, Brigitte Fichot, Nella Melega, Rebecca Peyrelon, Vincent Orssaud, Paul Bensimon, and Yves Bonnefoy.

ISABELLE BERMAN

Introduction

This book was born under the following circumstances: for several years (since 1985, to be precise), I had been working on a study of translation in France from the fourteenth to the seventeenth century, with a focus on the figures of Nicole Oresme, Jacques Amyot, Joachim du Bellay, and Perrot d'Ablancourt. But, as the French expression goes, the book was barely limping along. For all kinds of reasons, I lacked time to work on it continuously. It also required me to read many primary and secondary sources and, more fundamentally, to penetrate the worlds of the fourteenth, sixteenth, and seventeenth centuries, something that was not altogether obvious. Living in the world of German romanticism at the end of the eighteenth century had been much easier for me. The "archaeological" journey back toward Amyot, and even more so toward Oresme, did not allow for any immediate intimacy. Nonetheless, the book was progressing, slowly, year after year, each version enriched by new readings. My feeling of ignorance, or rather, of incomplete knowledge, was diminishing. But the amount of work remaining was considerable, and the time that I could devote to it still as limited. All along, a deep-seated feeling haunted me: would this book be the real "continuation" of *L'épreuve de l'étranger* [*The Experience of the Foreign*]? Wouldn't it be too erudite, too historical? When asking myself these questions, I was obviously thinking of the readers of *The Experience of the Foreign* whose reactions I had known. Wouldn't they expect a different book from the one I was laboriously preparing? So it sometimes seemed. But what book? I had no other book in mind, at least for the immediate future. But then, this was taking myself all too seriously.

Then, a year ago, I had to write for the university a synthesis of my research on translation, that is, of *The Experience of the Foreign* and the various texts and articles that I had published since 1984 and even before that. There again, at the beginning, things were quite slow. Synthesizing *The Experience of the Foreign* was particularly difficult. But everything changed when I came to one of the chapters of the synthesis dealing with my "translation analyses." In my seminars at the Collège International de Philosophie, I had done many analyses of translation, for instance, of Maurice de Gandillac's translation of Walter Benjamin's "The Task of the Translator," Chateaubriand's translation of Milton's *Paradise Lost,* Hölderlin's translation of *Antigone,* Klossowski's French *Aeneid,* and a Grimm's tale translated by Armel Guerne and Marthe Robert. Little by little, although in an improvised and embryonic way, I sketched, if not a method, at least a form of approach to translations. For my synthesis, I had chosen the last analysis I had done at the Collège International de Philosophie (1989), the analysis of a poem by John Donne, Elegy XIX, "Going to Bed," one of the most beautiful love poems I know. In the seminar, I analyzed the elegy and compared it to two French translations (one by Yves Denis, and the other Philippe de Rothschild), and a Mexican one by Octavio Paz.

When I started going over the text of my seminar and attempting to adapt it for my synthesis, something unexpected happened: the chapter began to grow and grow until it became clear to me that this part of the synthesis (originally titled "Translation Analyses") *wanted to become a book,* a book that, like the synthesis, was simultaneously a work about the criticism of translations, about the genre of "translation criticism," and about John Donne, the old translations and the (future and desirable) retranslations of his works.

At that moment, everything moved very fast, and the book was written with a sort of impatience that did not preclude, however, the patience required for multiple rewritings and numerous readings and rereadings that come to the support of the work of writing. Already, as I went along, I could see a number of interlocutors, of readers of the book, of whom, actually, several were mentioned many times in the book. I was not so much writing for them as *with them.*

I said that the book, while now deployed as a book, remained what it was in the synthesis. This refers to its division into two very distinct parts, the first one being, quite academically, the epistemological introduction to the other part. This introductory part, which was useful and even necessary in the synthesis, was not mandatory for a work on John Donne and his translations, but I preferred leaving things the way they had initially been set.

The first part of the book deals with translation criticism, presented as one of the genres of Criticism, with a capital *C*. For me, beyond the fact that it is a veritable institution, Criticism has been alive among the great Western critics since the eighteenth century, and especially since the founding father of modern criticism, Friedrich Schlegel. In the twentieth century, it is alive for me in figures like Walter Benjamin, Leo Spitzer, Hugo von Hofmannsthal, Ezra Pound, Boris Pasternak, Valery Larbaud, Maurice Blanchot, Roland Barthes, Gérard Genette, Octavio Paz, Jorge Luis Borges, Hans Robert Jauss, Roman Jakobson, Jean Starobinski, Giuseppe Ungaretti, Michel Deguy—I am citing at random the names that come to mind, mixing the greatest ones with the lesser figures, those who were "only" critics and those who were mostly poets or writers, those who wanted to be "scientific" and those for whom criticism was part of the movement of their own oeuvre. They all, with passion and rigor, wrote about other works; they all contributed to building the great edifice of Criticism, which exists in the service of the works, their survival and their illustration, and of the readers.

From these great critical works, which I have never stopped reading and rereading for the last thirty years, in particular from Schlegel and Benjamin, I draw in this first part the contours of a criticism of translation that constitutes one of the wings of the edifice of Criticism. I attempt to show its meaning, its necessity, and its positivity.

But one may ask, "Doesn't this criticism already exist, in the most diverse forms, and probably since the eighteenth century?" It does, and it does not. Since the classical age, there have been critical reviews of translation in which "criticism" or "critique" means *judgment* (in the Kantian sense) or *evaluation* (in the language of a modern school of translators). But if criticism means a rigorous analysis of a translation, of its fundamental traits, of the project that gave birth to it, of the horizon from which it sprang, of the position of the translator—if criticism means, fundamentally, *bringing out the truth of a translation*—then I must say that translation criticism has barely begun.

What we most often find are comparative analyses produced in various contexts. There are many, ranging from the most naive and simplest ones to the most detailed and extensive ones. But precisely because they appear in writing contexts that are each time different, they don't have any *specific form*. Thus they cannot help us to form a "genre."

We must look elsewhere, perhaps not for models, but at least for consistent examples of such a genre. There are two, as far as I know, that thus produce two forms of analyses or criticisms of translations.

The first one was started, as we know, by Henri Meschonnic with his well-known texts about the translations of Celan, the Bible, Trakl, and so forth. This form of criticism has here a negative form, one could say a polemical form, which corresponds to what Benjamin has called "the inevitable negative moment of this concept" (of criticism in general; *Le concept de critique* 89).[1] No doubt, Meschonnic has created a real form linked to a whole theoretical construct that is beyond the scope of this study (poetics, theory of rhythm, etc.). I will attempt to bring out the logic of this form and its fundamental characteristics. I will emphasize its positivity and, at the same time, what this logic involves (perhaps because of the very personality of the author) that is unilateral and sometimes unjust despite its very soundness.

The second form is the one proposed by the so-called Tel Aviv school (Even-Zohar, Toury), which develops a "semiotics" of translation, itself headed by a socio-critique of translations, or rather of what it calls "translated literature." It is within this socio-critical trend that we find analyses of translated texts, and a theoretical reflection on the analysis of translations. The Tel Aviv school is not well known in France, but it has had followers in other countries for a long time, in Belgium particularly (Lambert, among others) and in Canada (Brisset, etc.). Similar currents with the goal of a "cultural" theory of translation are also developing in Germany and Austria (Snell-Hornby, etc.), but to my knowledge, they do not provide analyses of translation per se.

Generally speaking, the analyses of the Tel Aviv school and their Belgian and Canadian followers are functionalist and deterministic. They attempt to systematically study what Meschonnic is content to hastily condemn, that is, the ideologies and the doxa that affect translation practice and make translations what they are. Whereas Meschonnic writes militantly, in a fighting position, so to speak, our semioticians/functionalists aim to be neutral and scientific observers, true "traductologists." Here again, I will analyze the fundamental traits of the form of analysis that is found in Toury and Brisset, in particular. And here again, I will emphasize the positive as well as the negative.

The third section of this first part lays out my own critical project, which

---

1. [In the standard English version of "The Concept of Criticism in German Romanticism," the translation reads: "Under the name of criticism, the Romantics at the same time confessed the inescapable insufficiency of their efforts . . . and so finally alluded, in this concept, to its necessary 'incompleteness of infallibility'" (143). The notes that follow provide partial bibliographic references and published English translations of quotes when they exist. Brackets indicate notes supplied by the translator. Trans. Note]

uses *hermeneutics* as developed by Paul Ricœur and Hans Robert Jauss on the basis of Heidegger's *Being and Time*. Like Meschonnic, who claims for his poetics the names of forebears such as Humboldt, Saussure, and Benveniste, and in the same way that Brisset uses various semiological, sociological, and structuralist discourses (Greimas, Foucault, Duvignaud, Jakobson, etc.), I call upon modern hermeneutics. This is my choice. Modern hermeneutics, in the sober version of Ricœur and Jauss, allows me to shed light on my experience as a translator, as a reader of translations, as an analyst of translations, and even as a historian of translation.

But as my analysis of translations is and aims to be a criticism, it is also based on Walter Benjamin, for he offers the highest and most radical concept of "literary" criticism and of criticism in general. Not only is Benjamin unsurpassable, but he is still ahead of us. We never cease trying to catch up with him, as in poetry we never cease trying to catch up with Hölderlin, Hopkins, and Baudelaire.

Thus here I am using post-Heideggerian hermeneutics and Benjaminian critique to clarify and order (but not systematize) my experience of the analysis of translation.

As this analysis is first and foremost constituted by *readings* and *rereadings*, my path starts there, with readings of the translation, and then, quite apart from them, readings of the original. The dialectic specific to these readings leads me to the *author of the translated text,* the elusive "translating subject," whom all translation theorists mention but do not manage to find. This part is logically titled "In Search of the Translator." It is in no way subjective. It seeks to know, of course, *who* the translator is concretely, but especially to determine *his translating position, his translation project, and his translation horizon*. In this section, I will discuss at length these three hermeneutic categories.

Following this discussion, I will then move to the comparative analysis of the translation and the original. How is the "confrontation" with the original done? What is the linguistic and scriptural ("textual") form of this confrontation? That is, how is this part of the criticism *written?* This is truly a crucial question, for many existing analyses of translation are characterized by their denseness, their obscurity, their arcane character, and their jargon (semiotic jargon especially)—even in part in the case of Meschonnic's and Brisset's analyses. I present four principles meant to make translation criticism readable and, if possible, fascinating, opening new horizons: "clarity of exposition," to use Hölderlin's expression; reflexivity; digressivity; and commentativity (the characteristic of a "commentary" in the traditional sense of the term).

If the analysis of a translation must also be a *judgment*, and by its very nature it must be (we can never be naturally neutral when dealing with a translation), what should the basis of such a judgment be? Is there a basis that is non-subjective and, most importantly, non-dogmatic, non-normative, and non-prescriptive—is there a *consensual* basis of judgment? I attempt to show that there is one, in spite of superficial oppositions like those between literalness advocates and sense proponents, or the opposition (which overlaps with the other) between source text proponents (*sourciers*) and target text proponents (*ciblistes*).

The following section is devoted to the study of the *immediate reception of the translation*. Here, the mediate criticism focuses on the immediate criticism, the reviews that followed the translation when it first appeared and that have partially shaped its image for the readers. For every important translation (or for the translation of an important work), this immediate criticism is gathered in the book review files of the publishers. The analysis of these files is a fascinating undertaking, but it can hardly be considered an end in itself.

The last section defines the tasks of "productive" criticism (to use Schlegel's expression) in the field of translations. When the translation is "good," "excellent," "great," criticism is productive in that its task is to reflect, to send back to the reader, this excellence or greatness. Schlegel says about "poetic criticism" that it "will present the representation anew, will once again form what is already formed. . . . It will complement, rejuvenate, newly fashion the work" (qtd. in Benjamin, *Le concept de critique* 112).[2]

Any translation, like any work of literature, always needs to be reflected in this way, *illustrated* in Dante's sense.[3] *At its core, criticism is illustrative*: illuminated by the work, it illuminates it in turn (hence the necessity of its having "clarity of exposition"). If the translation is "average," "insufficient," "wretched," "clumsy," "bad," "execrable," "false," "erroneous," "absurd"—all impressionist qualifiers that have some truth and that analysis generally *confirms*[4]—then

---

2. ["The Concept of Criticism" 154. Trans. Note]

3. "Par cela que nous nommons illustre nous comprenons ce qui, illuminant et illuminé, rayonne" (Dante, *De l'éloquence vulgaire* 30). ["Now when we call something 'illustrious,' we mean that it gives off light or reflects the light that it receives from elsewhere" (Dante, *De vulgari eloquentia* 41). Trans. Note]

4. Unlike qualifiers like "brilliant," "elegant," "masterly," and "beautiful," they generally reflect not the surrounding doxa (common beliefs), but the being of the translation text.

we must not be content, as Meschonnic is, with a simple work of destruction. The critic must shed light on the reasons for the translation's failure (here we join, in a certain way, our socio-semio-critics, but without their concepts and their discourse type) and prepare *the space for a retranslation* without acting as an advice giver. This space is itself caught in a larger space, that of the *transfer [la translation]*[5] of a foreign work into a language culture. This transfer does not only occur with translation alone. It also occurs through criticism and many forms of textual (or even nontextual) transformations that are not strictly translation related. *All of them taken together constitute the transfer [la translation] of an œuvre.* There is a dialectic between the *transfer* that does not involve translations and translations [*traductions*] per se. One may consider that a body of work is really "transplanted" and "implanted" (which does not mean integrated or naturalized) only when it is translated in the strict sense of the word (and not, for example, adapted). But a translation can be deployed and affect this language culture only if it is supported [*étayé*] and surrounded by critical works and transfers that do not involve translations.

In turn, the *transfer* of works itself belongs to a larger whole of *transfers* or circulations (as the journal *Change* called it) going in two directions that are opposed to a certain extent: the first direction is that of *communication*, hence of humanity as productive of communication (a word coined in the fourteenth century by Nicole Oresme, one of the theoreticians and practitioners of the medieval *translatio studii*); the second direction is that of *migration* and involves humanity as migrant reality, a migrant *mutating and cross-breeding* reality. Between communication and migration, there is another whole that also concerns translation, and that is *tradition* and humanity as productive of *traditionality*. That translation is at the heart of communication, migration, and tradition is visible historically in the West in the fact that its figure belongs to the network of fundamental Latin words like *traditio, translatio, augmentatio*. Western translation is traditionalizing,

---

5. [Berman uses the term *la translation* to signal a difference from *la traduction*, the standard French term for the concept of translation. The word "translation" exists in French. It refers to the action of transferring from one place to another (for instance the seat of a court or the headquarters of a company, a property or a title, or the date of a feast day). It is also used in physics, computing, and mechanics (in this case, the English equivalent is also "translation") and in linguistics (where it refers to the relation of words that have the same function but a different nature). Berman uses this semantically rich term to focus on the movement, the transfer, of a work into a different space, its settling into the foreign culture, which involves the whole reception of a foreign work in another culture rather than the actual act of translation. Trans. Note]

translative, and augmentative. And it is, first and foremost, a *res latina*, a *res romana* (a fundamental element of Latin and Roman culture). Translation took on or started to take on its specific shape in Rome, and not only among the authors who are always cited—Cicero, Horace, and Saint Jerome.[6] All of Latin culture, at a specific time, and because it was based on *traditio* and *augmentatio*, became "translative." This was so new, and implied such a different relation to language, that there was no *name* for it yet, as J. Lohmann shows us revealingly:

> The concept of translation presupposes the possibility of the identity of content of what is linguistically intended in the different forms of linguistic expression. This concept of "translation," to put it precisely, did not exist until Cicero, in whose philosophical and rhetorical writings we witness to a certain extent the birth of this concept (which represents a totally new relation of man to language). . . . This [event] is also expressed, among other ways, by the fact that Cicero does not yet have a verbally fixed concept for this thing (he says for example: *verter, converter, aliquid (Latine) exprimare, verbum e verbo, ad verbum exprimere, (Graece, Latine) reddere, verbum pro verbo reddere* . . .). Latin is thus the place where this new relation of man to language was initially formed in Europe, which is why we can designate Latin as the first "language" in the strict sense of the word (that is, language that, for its speakers, consists of *mots [words]*—not of *paroles [utterances]!*—which to a certain extent are presented as sense-transcendent and which, as a result, become in principle "convertible" with respect to this sense. (85)[7]

 6. The vision Nietzsche gives of translation in Rome in "Die fröhliche Wissenschaft" (1882), which is summarized by "In those days, indeed, to translate meant to conquer" (68), goes back to Saint Jerome speaking about another Roman translator: "Sed quasi captive sensus in suam lingua victoris jure transposuit." [But he (the translator) "considers thought content a prisoner which he transplants into his own language with the prerogative of a conqueror" (qtd. by Friedrich 12–13). Trans. Note] But neither the Latin figure of translation nor Saint Jerome's practice is limited to an "act of conquest." The relation of the Romans to translation cannot be separated from their link to tradition, to the founding fathers, and to Greece. When I wrote that "Romanness is defined in great part by a conquering and unscrupulous traductionism," it was really a sin of ignorance and prejudice on my part ("La traduction et la lettre" 50–51). In this book, I must recognize many errors of this kind.
 7. [In his translation from German, Berman uses the word "term" to render *wörten*. However, as terminologists point out, in English, "terms" are special language words that have assigned meanings, whereas *wörter* are the forms of words. In this context, *mots* (words) seems a more accurate rendering of Lohmann's *wörter*. Trans. Note]

In-named and pluri-named, *translatio,* a fundamental word in Latin culture, was everywhere, as Frederick M. Rener, another German author, showed us in his book on the history of Western translation, *Interpretatio: Language and Translation from Cicero to Tytler* (1989). One must read the whole work to realize this. But here, it will suffice to report the following surprising fact, which shows the extent of the *spirit of translation* in Rome: "In late Roman times, Virgil's three works, the *Bucolics,* the *Georgics,* and the *Aeneid,* were regarded as 'translations' of three Greek poets, Theocritus, Hesiod, and Homer, in that order. This notion is found in Aulus Gellius when he mentions the Roman comedies which were 'translated' ('versas') from Greek: 'sumptas ac versas de Graecis'" (309–10).

More originarily, the famous "Roman values"—*fides, constantia, severitas, gravitas, auctoritas* (see Momigliano 27)—can themselves be considered the primary virtues of the translator being born. Much later, Luther, the enemy of Rome, would probably remember it when he exclaimed, "Translation is not an art for everyone as some mad saints think; it requires a heart that is really pious, faithful, zealous, prudent, Christian, learned, experienced, practiced" (*Œuvres* 6:198).[8]

Waves of translation probably existed in ancient times well before Rome—there were translations in the Mesopotamian region, the Septuagint Bible, et cetera. The Septuagint Bible was an event—for Jews.[9] But the fact remains

---

8. The German says for the "predicates" of the heart "ein recht/frum/trew/vleissig/forchtsam/christlich/gelert/erfarn/geübet hertz" (Räkel 93). [The English version reads: "Ah, translating is not everyone's skill as some mad saints think. A right, devout, honest, sincere, God-fearing, Christian, trained, educated, and experienced heart is required" (Luther, *An Open Letter*). Trans. Note] Räkel translates in reverse order: "A trained, experienced, informed, Christian, respectful, diligent, faithful, pious and right heart." There are nine attributes for the translating heart, whereas the French edition by Labor and Fides list only eight, translating *recht/frum* as "really pious" [*vraiment pieux*] instead of "right/pious" (198). Rener, who is the only one to take this list of qualities seriously, says, "It is unlikely that this list is of Luther's invention. Most likely, Luther used a traditional matrix which he adapted to fit his own situation. Traces of such a matrix which may have served as model can be found in Quintilian" (316). In his *Interpretatio Linguarum Seu de Ratione Convertendi et Explicandi Autores Tam Sacros Quam Prophanos,* Lawrence Humphrey asks the translator, as Luther does, to have "fidelitas et religio" (qtd. in Rener 320). As we can see, all the "qualities" of the translator are Roman. [The title of Humphrey's work translates as *The Translation of Languages, or About the Theory of Translating and Freely Translating Sacred as Well as Profane Authors.* In Latin, *interpretatio* (translation), *convertere* (to translate), and *explicare* (to translate freely) all refer to the same thing. Trans. Note]

9. "Sacred books had become accessible to those interested in Judaism. Nothing proves, however, that Gentiles, generally, ever knew the Bible: it was bad Greek. No poet, no Hellenistic

that it is only in Rome, in pagan Rome, then in Christian Rome (in any case, a Rome dominated by *religio*), that translation took its shape, figure, and stature, if not yet its status and proper name. When Leonardo Bruni, in the fifteenth century, created the Renaissance form of translation, which is its first *modern form* before that of German romanticism, and at the same time created the very word *traduction* (see Berman, "Tradition-translation-traduction"), he did it from the rhetorico-grammatical totality of the Roman form of translation, whereas the Middle Ages had only retained of this form the transfer of the "sentence" (of sense), in other words, *translatio*.¹⁰

Thus translation, as a form, is not at all, as people keep repeating somewhat stupidly, "the oldest profession in the world." For us, in Western Europe, it has an origin, a place, and a date of birth. Outside of Rome, there is only babbling, pragmatic translations, closed translative acts, in a word, everything that took place before the Beginning.¹¹

We, translators, are and shall remain Roman, even if we must fight

---

philosopher ever quoted it.... The text of the Septuagint remained an exclusively Jewish property until Christians adopted it in turn. We do not even know if the work was deposited in the great Ptolemeic foundation of the library of Alexandria" (Momigliano 103–4).

10. For a discussion of the medieval concepts of *translatio, translatio studii*, and the like, see Serge Lusignan, *Parler vulgairement*.

11. This sheds a sobering light on the comments about the "paradigmatic role of Bible translation" and "the theological *impensé* [unthought thought] of translation" (Ladmiral 121). There is absolutely no historical foundation for this type of statement; Bible translation, which indeed starts with Saint Jerome, is already in itself a Roman phenomenon, structured according to the Roman figure of translation. It is something else to say that any translation of a literary work (whatever it may be: Pindar, Plato, or the Bible) presupposes a spirit, a "heart" steeped in *religio*: Saint Jerome, Oresme, Luther, Amyot, Perrot d'Ablancourt, A. W. Schlegel, Tieck, Hölderlin, Voss, Chateaubriand, Baudelaire, George, Celan, to list names of great Western translators at random, without distinction of genres, all have a "religious heart" (no matter what their denomination is). This has nothing to do with a "theology" to "secularize." "Religious," here, cannot be thought apart from ethics and poetics. *The translating heart is poetic, ethical, and religious.* Rilke also spoke of the "practiced heart" of the poet. With regard to Ladmiral's "theological *impensé*," broadly speaking, biblical translation—Christian, Jewish, or any other—has lately been giving itself more importance than it deserves. It is true that three of the greatest translations in the history of the West are Bible translations: the Vulgate, the Authorized Version, and Luther's Bible. But if these translations are great, it is because they are great *œuvres* (literary works). Next to these Bible-works, there are hundreds (thousands?) of Bible translations that are without any interest. To build a "theory of translation" based on Bible translation "problems" does not make particular sense. This idea is founded—among our secularizers—on a "religion of the Book," of the "unique Book," and we know its negative effects. In this regard, see the essential comments of J.-C. Bailly in *Le paradis du sens* (62–66).

against some aspects of Romanness within us; even if, in some way, we must become Greek and Jewish. The first part of my book ends with these considerations.

The second part is devoted to John Donne and to the translation of his works. It can be considered the "application" of the first part.

To deal with John Donne and his translations *in France* is to mention an appalling situation. A person wishing to read the "Great English Poet" is reduced to consulting the out-of-print bilingual anthologies in libraries, and they are in any case unsatisfactory. To my knowledge, there are *today* only two accomplished and accessible translations of isolated poems by Donne: Yves Bonnefoy's translations of "A Hymne to Christ, at the Authors Last Going into Germany" and of "Hymne to God my God, in my Sicknesse" in the journal *Palimpsestes*. A third Donne poem may be read in the beautiful translation of "A nocturnall upon S. Lucies day, Being the shortest day" by Robert Ellrodt, which is presented as an essay in the middle of an article. If it can be found, this poem is in the study on John Donne published in 1983 by L'Âge d'Homme, to which I shall return in a moment. In summary, it is almost impossible to find Donne's works in France. Only his name is in circulation.

There is indeed the splendid book by Ellrodt, *L'inspiration personnelle et l'esprit du temps chez les poètes métaphysiques anglais* (1960), which devotes many pages to Donne and quotes him extensively (using Ellrodt's beautiful translations). Issue 45 of *Poésie* also published a chapter of the equally wonderful book by John Carey, *John Donne: Life, Mind and Art* (1981). These two critical masterpieces support well enough by themselves an absent translation. Finally, the John Donne special volume published by L'Âge d'Homme is divided in two parts, as is customary: critical studies and texts by the author. There are translations of Donne's poems taken from one of the out-of-print books (*Poèmes de John Donne*, translated by Jean Fuzier and Yves Denis, the inadequacy of which I will show) and a few "attempts" at translation by Philippe de Rothschild that are absurd, as we shall also see. The second part of the dossier, except for a rare article, is so pedantic that it will turn away any reader wanting to get to know John Donne's works.

The fact that Donne, in spite of the efforts by many people since, it seems, the beginning of the twentieth century, has been unable to achieve his *transfer-translation*, to become established in France, is the result first of this string of faulty translations. Even if they were talked about when they were first published, they have nonetheless *closed all access* to the poet in French.

These translations, in particular those by Jean Fuzier and Yves Denis, are all the more pernicious in that, not having been criticized in their principles, they risk generating other similar translations ad infinitum. Consequently, there is a need to carry out a basic critical work meant to end this pattern of bad repetitions and to think about the conditions and presuppositions for a new retranslation.

For reasons that will be described later, my analytic trajectory will focus on Elegy XIX, "Going to Bed," and four translations (there were only three in my seminar): the translations of Auguste Morel (1925), Yves Denis (1962), and Philippe de Rothschild (1983), and of Octavio Paz in Spanish (1971).[12] Because Denis' translation is part of a project and is not isolated, we give it priority. In addition, it represents a trend in the translation of traditional poetic works that I think is mistaken and dangerous.

After a brief presentation of Fuzier and Denis (thus answering my question: Who is the translator?) and of their anthology, I will move on to the examination of their project, which, as we shall see, is easily reconstituted. It is an anthology, a selective and hierarchical anthology, that presents the Donne poems selected in the direction of a "spiritual ascent" and excludes the commissioned poems, which it considers "conventional." Then, it is a translation that aims to be poetic, that is, versified, and that attempts to produce a "French Donne." This means two things: a Donne for whom the translators tried to find, even among several more or less contemporary poets, the French equivalent (from Scève to Ronsard, Desportes to Sponde, etc.), and a Donne such as he would have been if he had been translated at the time or, according to the hypothesis of the author of the anthology's foreword, J.-R. Poisson, as he would have written in French (as Rilke did, Poisson says[13]). That is to say, a Donne translated in an archaizing language and archaizing forms.

To begin, I will offer several criticisms of this project. First, I will question the self-evidence of translating a poet from the tradition, a poet subjected to prosodic and versification rules (but who obeys these rules effortlessly), by obeying similar rules or equivalent rules. Is it not going against a certain "crisis" of verse in France, announced by Mallarmé (I'll return to this later), and about which Roubaud (in *La vieillesse d'Alexandre*), among others,

---

12. In fact, Paz's translation dates from about the same time as Denis'.
13. This hypothesis is all the more absurd since Rilke did not write in French the same way he did in German.

speaks at length?[14] The problem is not whether to translate in verse or in prose, but knowing how to translate in verse. The second criticism has to do with the idea of a "French Donne." Does it make sense to speak of, and a fortiori to look for, a French Donne? It is quite obvious that no French poet, neither in Donne's time nor now, resembles Donne, even from afar. It is also obvious that Donne himself is quite different from the other English metaphysical poets of his time. Finally, it is obvious that the English poetic field past and present is fundamentally different from the French poetic field past and present. The idea of a French Donne is thus inconsistent. However, the idea of a Donne translated in the language and the forms of the poetic French of the times is not so inconsistent a priori. But it invites criticism, varied and substantive criticism, which I will present in turn.

After this criticism of the project, I will prepare for the confrontation between "Going to Bed" and its translations with a first confrontation between the poem "Sapho to Philaenis," a lesbian poem (the first one in England), and the translation given by Fuzier and Denis. This allows us to see how the translator follows through with his project and what the consequences are.

The following section is devoted to the long analysis of "Going to Bed" without reference to the translations. Only this analysis, which is also a commentary, an interpretation, and a historical contextualization, can allow for a rigorous confrontation. "Going to Bed" is not only a "very beautiful" love poem. It is also a unique poem, unique in Donne's oeuvre, unique in Western poetry, which does not mean that it is the "greatest," the "most beautiful," and so forth. It seems unique to me because of a number of traits that can be quite easily defined.

"Going to Bed" is not alone in being unique. As a poem of joy, love, and nudity, it is inscribed in a whole line, a whole constellation of Western poets that includes Pindar, the troubadours, Blake, Hölderlin, Hopkins, and many others. But in Donne's oeuvre itself, the poem is inscribed in a very specific constellation: some poems form its core, its "seed," so to speak; other poems are, each in its own way, its inversion; while yet others develop some of the constellation's aspects. This well-defined constellation, in turn, belongs to a network of other poetic constellations in Donne. The whole, as Benoist tells us, forms "an extraordinary topology, the richness of which consists in an

---

14. This crisis has been also studied, from a very different angle (close, in part, to Fuzier's), by Efim Etkind.

endless referral from one poem to the next in a network of mutual *translation* [*traduction*]" (12). It is obvious that the translator must take into account this "network of mutual translation" in his work, which corresponds to the a priori translatability specific to Donne's poetry.[15]

The profound uniqueness of "Going to Bed" lies in that these lines, addressed to the loved one and speaking of the soul, the body, joy, nudity, woman, move at breathtaking speed from the rhetorical to the lyrical, then from the lyrical to the metaphysical: at the center of gravity of the poem, two or three lines take on the value of *poetic enunciations that have truth as their purpose*. These enunciations summarize Donne's metaphysical thinking and show its intimate connection to the mode of metaphysical thinking itself (somewhat like in Hopkins). What bears witness, so to speak, to this metaphysical character of the enunciations is the extreme precision of the vocabulary used by Donne in these lines: every word has its own necessity, as I will attempt to show.

Once this long analytical and interpretative work is done, I will move "at last" to the confrontation between Fuzier/Denis and Donne. At this stage, it is true, we already know what the result of this confrontation will be—something that, certainly, is not pleasant. The title "Le coucher de sa maîtresse" ["The Going to Bed of His Mistress"], a title that adds and emphasizes "of His Mistress" (which, it would seem, does not appear in all the English editions), already indicates that the translators want to make of this poem something that it is not—that is, an erotic poem in the French style—and everything that follows shows this eroticization at work. Line by line, we see how the translators, primarily preoccupied with formal issues and archaism, have neglected colloquial tonalities, have destroyed—this is the right word—the subtle networks of images and terms and, it goes without saying, haven't even noticed the poetico-metaphysical weight of the lines mentioned above. The whole translation is thus a disaster, a disaster more striking than for other poems, because of the uniqueness of "Going to Bed."

This disaster should not be attributed to a lack of talent on the part of the translators, but to the project itself, the consequences of which inexorably

---

15. This corresponds to a principle I stated in "La traduction et la lettre" about Milton: "The internal relation that a work has with translation (what it contains within itself of translation or of non-translation) determines ideally its mode of interlingual translation, and the translation 'problems' that it may present" (113). Every work *anticipates* its translation in its own structure.

unfold. The same can be said about Rothschild's translation, with the difference that it seems carried, if I may say so, more by a childish vision of poetic translation (albeit full of love and sincerity) than by an actual project.

At this stage, I will come back to an older translation of "Going to Bed," which I thought was almost impossible to find, and which Pierre Leyris was kind enough to share with me: it is Auguste Morel's version (1925).[16] This translation, which is even less accessible than the others, since it can only be found at the Bibliothèque Nationale [the French National Library], was mentioned, rather strangely at that,[17] by Pierre Legouis and Léon-Gabriel Gros in their anthologies. It is a version in verse, without rhyme, and also archaizing, but its archaism is quite different from that of Denis and Rothschild. It is a happy archaism; first, because it is effortless, it does not sound laborious; second, because it seems it took Ronsard as a model of French poetry. Obviously Donne is not Ronsard, but we read a happy, pretty (without affectation) poem, and "Going to Bed" is also a happy poem.

Moreover, this translation is happy in that it easily resolves the specific difficulties offered by the original where, I must say, the other translators fail miserably. Here is an example. When the poet tells the woman he loves in daring and inimitable lines (lines 25–26):

> Licence my roaving hands, and let them go,
> Before, behind, between, above, below (Fuzier and Denis 76)

Denis renders it as:

> Laisse, laisse quêter ma main buissonnière
> Par-dessus, par-dessous, entre, devant, derrière! (Fuzier and Denis 77)[18]

---

16. Morel, as we must remember, is the translator of James Joyce's *Ulysses*.
17. Legouis says: "A translation in prose [?] in the language of the sixteenth century of the most erotic of the Elegies" (*Poèmes choisis* 51). But this poem was translated in verse.
18. [Literally,
> Let, let seek my truant hand
> Above, beneath, between, in front, behind.

I will provide close translations into English of the French and Spanish translations of Donne. Trans. Note]

And Rothschild says:

> Licence veut ma main rôdeuse, qu'elle erre
> En haut, en bas, entre-deux, devant, derrière. (Benoist 83)[19]

Perhaps it has to do with the fact that, in Morel's version, *dessous* [under] is written as *dessoubs*. Be that as it may, line 26 in his version avoids the silliness of the other two translations:

> Donne à mes mains errantes congé, qu'elles aillent
> Devant, derrière, entre, dessus, dessoubs. (Morel 98)[20]

Naturally, as happy as it may be, this version remains subjected, in terms of its archaism, to the same criticisms waged against Fuzier and Denis. And it has remained isolated. But it seems as close as possible to what a translation of "Going to Bed" would have been at the time of Donne's life (or a little before), if it had been possible, as is shown in the version that Morel proposes for lines 13 and 14:

> Your gown going off, such beautious state reveals,
> As when from flowry meads th'hills shadow steales. (Fuzier and Denis 76)

> Vostre robe en tombant suavité révèle
> Autant qu'ombre des monts quittant la prée en fleur. (Morel 98)[21]

I will then move on to the second successful version of "Going to Bed,"[22]

---

19. [Licence wants my roaming hand, let it wander
    Above, below, in-between, in front, behind. (Trans. Note)]
20. [Give to my roaving hands licence, let them go
    Before, behind, between, above, below.

Dessoubs is the seventeenth-century spelling of the modern *dessous*. It means "underneath," "below." Trans. Note]

21. [Your dress falling suavity reveals
    As shadow of the hills leaving flowery field.

The word order, spelling, and grammatical gender reflect seventeenth-century usage. Trans. Note]

22. There is another one by the great Brazilian poet-translator-critic Haroldo de Campos; it came my way, but I don't know Portuguese. It has also been set to music.

which is no longer French but Mexican. It is Octavio Paz's version. This translation, presented by its author as a "free adaptation," is fascinating in several respects. The use of the word "adaptation" by Paz is baffling. On the contrary, his work follows the principles stated by Pasternak in his "Notes of a Translator," in 1944:

> Translations either have no meaning at all, or else must have a closer relation to their originals than is usually supposed. Correspondence of text to text is too weak a link to guarantee a translation's expediency. Such translations fail to do what they promise. Their pale re-tellings convey no sense of the most important thing about the object they undertake to reflect—its power. To achieve this aim, a translation has to be connected with its original and a translation must be the relation between a function and its derivative, between a tree-trunk and the new shoot struck from it. ... Translations are conceivable because ideally they too must be works of art, and must, by virtue of their own unrepeatability, stand on the same level as the originals, even while sharing their text. (*Œuvres* 1343–44)[23]

That is what happens in Paz, but in a singular way. On one hand, his translation is indeed a poem that is completely autonomous. On the other hand, it reaches a "more real dependency"; it expresses, as I will show, the power of the original and—what is even more powerful—it succeeds in keeping and restituting most of the fundamental "signifiers of the original." Last, Paz's translation reaches the same level as the original—I mean its ultimate, metaphysical, level—by paradoxically replacing its central signifier, "joyes," *joies* in French—which is a central signifier in Donne's poetry and in Western poetry—with a central signifier of the Hispanic *universum, goce,* itself untranslatable (*jouissance?*). Where Donne says in lines 33–35,

> Full nakedness! All joyes are due to thee,
> As souls unbodied, bodies uncloth'd must be,
> To taste whole joyes (Fuzier and Denis 78)

23. [From "Notes of a Translator" 96–97. The English translation of Pasternak's essay is much closer to the Russian than the French one (instead of "expediency," the French uses "legitimate," and the last sentence is quite different: "If translation is conceivable, it is in nature where, ideally, it must also be a work of art, and reach, from a common text, the level of the original thanks to its own uniqueness." The Russian uses "paraphrases" in the plural instead of "re-tellings." In the French version, we find "paraphrase" in the singular. Trans. Note]

Paz radically hispanizes it:

> La plena desnudez es goce entero:
> Para gozar la gloria las almas desencarnan,
> Los cuerpos se desvisten. (*Traducción* 31)[24]

This is how he joins "the level of the original by virtue of its unrepeatability."[25]

. . .

The analysis of the French translations of Donne proved negative. The time has come to think about a *new transfer-translation* and a *new retranslation* of Donne in France; we are in the midst of a "productive" criticism. Before any new translation comes the question: Who is Donne? *Who is this Donne whom we want to introduce and translate?* If the anthology by Legouis attempts to present him in all the variety of his poetic works, if the anthology by Léon-Gabriel Gros does the same (but in a more confused way), Fuzier and Denis show him as a profane and libertine poet who, rather abruptly, becomes a stern "spiritual" poet. Poisson speaks of "spiritual ascent." But if there is indeed a turning point of this kind in Donne's life and work, it occurs against the background of a great permanence of being. Donne remains the one who wrote: "Antes muerto que mutado" [Rather die than change]. One of the aspects of this permanence of being is its Christian spirit. Donne is foremost a Christian poet, a religious poet. "Going to Bed" is a religious poem, innervated by religious images and representations.

However, Donne is not only a Christian poet; like Bossuet, like Kierkegaard, he is (to use Heidegger's expression) a *Christian author*. He is the author of homilies that, as we well know, held all of London spellbound. Besides the sermons, there are various works (*Pseudo-Martyr, Ignatius's Conclave, Biathanatos,* and *Essays in Theology*) and letters. In a word, Donne is also a prose writer, a great prose writer at that. In all the anthologies, Donne does not appear as a Christian prose writer, or as a Christian poet and author! In

---

24. [In English a literal translation of Paz's lines would be:

Full nakedness is entire joy,
To enjoy glory souls unbody
Bodies undress. (Trans. Note)]

25. [Pasternak, *Œuvres* 1344. Trans. Note]

his *Reliquiae* in 1957, Leyris carefully presented Hopkins as what he was: a poet, a prose writer (letters, journal, etc.), and an "illustrator."

Once the form of the new translation is settled, there remains the question of the paths of a retranslation of Donne's poetry. In my opinion, these paths are already, in an embryonic stage, suggested by the three translations mentioned earlier (Ellrodt's and Bonnefoy's translations).

Ellrodt presents his translation, very modestly, as an "attempt." It is a translation in rhymed verse sounding slightly classical, not at all like a sixteenth-century poem, and not archaizing. It follows closely Donne's networks of images and terms but does not quite sustain some of the more colloquial lines. Applied to all of Donne the poet, this translation mode might run the risk of uniformity. But it is a possible path.

The other path is the one taken by Bonnefoy. Following what he said about poetic translation and the translation of Shakespeare, Bonnefoy intends to go beyond "classical forms, closed prosodic forms," without necessarily abandoning a "concern for the real laws of verse" ("L'idée de la traduction" 244). It seems to me that his translations have three characteristics: a slight *condensation* of the original (as in Celan), a noticeable *rejuvenation* of the original, and the production of a *slightly "prosaic" poeticality*. This rejuvenation results from the abandonment of "closed prosodic forms" (rightly or wrongly perceived as old), from the slight condensation (which de-rhetorizes Donne, and rhetoric is also perceived as old), and, naturally, from the slight prosification. To rejuvenate the original is the ultimate goal that Goethe assigned to a translation.[26] This does not necessarily mean to modernize it, although rejuvenation is incompatible with any form of archaization. Translated by Bonnefoy, the two poems by Donne (poems of illness and death) seem young, diaphanous, and new. It is a very powerful appearance [*paraître*], which cannot be avoided.

---

26. Goethe used the concepts of *Verjüngung* (rejuvenation) and *Auffrischung* (regeneration). [*The Experience of the Foreign* 65. Trans. Note]. In the introduction to his translation of the book of Genesis, Grosjean states: "The original text will always be examined in its context of origin, but to translate it is to attempt to bring its youth to another people of another time" ("Note du traducteur" 15). It is true that Grosjean concludes that translation "must speak without making the reader feel disoriented to hear it." In fact, the more a work is rejuvenated by translation, the more it seems both close and distant and, if it is a work from the past, young and old. Any work, indeed, is disorienting. A really ethical translation must avoid the excessive "effect of foreignness" as well as an excessive effect of naturalization. Here, every translator must find his way, must go between Charybdis and Scylla.

But how is the poeticality of Bonnefoy's translations slightly *prosaic?* I cannot summarize here the long developments that are required to provide an appropriate answer to these questions, and that have to do with the relations between poetry and prose, since German romanticism and before, during all great periods of poetry. For these developments I will invoke the comments of Novalis, Hölderlin, Baudelaire, Mallarmé, Hopkins, Alain, Hofmannsthal, Pasternak, Benjamin, Roubaud, and others.

If the "prosaic" is in a certain way one of the destinies of modern poetry, a destiny through which, paradoxically, poetry meets its pure poeticality, a destiny through which the "joyous verse" finds itself through "somber prose,"[27] it is obvious that the translation of poetry, as poetic act, is affected and reoriented by it.

The influence of prose on the translation of poetry is even stronger in the Anglo-Saxon domain because, in English poetry, there has been a tradition of prosaic poetry totally opposite to the French tradition of mannered poetry.[28] For a translator of English language poetry, there is today a *fundamental circle:* in order to be able to translate this poetry in its specificity, he must accept a certain degree of prosaicness (colloquialisms, triviality, etc.). But for this prosaicness to be accurate, it must be taken from Anglo-Saxon poetry, and this can be done only through translation. This circle is not a vicious one; it is simply the circle in which the translator must fight and struggle. The important thing is to remain in the circle.

All these reflections on prose, poetry, and English literary works lead us, through a progression from the general to the particular, to the specific tasks of a retranslation of Donne today—Bonnefoy's versions function here as an inspiration rather than a model.

27. I quote Roubaud: "L'amour lumineux s'écorce dans le désir sombre ..., l'amour de la langue dans le sombre de la langue, le vers joyeux dans la sombre prose, le non-vers.... Je dis que le vers joyeux s'écorce dans l'obscur non-vers, c'est que la prose est cette basse de basalte et de laves" ("Le silence" 114). ["Luminous love strips off its bark in dark desire ..., love of language in the darkness of language, joyous verse in somber prose, in the not-verse.... I say that the joyous verse strips off in the obsure non-verse, for prose is this *base of basalt and lava.*" "Basse de basalte et de laves" is a quote from Mallarmé's well-known "À la nue accablante" ("Shipwreck Sonnet") of 1894, translated as "To the Overwhelming Blackness" by Roger Fry (Mallarmé, *Poems* 123), or as "Hushed to the Crushing Cloud" by Henry Weinfield (Mallarmé, *Collected Poems* 83). Trans. Note]

28. Hopkins himself bases the use of "sprung rhythm" on the fact that it is "nearest to the rhythm of prose, that is, the native and natural rhythm of speech, the least forced, the most rhetorical and emphatic of all possible rhythms" (*Letters* 46).

The last part of this study analyzes the reception of the translation by Fuzier and Denis, that is, the articles published in 1962 in newspapers and journals. It seems that the reception has been globally positive apart from a few reservations. What can explain such a positive reaction? I examine here in turn the *yes* of an "authority" on poetry like Jean Grosjean; the *yes* of the eminent English literature scholar Legouis, along with reservations quickly toned down; and the various mirages that, here and there, may have led to a judgment that was a priori positive: the mirage of ignorance, of archaism, of the "pure poetic." Finally, I study the *translation horizon and the poetic horizon* of the 1960s, which obviously guide any critical evaluation.

Thus ends the long path along which criticism has attempted to fulfill, moment by moment, its hermeneutic, analytic, reflexive, digressive, commentative, historical, and productive essence. I would add its citatory (or citational) essence. In this book, I have provided many, many citations. This has been a deliberate, desired, cultivated gesture felt to be a necessity. I hope that the reader will not experience as heavy what seemed to me to be the *dialogic* life of this work, and one of the principles of its composition.

Antoine Berman
Paris, October 28, 1991

PART I

The Project of a "Productive" Criticism

In my research and my seminars, I have been led to analyze or criticize a number of translations. It goes without saying that no traductological research can be done without such analysis or criticism,[1] which doesn't necessarily mean that it occupies a central place in translation studies: "going to the concrete" is justified only when it is carried by a conceptual reflection.

In my 1984 seminar, I analyzed Hölderlin's *Antigone,* as well as the translations of Sappho by Edith Mora and Michel Deguy, Klossowski's *Aeneid,* and Chateaubriand's *Paradise Lost.* In 1985, the commentary on Walter Benjamin's "The Task of the Translator" (*Mythe et violence*) was also the occasion to examine the French version by Maurice de Gandillac.[2] In 1988, I studied two French translations of Grimm's last tale, *Der goldene Schlüssel* [*The Golden Key*], one by Armel Guerne, the other by Marthe Robert. In 1989, I analyzed French and Mexican translations (by Rothschild, Fuzier and Denis, and Octavio Paz) of John Donne's poem "Going to Bed," as well as three French translations of Hölderlin's poem "Wenn aus der Ferne" ["If from a Distance"] (by Jouve, Bianquis, and Roud). That same year, in a seminar I gave in Buenos Aires, I studied a recent retranslation of Plato's *Phaedrus* (see Brisson). Last,

---

1. We shall see later why I privilege the term "criticism."
2. A retranslation of this essay by Martine Broda (who had attended my seminar) came out in 1991 in *Po&sie.*

in my book on Amyot, I examined the translation of Aristotle's *Nicomachean Ethics* by Nicole Oresme and, of course, Amyot's Plutarch.³

The form and the framework of these analyses vary. In the case of Hölderlin, Chateaubriand, and Klossowski, my goal was to show "the work on the *letter*, on the word" to which their translation bears witness. For Benjamin, the analysis came to be inserted in a commentary on the content and the language of the original. For Grimm, the comparative analysis of Guerne's and Robert's translations took place within the context of a reflection on the principles that direct, or should direct, the translation of so-called children's literature. For Donne and Hölderlin, as for Benjamin, the comparative analysis of the translations accompanied a line-by-line commentary of the original poems.

With the retranslation of the *Phaedrus*, my analysis focused on the translation of fundamental words in the dialogue (such as *eidos*, idea or form), and especially on the paratextual matter (introduction, afterword, notice, notes) that *support* [*étayent*] the translated text.⁴

The analyses of Oresme and Amyot, largely based on studies by specialists, are linked to the historical work mentioned earlier, and their goal is to grasp the fundamental traits of the entire creative production of translators, rather than one of their translations in particular.⁵

Finally, my remarks about the translation of Freud's *Œuvres complètes* for the Presses Universitaires de France—remarks that are so brief that one can hardly speak of analysis—originated in the fact that the authors of this translation, Jean Laplanche in particular, referred several times to *The Experience of the Foreign* when speaking about their translation project.⁶

---

3. To this list I must add a brief review of the French translation of Mário de Andrade's *Macunaíma* by Jacques Thiériot ("Rescension de la traduction") and my notes on the translation of Freud's *Œuvres complètes* in the Presses Universitaires de France edition (see "Observations sur la traduction").

4. The notion of translation support is examined in my book in progress on Amyot.

5. The oeuvre of a translator is not the sum total of his translations. And not all translators author an oeuvre, a creative production. The creative work of the sum of the translator's translations results from the constant coherence in the choice of translated works (and consequently from the minimal proportion of accidental translations); from the coherence in the mode of translation developed, often progressively, by the translator; and, of course, from the important part of "successful" translations. One can thus speak of creative work of translation about Amyot, Perrot d'Ablancourt, A. W. Schlegel, Armand Robin, Paul Celan, Pierre Leyris, and so forth.

6. "Even if he did not inspire our work, Antoine Berman's book on the history of translation in Germany, *L'Epreuve de l'étranger*, provides us with useful benchmarks" (Bourguignon, Cotet, Laplanche, and Robert). But the authors also quote passages relative to "ethnocentric translation" (9), in which they see an obvious confirmation of their own project. With regard to my position on their project and their work, see my "Observations sur la traduction" (112–22).

As varied as these analyses may be, they all have some characteristics in common. Fundamentally, and this is where they differ from Meschonnic's own analyses, they do not have first in mind a *negative* objective, that is, destroying translations that are thought to be "bad" or "insufficient." Even if I sharply question some translations of Donne, Plato, Benjamin, and so forth, even if the work of analysis uncovers serious errors, I have always wanted to avoid systematic attacks and rather, when possible, look for the reason or reasons for these errors. In the total count, nine of my analyses are positive "evaluations" (Hölderlin, Chateaubriand, Klossowski, Deguy, Paz, Jouve, Roud, Amyot, Oresme); three are mixed (Robert, Guerne, Thiériot), that is, according to the analysis, these translations possess some weaknesses; and four are negative (Mora, Gandillac, Fuzier/Denis, Rothschild). In this last case, the analysis suggests that they are not "bad" translations, but seriously defective (Gandillac), poetically insufficient (Mora's Sappho), or based on a misguided project (Rothschild, Fuzier/Denis). The translations of Brisson, Bianquis, and Freud must be evaluated on the basis of other criteria. Brisson's work is sharply attacked, but solely from the point of view of the paratexts. Geneviève Bianquis' is not so much a translation as an introduction (I personally discovered Hölderlin, *received* him, through this introduction), and as such, it is a positive one. Finally, Freud's translation with PUF [Presses Universitaires de France] is a *work in progress* [in English in the text] based on a project that I think is positive, but that would need to be completed (see my remarks in "Observations sur la traduction" 120–21).

THE CONCEPT OF TRANSLATION CRITICISM

The very expression "translation criticism" may lead to misunderstandings, for it seems to suggest only the negative evaluation of a translation. Such are the analyses made by Meschonnic about Celan's translation by du Bouchet[7] and the translation of the Bible by Chouraqui. And when Pierre Leyris, with a softer tone, examines with a fine-toothed comb the translation of a T. S. Eliot poem by Saint-John Perse, or that of a Thomas Hardy poem by Paul Valéry, it is mostly in order to reveal serious changes of register, in a word, processes of loss (see Leyris, "Notes sur un poème").

---

7. His analysis remains a model of its kind, as much for its rigor (in the dual sense of the word) as for the scandal it caused in Parisian poetic circles at the time.

This situation refers us, beyond translation, to a duality inscribed *in the very structure of the critical act*. We will never be able to remove all negativity from this act. Benjamin speaks of "the inevitable negative moment of this concept" (*Le concept de critique* 89).[8]

Since the Enlightenment, criticism, what it tends to, has been a work of the negative. But this fact should not make us forget that, just as essentially, this negative work is the flip side of a work of the positive. In its essence, criticism is positive, whether it is the criticism at work in the domain of language productions, of art in general, or in other domains of human life. Not only is criticism positive, but this positivity is its *truth:* a purely negative criticism is not a true criticism. This is why Friedrich Schlegel, the founding father of modern criticism, and not only German criticism, reserves the use of the word "criticism" or "critique" for the analysis of high-quality works and uses the term "characteristic" for the study and the evaluation of mediocre or low-quality works.

Let us examine the nature of this positivity in the criticism of works of language, then in the criticism of their translations. The criticism of works of language, whatever form it may have taken since the beginning of its modern configuration at the dawn of the nineteenth century, and whatever its inevitable deviations and deteriorations (compensated by continual revivals) in its practice and theory, is clearly something that is *necessary*—that is, something that has an a priori necessity founded in the works of language themselves. For it is these works that call for and authorize something like criticism because they *need* it. They need criticism to communicate *themselves,* to manifest *themselves,* to accomplish *themselves* and perpetuate *themselves.* They need the mirror of criticism. It is true that the many paratextual forms to which this need gives rise often produce the opposite result: criticism makes the works more distant; it obscures, smothers, almost kills them. (Here one thinks of those students who only read studies of a specific work without ever reading the work itself.) But regardless of this peril, and it is an inevitable one, *criticism is ontologically bound to the work.*

Obviously, this doesn't mean that in order to understand Proust, *it is neces-*

---

8. [In the standard English version, "The Concept of Criticism," the translation reads: "Under the name of criticism, the Romantics at the same time confessed the inescapable insufficiency of their efforts ... and so finally alluded, in this concept, to its necessary 'incompleteness of infallibility'" (143). Trans. Note]

sary to have read Poulet, Blanchot, Deleuze, Genette, or Henry (critics who have produced great critical texts on Proust's works). Nothing forces us to do so. But the existence of this critical work modifies *À la recherche du temps perdu*. It is now—and because of the *criticisme* that it carries within itself, the oeuvre that has produced its criticisms—a thing it wasn't at its beginning, and these criticisms shed an ever-renewed light on it. In the case of Proust, we are dealing with accomplished criticisms, true *critical works*. Criticism of this kind makes the works fuller by revealing their infinite signifiance.[9] And correspondingly they enrich the reading done by the readers. It is always gratifying to read a critical work that brings new light to a work we love.

The criticism of works of language is thus a vital thing for the works, and consequently a vital one for human life in that it is also, and essentially, a living in and through the works (see Ricœur, *Du texte à l'action* 115 and following; also Arendt, *The Human Condition,* chap. 4).[10] Naturally, this high mission of criticism is not always easy to undertake, and the critic must always struggle against an erudite, pseudo-scientific, or purely formalist degradation of his practice. The level at which this mission is situated received its original definition from Schlegel: "This poetic criticism . . . will present the representation anew, will once again form what is already formed. . . . It will complement, rejuvenate, newly fashion the work" (qtd. in Benjamin, *Le concept de critique* 112).[11]

Among the multiple forms of criticism of verbal works, there is the criticism of the works that "result" from the transfer, the translation of a work from one language to another: what has been called, since the time of Leonardo Bruni, *translations*. We know that translation is no less necessary to the works, to their expression, fulfillment, survival, and circulation, than is criticism, not to mention the fact that translation has a more obvious empirical necessity.[12]

---

9. [For a discussion of the difference between signifiance and significance, see Richard Harland's *Superstructuralism: The Philosophy of Structuralism and Post-structuralism.* Julia Kristeva and Roland Barthes separate out "two distinct levels of language: a level of 'signifiance' or creative transgressive meaning, and a level of 'signification' or socially instituted, socially controlled meaning. . . . Whereas the 'signification' of a word is held fixed and self-identical within a system, the 'signifiance' of a word opens out centrifugally" (168). Trans. Note]

10. [*From Text to Action* 87 and following. Trans. Note]

11. ["The Concept of Criticism" 154. Trans. Note] "To rejuvenate" the work is exactly what Goethe asks translation to do. See my chapter on Goethe in *The Experience of the Foreign: Culture and Translation in Romantic Germany.*

12. Benjamin even calls criticism "another, if lesser [than translation], factor in the continued life of literary works" in "The Task of the Translator" (77).

What is important to note is that criticism and translation are structurally related. Whether he feeds on critical works or not in order to translate such-and-such a foreign book, the translator acts like a critic at all levels.[13] When translation is retranslation, it is, implicitly or not, a "criticism" of previous translations in two senses: it is a *developer,* in the photographic sense of the term of making the image visible; it makes translations visible as what they are (i.e., translations belonging to a specific time, a specific state of literature, language, culture, etc.), but its existence can only attest that these translations are either deficient or obsolete. Here again we encounter the duality of the critical act.

That said, there seems to be a certain tension between criticism and translation,[14] as evidenced by the frequent lack of interest that critics show in "translation issues" and the dearth of great translators who are also great critics (and vice versa).

The criticism of a translation is thus that of a text that itself results from a work of a critical nature. This is a delicate operation that developed only very recently[15] into its "modern" form, that is, a form similar to that of the criticism per se of literary works. The criticism of translations may have existed for a long time (since at least the seventeenth century) in the form of judgments, but it has never been as developed as the criticism of original texts.

As we know, most of the time, critics study translations either in their source language or in some French version, "forgetting" that the text is a version. They study "foreign works."

Not only has the criticism of translations been slow in developing, but when it has been developed, it has mainly been in an essentially negative direction, which consists of identifying, often obsessively, the "defects" of translations even when they are successful. Positive criticism has remained

---

13. This critical nature of translation has been mentioned many times. For example, Steiner states: "There are translations which are supreme acts of critical exegesis, in which analytic understanding, historical imagination, linguistic expertness articulate a critical evaluation which is at the same time a piece of totally lucid, responsible exposition" (*After Babel* 429).

14. See my article "Critique, commentaire et traduction." Today I am inclined to think that I exaggerated this tension on the basis of a questionable concept of the critical act, and that this indifference, this distance of critics from translation, belongs to an era that is ending.

15. This modern form of criticism is dual: first, the critic's work takes the form of the *essay,* and secondly, that of a *scientific analysis.* Literary criticism is based on this dual model, and it is the same, as we shall see, for the criticism of translations. "Literary" criticism and "scientific" criticism can coexist in the same body of criticism, as the work of Roland Barthes, for example, shows.

an exception up until very recently, especially when it is pure, that is, without negative elements. But the two forms of criticism move most of the time—moved until recently, except for the erudite studies of ancient translations—in the same space, the space of judgment, whereas the criticism of literary works, while keeping this possibility (for instance, in the press), is deployed in a multiplicity of dimensions and discourses that constitute all its strength and richness.

This tendency to want to judge a translation, and *to want to do this only,* refers back to two fundamental traits of any translated text, one being that this "secondary" text is supposed to correspond to the "primary" text, is supposed to be truthful, true; the other trait being what I will call *defectivity,* a neologism attempting to gather all the possible forms of defects, failings, and errors that affect *any* translation. The translated text *calls for* judgment because it gives rise to the question of its own truthfulness and because it is always (which brings into question this truthfulness) defective somewhere. Every translation presents defects [*présente des défauts*], as the French expression goes, even if many attempt to hide them; the best translators are sometimes caught by moments of inexplicable drowsiness next to which those of the "good Homer," which filled Horace with indignation, seem minor.[16] Without dogmatic a priori, one can safely say that most translations are insufficient, mediocre, average, even bad, and this without *at all* questioning the talent or the professional ethics of their authors. Finally, the translated text seems affected by an originary flaw, its *secondariness.*[17] This very old accusation, of *not* being the original, and being *less* than the original (it is quite easy to move from one accusation to the other), has been the bane of the translating psyche and the source of all its guilt: this defective labor is claimed to be an error (one *must not* translate literary works; they do not want to be translated) and an impossibility (it is *not possible* to translate them).

It is true that this morose discourse on the defectivity of translations has

---

16. "At idem indignor quandoque bonus dormitat Homerus" (*Art poétique,* qtd. by Steiner, *After Babel* 327). ["But am more Angry, if once I heare good *Homer* snore" (trans. Ben Jonson, qtd. by Steiner, *After Babel* 328). Trans. Note]

17. Georges Mounin opens his *Belles infidèles* with the following sentence: "All arguments against translation are summarized with one: it is not the original" (7). The self-evidence of this sentence begins to be shaken when we remember that the very concept of the original only goes back to the sixteenth century, and that the possibility, the obligation, of translation comes under the innermost essence of the "original." Translation may not be the original, but it is not exterior to it: translation is a metamorphosis of it.

always been accompanied by another more positive discourse: defective or not, translations have an obvious communicative use, and they contribute to "enriching" the translating language and literature. But until Goethe, Humboldt, and Schleiermacher, this positive discourse was never able to go beyond the phase of a—just—apology of the collateral beneficial effects of translation; without attending to the ontological link between the original and its translations, this positive view has easily been dominated by the negative discourse that disregards (or negates) this link.

But isn't a translation's purpose not only to "render" the original, to be its "double" (thus confirming its secondariness), but to become, to be, a work [*œuvre*] as well, a legitimate work? Paradoxically, this purpose of reaching the autonomous, durable status of a work doesn't contradict the first purpose; it strengthens it. When it achieves this double purpose, a translation becomes a "new original." It is certain that few translations achieve this status. A certain number do; a few, the "great" translations, reach the rank of major works and exert an influence over the receiving culture that few "native" works have.

Thus the criticism of translations focuses on texts that are also "critical" and that are, moreover, either simple muted echoes of the originals (the most frequent case), or (more rarely) authentic works that tower over them.

If we think that literary criticism is essential to the life of literary works (and of the reading that is a moment of this life), we must consider, based on what has been said, that the criticism of translations is as essential and thus give this part of criticism all the serious attention given to the criticism of the works themselves. I said that the criticism of translations is still underdeveloped. However, we are going to see immediately that it is in full expansion, and in a plurality of forms and modes that are increasingly differentiated and rich. What it lacks, as translation does too, is a certain symbolic status, the secret dignification without which no "discursive practice" can literally be established as legitimate. Contributing to this dignification, which the criticism of literary works achieved in the nineteenth century, is one of the goals of translation studies. It almost goes without saying that this dignification would contribute to the dignification of translations, of translation in general, and perhaps of the translators themselves.

THE DIFFERENT KINDS OF TRANSLATION ANALYSIS

At first glance, the diversity of translation analyses is such that it discourages any classification or seems to be a futile effort. Translated texts are examined from every possible point of view, in the most varied contexts, with different goals every time.

First, there is a large group of studies, articles, and the like, that are content to directly compare the original with its translation or to compare translations to each other, to inevitably identify disparities, "changes." These studies all have, whatever their form, their goal, or their context may be, the *same formal structure*. Most of the time, they function at the micro level. They lead up to an "acknowledgement of differences," which is almost never to the credit of the translator. Here, there is no study of the *system* of these differences or of the *reasons* for this system. There is no reflection about the concept of translation that, invisibly, plays the role of *tertium comparationis*. Thus most of the time these studies, which range from direct evaluation (good/average/bad) to more neutral, more objective analyses, do not have any particular ambition. They aim neither to adopt a *rigorous form* that would define their specificity, nor to claim a methodology (they probably do not even consider it). They naively compare and confront.

Then, there are detailed, erudite analyses of the transformation systems that govern *some*, generally high-level, translations. Part of Hölderlin's translations has thus been carefully analyzed in Germany; for France, I can mention two exemplary cases: Robert Aulotte's work on Amyot's translation of Plutarch (*Amyot et Plutarque*) and that of Roger Zuber on Perrot d'Ablancourt's translations (*Les "belles infidèles"*). These analyses are global; from typical examples and privileged passages, they reconstitute the *fundamental traits* of a translation, and even of the whole work of a translator. In the case of these two works, the translation under study is situated in its entire historical context and compared to other translations from the same period. These analyses are obviously so specialized that they are reserved for a very small number of people, which raises the problem, to which I shall return, of the "readability" of a translation analysis. Moreover, these analyses are not autonomous and are part of a whole that encompasses them: Beissner's studies on Hölderlin's translations are part of the German institution constituted by the Hölderlinstudien, Aulotte's work focuses on the "renaissance" of Plutarch in sixteenth-century Europe, Zuber's treats all the contributions of translation to the formation of classical prose in France. These analyses are thus integrated into already constituted "disciplines," that is, into the study of literatures and their history. In this sense, not only do these analyses lack autonomy, but they have neither a specific form nor a specific methodology.

All the analyses and types of analyses described up to now are characterized by their heterogeneity and their lack of autonomous form and methodology. By *form of translation analysis,* I mean a discursive structure *sui generis,* adapted to its subject (the comparison between an original and its translation[s]), a form sufficiently *individuated* to be distinguished from other types of analysis. I also mean a form that is self-reflecting, that thematizes its specificity and, thus, produces its methodology; a form that not only produces its methodology but attempts to found it upon an explicit theory of language, of the text, and of translation.

From the current translation analyses that seem to have a form, and a *strong* one at that, I have first chosen Henri Meschonnic's, and then the analysis of the traductologists linked to the functionalist Tel Aviv school (Toury for Israel and Brisset for Quebec). Since I do not aim to be exhaustive, I did not include Germany, where, however, *Übersetzungskritik* (see Paepcke) is not a neglected field.

Henri Meschonnic's Engagé Analyses

By "engagé analyses," I mean the analyses that, solidly supported by "modern" fields of knowledge (linguistics, semiotics, poetics, etc.) and by an explicit theory of translation and writing, examine translations in the name of an entirely predetermined idea of translation and its tasks. These analyses can rightly be called "engagé" in that they are not satisfied with evaluating a translation from the vantage point of this idea, but they *attack* translations that do not conform to it. The orientation of these analyses then takes a turn that is, if not polemical, at least quite militant. It is possible to find analyses of this kind that have a positive orientation, in the sense that they focus on translations corresponding to this idea, but in fact they are rare. That is what I have attempted with Hölderlin, Chateaubriand, and Klossowski, without, however, bringing into play a methodology as rigorous as the one structuring "negative" analyses. Henri Meschonnic is the representative of this type of analysis, and in a certain way he created its form.[18] His criticisms of translations of Celan, Trakl, Humboldt, Kafka, and the Bible are well known.

In this case, the analyses are not autonomous; in Meschonnic's work, they belong to the poetics of translation, which "can only depend on poetics" (*Pour la poétique* 325). However, they have a specific form, the best example of which is the structure of the study "On appelle cela traduire Celan" (*Pour la poétique* 369 and following), which has one part about the translated poet ("Celan dans le language"), and a part on the translations ("Celan dans *Strette*," *Strette* being the general title given by the translators to their collection. It is the title of one of Celan's collections, but other poems by Celan are also included in the *Strette* by du Bouchet). One clearly sees then how the first part, which belongs to poetics, supports the second one, which belongs to the poetics of translation.

The analysis just mentioned systematically points out all the failings of the incriminated translations, seeing in them most often the effect of ideological biases (in the largest sense of the term), aesthetic and literary fashions, conventions,[19] and so forth, and of subjective faults of the translating psyche. If Meschonnic identifies quite well the "causes" of the defectiveness of the translations that he is attacking, he doesn't waste his time analyzing them. What matters for him is *denouncing*, denouncing with *precision*. Hence a meticulous tracking of the incoherencies, poor systematicity, and biases of the translators. This denunciation goes with specific retranslations showing, convincingly for the most part, how the translators could have respected without difficulty a form of significance of the original: the obstacle was in their heads, in their biases, not in the original. All this detailed criticism never ceases to be *self*-reflective, to be accompanied by often injunctive assertions about the task of the translator, the meaning of translation as a work of writing [*travail d'écriture*], as "work in the chains of the signifier" (*Pour la poétique* 314).

---

18. In his dissertation, "L'homme décentré. Culture et traduction, traduction et culture," Jean-Louis Cordonnier analyses the translation of Alejo Carpentier's novel *El arpa y la sombra* by René L. F. Durand, his regular translator, taking his inspiration from Meschonnic. The analytic "methodology" proves to be perfectly transferable and demonstrates once again, if there was any need, its own necessity.

19. About the translation of Celan, Meschonnic speaks of a "cluster of tics" (385), of "poetisms" (389), of "hackneyed affectations" (388), of "epigonic writing" (390) and "epigone's tics" (403), of "antiquated conventions" (403), and so forth.

Meschonnic's criticisms are most often unanswerable. The analyst's eye tracks down in the darkest corners the many forms of translation failings. There is more, and more striking still, the analysis of the translators' work reveals that (almost) all of them have a certain self-satisfaction; a certain carelessness; a certain casualness verging on objective scorn for the author (and the public); a narcissistic complacency; and, *last but not least* [in English in the text], a lack of consistency (which is displayed, for instance, in the curious mix of a-systematicity and bad systematicity in their work, something that had already surprised Mounin, who spoke of "disparate"), characteristics that are rather surprising. These lackluster but undeniable traits of the translating psyche are not analyzed or ever taken into account by the analyst; I think they are linked, among other reasons, to the fact that this *psyche* has always acted in the shadows. No one looks closely at what it does: the translator has *a certain impunity* that is ironically guaranteed by his solitude and his dereliction. Consequently, the translator, left to his own devices, can also do what he wants. That is, he deals with the original as he likes, in the name of his freedom.[20] It is true that

---

20. The translator's "freedom" can mean two things. First, it means claiming a certain freedom as necessary to his psyche (not to be a "slave") and to his work of transmutation when facing a work. Jean-Yves Masson says that one must know how to "stand up to" the original so that translation can blossom as an ethical relation" ("Territoire de Babel" 158): Isabelle Berman writes that sometimes one must be able to say no to a work, to respect in it "the black, inaccessible zones of a culture." She adds, "The translation of *Sept fous* was going to suffer our censorship, bear the mark of our place, our history . . . for this writing, which was so brutal, hurt our own tolerance. We had to love and hate the translating language, love and hate the language to be translated" (Arlt 11–12).

The work of translation thus requires a free subject who is free in his fundamental choice of translation, in his specific choices, free in the mastery of this chain of "blow by blow" (Ladmiral) constituted by translation when practiced close to the text. This freedom is the same as fidelity, and it is up to each translator, not without risk, to define the boundaries of the playing field of this freedom-fidelity.

But, unfortunately, the demand for freedom has another, quite different, side: there is a bad freedom, as there is a false fidelity, a false respect. This is what happens when the translator's freedom, his liberty, takes the form of liberties. On the pretext of not being a "slave," of being "creative," of meeting the demands of the "public," and so forth, the translator takes liberties with the original. The most arrogant of these liberties is that of the poet who, in the name of "Poetry," forces his own poetics on that of the original (as is the case of du Bouchet with Celan, of Jouve with Shakespeare, etc.). Freedom then runs into pure and simple manipulation. This freedom in order to manipulate is the refuge and the expression of all weakness, all laziness, all infatuation, and it expresses, among too many translators, a psyche that is lying, untruthful, since this freedom betrays the principles of "fidelity" that at the same time it always trumpets loud and clear. Hence the Italian saying *traduttore traditore* (poorly translated in French as *traduction trahison* [translation betrayal], since it only applies to translators, and not to translation as betrayal, as Maurice Pergnier [xvi] has rightly observed).

he doesn't owe any explanations to anyone.[21] He can be a-systematic; all he is asked is to appear systematic. He can embellish, make more aesthetic if he feels like it: Who will care? Who will look? He can surreptitiously disregard problems: Who will suspect it? In a word, *the translating psyche sinks into the space of deceit* and soon (something that should make us more understanding) becomes *self-deceit*, believes it is faithful, exact, creative, and so forth. There is here *the revelation, expressed so strongly, perhaps for the first time ever*, of something very serious. The "method" or "form" created by Meschonnic brings to an end the anonymity of the unfaithful and manipulative translator. One can never underestimate the importance of this event. And still, there is in all this something that is disturbing yet difficult to pinpoint at first.

At this point it is important to be clear: the few "critical remarks" that I will make must not make us forget the immense debt we owe to Meschonnic's poetics. With regard to my translation research, even if it hasn't been inspired or influenced by Meschonnic's poetics, it has been constantly nourished by them, and on many issues we share fundamental intuitions (for instance, on the theme of orality). What seems open to criticism here are rather certain stereotypes of Meschonnic's writings. The aggressive orientation that is present in all his writings, and that, with the exception of poets, seems only to spare figures like Humboldt and Benveniste, is one such trait that he sometimes seems unable to escape. It is true that some authors can only show what they are capable of in polemics and in a "fighting position," like Leo Spitzer (14). Of course, the negativity of Meschonnic's criticism has its positive side. Moreover, it attacks only translations that mistreat works crucial to our culture: the Bible, Celan, Kafka, and so forth. It attacks only the translations of great works. It defends originals as much as it attacks their translations. But our unease remains. Where does it come from? From the impression that a "just verdict" has been pronounced but that the accused have not had a chance to defend themselves, or even that elementary procedures haven't been quite followed. Everything happens too fast. The hasty character of the trial leaves doubt as to the complete accuracy of the verdict. And it is now *the nature of the error committed* that becomes uncertain, in spite of the overwhelming character of the "evidence." One wonders, finally, whether the

---

21. Except, of course, to the "Great Other" constituted by the sponsor, the publisher, the series editor. But there is always a way to fool him, or to act in connivance with him (they often share the same doxa). The subservience toward this "Great Other," found so frequently, does not contradict—on the contrary—the unconscious scorn for the author and the public.

punishment meted out was not based on almost mechanical criteria. And indeed mechanicalness is the greatest danger facing all translation analysis, as we shall see later with the Tel Aviv school. We now understand, even if we don't share their hostility, why many prominent translators whose ideas are, in the end, close to Meschonnic's own reject his writing outright.

The translation critic who, like me, feels some unease at the virulence of these analyses should keep in mind these lines by Derrida, even if, here again, he does not embrace them: "When quoting the existing translation [of Celan], I would first like to express my great debt and to pay homage to those who took the responsibility or the risk to translate.... In general I have refrained from translating, and especially from retranslating. I did not want to appear to be trying, however slightly, to amend a first attempt. In the proximity of such texts, lessons or polemics have no place" (115–16).

Descriptive Socio-critical Analyses (Toury, Brisset)

All the analyses that we have mentioned up to now are what the translation specialists whom I am going to present call "source oriented," that is, focused on the original texts. The goal of the description and characterization of a translation is to establish (hence the tendency to evaluate, positively or negatively) whether it has "rendered" the original well and whether or not it has rendered it on the basis of an explicit or implicit concept of translation. They are thus, except for the analyses inserted into literary history studies, tendentially prescriptive.[22] In contrast, the so-called Tel Aviv school, founded by Even-Zohar, is currently represented most prominently by Gideon Toury, a translator and the author of a very interesting work titled *In Search of a Theory of Translation*, and by those who, mostly in Belgium (Lambert et al.) and in Canada (Annie Brisset), follow or develop their point of view and are *target oriented*. From the outset, they want to avoid analyzing translations with a prescriptive frame of mind, and they want to study in a neutral, objective, and "scientific" way what they call "translated literature," which is an integral part of the literary "polysystem" of a culture or a nation. The phenomenon of "translation" must be apprehended through the study of the "translated literature" in its empiricity, without being led by the presuppositions of linguists or philosophers. To analyze a translation is no longer

---

22. Translation "theories" share the common trait of being prescriptive, normative, even when they claim to remain neutral and objective.

to judge it and is no longer only to study the system of transformations it constitutes. Rather, this study, done with rigor, with all the resources of linguistics and textual analysis (semiotics, as Toury says), must proceed to an examination of the socio-historical, cultural, and ideological conditions that made a translation what it is (similarly, the representations of translation that support or accompany the act of translation during each era must be subjected to the same approach). Here Toury does not speak of conditions or of factors but uses the term "norm":

> Like any other behavioral activity, translation is necessarily subject to *constraints* of various types and degrees. A special status among these constraints is enjoyed by *norms*—those inter-subjective factors which are the "translation" of general values or ideas, shared by a certain social group, as to what is right and wrong, appropriate and inappropriate into specific performance-instructions which are applicable to specific situations, provided that these instructions are not yet formulated as laws.... Thus, *translational* norms may be said to serve as a *model*, in accordance with which texts are selected for translation, and translations are actually formed and formulated. (141)

Among these "translational" norms, we find what Toury calls "the initial norm":

> Before turning to discuss the implications of the translator's commitment to the operational norms for his translation, I would like to introduce one additional concept which, for the time being, I shall call, for lack of a better label, the *"initial norm."* This most important notion is a useful means to denote the translator's basic choice between two polar alternatives deriving from the two major constituents of the "value" in literary translation mentioned earlier: he subjects himself either to the original text, with its textual relations and the norms expressed by it and contained in it, or to the linguistic and literary norms active in TL [target language] and in the target literary polysystem, or a certain section of it. (54)

It is easy to see that this initial norm, which places all translators in front of a forced disjunctive, is but the reformulation of the old dilemma so clearly formulated by Humboldt: "Every translator must invariably meet one of the two following hurdles: he will stay too close to the original, at the expense of the taste and the language of his people, or to the originality of his people, at the expense of the work to be translated" (qtd. in Berman, *L'épreuve de l'étranger* 9).[23] Thus, with Toury, translation analysis stops being *source oriented* (i.e., basically evaluative) and is based on an explicit methodology and theory: "An indispensable prerequisite for the analysis of translated texts (and consequently also for a systematic study of translational norms) is therefore the development of a theoretically based and explicit method for the comparison of one translation and its original, taking into account general linguistic and literary theories (including some theory of the literary text) and involving complete and accurate systematic descriptions of SL [source language], TL [target language] and the two respective literary polysystems" (58).

In his book, Toury analyses the Hebrew translations of a famous German children's book, *Max und Moritz* by Wilhelm Busch, from the nineteenth century to the present (140–51). Even for someone who does not know Busch or German or Hebrew, this analysis is quite instructive. For it places the various Hebrew translations in the *complex whole of interactions between languages and cultures,* which constitutes their historical space and makes them what they are.[24] The analysis explains the idiosyncrasies of each translation, the canonicity of some that, in this specific case, involve the use of a third language (Russian) playing for Hebrew the role of *langue-de-formation* (language of training) in its evolution toward a "modern" language. Far from being bound to local comparisons, Toury's analysis is globalizing, and the translation examples given fit into this globality. The result is extremely interesting and puzzling: here is a socio-historical analysis that does not judge, that also shows the reasons for the transformations made by the Hebrew translators of *Max und Moritz* (they vary according to the period and are also a function of the tendency to adapt that is characteristic of children's book translations). The "why" of these transformations, as you may have

---

23. [Letter to Schlegel, July 23, 1796. *The Experience of the Foreign* ix. Trans. Note]

24. This is similar, in a certain way, to the program for a history of translation that I proposed in *The Experience of the Foreign* "showing how in each period, or in each given historical setting, the practice of translation is *articulated* in relation to the practice of literature, of languages, and of the several intercultural and interlinguistic exchanges.... To write the history of translation is to patiently rediscover the infinitely complex and disconcerting cultural network in which translation is caught up in each period or in different settings" (2–3). [Modified translation of *The Experience of the Foreign*. Trans. Note]

guessed, are those "norms," in this case, the norms specific to Jewish culture in the nineteenth and twentieth centuries. These norms force the translator to make transformations at all levels if he wants his work to be accepted. The "transformation system" presented by any translation is thus the result of the internalization of these norms, which indeed the translator doesn't apply as if they were external directives. In turn, the content of translation norms can vary according to the demands of the receptor literary and cultural polysystem. If Toury considers that generally translation norms prescribe the *adaptation*, the *naturalization* of foreign works, it is possible that during specific periods, in specific cultures, and so forth, these norms prescribe the opposite: that would be the case of romantic Germany, for instance, if *The Experience of the Foreign* were to be rewritten in Toury's style.

To analyze a translation without going back to the system of norms that shaped it, then to judge it on this basis, is thus absurd and unjust, since the translation *could not* be otherwise, and since, as an act of translation, it only had *meaning* insofar as it was an operation subjected to these norms. Vialatte could not translate "as it was" the spare writing of Kafka because he was obeying, unconsciously, certain anesthetizing norms of the French polysystem and did so independently of his personal taste in this regard. When G.-A. Goldschmidt and Lortholary retranslate Kafka today, each in his own way, they do it according to the new norms that govern the French literary polysystem. In thirty years, Kafka may be retranslated according to other norms that are not yet known.

This theory of translation analysis seems as self-evident as the sociological concept of norms that it uses. It is applicable, as I have just shown, to any example. Before taking up the advantages and dangers of such an easy applicability, it is important to stress that Toury, in his eagerness to arrive at a scientific, or even functional, traductology, built schemata or laws that not only are questionable historically but also contradict his own sense of history. Moreover, these schemata reveal that, with regard to the role of "translated literature," the Tel Aviv school shares uncritically the current prejudices concerning translation's "secondariness." The axiom common to all historians of literatures, that is, that translated literature is important but secondary, is here, astonishingly, transformed into a *law*. The result is, as usual, the negation of the creative and autonomous role of translation in Western history, which for me amounts to saying that, like all functional theories, this translation school, despite its sociologizing historicism, is blind to the uniqueness of history. In his book, Toury adopts the assertions of his teacher Even-Zohar about the "peripheral" or "epigonic" character of translated literature in the French polysystem:

> In principle, as well as in practice, translated literature—including translated *children*'s literature—can occupy any position and serve any function in the target literature. However, it is a fairly safe hypothesis that its "normal" position tends to be *secondary* . . . [cf. Even-Zohar 124], that is, that it "constitutes a peripheral system within the [target literary] polysystem, generally assuming the character of epigonic writing. In other words, . . . it has no influence on major processes and is modeled according to norms already conventionally established by an already dominant type. Translated literature in this case becomes a major factor of conservatism." . . . [Even-Zohar 122]. This is so because the conditions in which translated literature tends to assume a *primary* position and to "participate actively in *modeling the centre* of the [target] polysystem" [Even-Zohar 120] . . . require that the latter be *weak,* and "in the long run no system can remain in a constant state of weakness" . . . [Even-Zohar 124]: it either gets stronger, or gradually passes away. (142)

Here again, the assertions seem self-evident. But the whole of Western history shows the opposite, even during the period in which ethnocentric translation dominates (the seventeenth and eighteenth centuries). The whole schema periphery/center needs to be revised. The fact that translation has always had a problematic status within the center does not mean that it is at the periphery. Translated literature is neither at the periphery nor at the center; it has been and remains that without which no indigenous literature can exist in the space of *colinguism* (see Balibar 75–81) constituted by the West.

From the law that he has just stated, Toury infers another law, which turns out to be equally false or rather shows that, in the history of translation, there is no law:

> Usually—that is, when translated literature occupies a secondary position—the first and foremost aim is acceptability in the target system (or part of it). This preference for acceptability is usually "translated" into the translator's subjecting his decisions and solutions to the norms which draw on what has already become institutionalized in the target pole, with

an almost automatically lessened extent of heed to the source's textual relationships. On the other hand, in the rarer cases when translation does occupy a primary position in the target polysystem, the translator feels free to deviate from the target-oriented norms, which often finds its expression in greater approximation to the reconstruction of the features of the source text, that is, to aim for adequacy, at the cost of a growing incompatibility of the resulting translated text and the norms governing the acceptability of texts (or even of translations) in the target literary and/or linguistic system. (142)

The assertion that translated literature occupies a secondary position, and that the translator submits to norms of "acceptability," may be true on occasion. But in the case of sixteenth-century France, we have an inverted relation: translation clearly occupies the center of the polysystem (see Naïs), which does not prevent most translations of that period from going in the direction of acceptability.

All this seems to take us away from the analysis of translations but in fact leads us back to it: for the members of this translation movement, translated literature is going to be systematically considered a phenomenon that is mostly secondary and expected to conform to norms that are completely *external* to it. And consequently, translation analyses will be limited to the search for these norms and to the study of their ascendancy over translators and translations—hence a growing mechanization, which is probably not intended by Toury, but which is displayed in full light when comparatists analyze translation on the basis of his ideas.[25]

There is a more serious problem. If, as a result of "translational norms" (which, in fact, are not norms specific *to* translation, but norms valid for all writing practices and beyond, such as French classical *bon goût* [good taste]), Madame Dacier could not have translated Homer differently from the way she did, *the question of the truth of her translation cannot, must not, even be asked.* The same is true for the bowdlerized translations of Dostoyevsky in France at the end of the nineteenth century, and so forth. But if indeed it may seem absurd or useless to judge Madame Dacier—even

---

25. During an international comparative literature conference at the Sorbonne in August 1985, most papers on translation were norm oriented. Comparatists had found a safe conceptual and methodological mine in order to integrate translations into their field of study, something they should have done long ago.

though romantic Germany did so and believed that classical France had *not translated* ancient authors—the case becomes even more difficult for those translations of Dostoyevsky, which are closer to our time. In the end, there is something resembling confusion here: after the translations of Chateaubriand, Baudelaire, Leconte de Lisle, Mallarmé, and so forth, the translations of Dostoyevsky can only be described as adaptations, introductions (in Meschonnic's sense), not as translations or even "first" translations (Berman, "La traduction," 116–17).

What is lacking here, and what is buried under the analysis of norms, is a general theory of literary transfer, of the passage of a work from one language culture to another.[26] The transfer in question has its forms and its moments: a foreign work is read, for instance, in France or becomes known there; it is noticed, and perhaps even integrated into a corpus of foreign literary texts that are taught without being translated; it can be published as an "adaptation" if it clashes too much with the native literary "norms." Then comes the time of a courageous introduction without literary pretension (generally aimed at those who are studying the work). Then comes the time of the first translations with a literary ambition, which are generally partial and, as we know, the most defective; then it is followed by (multiple) retranslations and, after that, by the translation of the whole *œuvre*. This process is accompanied, supported, by a whole body of critical work. Then comes, or may come, a canonical translation that will stand out and sometimes stop the cycle of retranslations for a long time.

The literary transfer-translation has been realized in its major phases, which, of course, can be arranged in different ways according to the works,

---

26. Literary transfer [*la translation*] is itself only one form of transfer among the whole space of translations that Western space since Greece has been, as is shown in the two related medieval expressions *translatio studii* and *translatio imperii*. All *transfers* are linked and support each other. Thus there would be reason to construct a vast history reflecting this translational space, a long-term collective task. And, more radically, this study of translational space would rest on *a history of migrations*, and a theory of human beings as *migrating-being* (migration founds *transfer-translation*) and, in this, as *mutating-being* (any migration is a mutation, as the fundamental phenomenon of the colony shows). Naturally there are other translational spaces, and a fortiori migrating spaces besides the West. For instance, there is the space of the Far East (see Octavio Paz, *Lecture et contemplation*).

In all these spaces, insofar as there is written matter, translation—which we can also define as a transfer-translation, a migration, and a mutation—plays a primary part. It would be necessary to examine whether each of these spaces, and it is quite likely, has its own specificity, and to ask why the Western translational system has become global.

the domains of the works, the periods, and the receptor language cultures. One can easily see that the sense of this transfer-translation is the "revelation" of a foreign *œuvre* in its very essence to the receptor culture. *The full revelation of this work is itself the work of translation and of translation alone.* And this revelation is possible only if the translation is "true." Before this occurs, there is no revelation; there are only steps leading (or not leading) to it. The concept of translated literature clouds the issue because it confuses literary transfer-translation with the essential moment of transfer-translation constituted by translation. For the Tel Aviv school, translation is whatever presents itself, names itself, as such. This is why, quite logically, Toury includes "pseudo translations" (such as Voltaire's *Candide*) in translated literature. If there is no reason to bring up the question of truth about all the forms of literary transfer-translation, there is good reason to bring up the question about translation, and then, to do it in a differentiated way, or you cannot judge in the same way a first translation and a retranslation, a partial or a complete translation, and the like. By ignoring these necessary differences and interpreting the literary *translatio* phenomenon as a process of *integration* into the literary polysystem of a culture, Toury is led to make very serious errors. First, translated foreign literatures are not generally integrated into a native literature, except for great translations, and by virtue of nongeneralizable specificities: Luther's Bible, the Authorized Version [in English in the text], Amyot's Plutarch, Galland's *Mille et une nuits* [*Arabian Nights*], and Schlegel's Shakespeare. They remain "foreign literatures" even if they mark the native literature. Leyris's Hopkins, as wonderful as it may be, is not a French poem but an English one, even if its high poeticality makes it a "true" poem in French. There is not even any need for a translation to be good for it to influence the receptor culture (as in the case of Dostoyevsky influencing Gide, the case of Kafka, etc.).

Translated literature is thus not integrated into native literature, as bookstore sections show us. It forms a *separate,* autonomous domain, in which pre-translations, introductions, and all the kinds of translation mentioned coexist helter-skelter. But if we interpret *translatio* in terms of integration (naturalization), we are led to see in it only a process of adaptation, in which the literary norms of the receptor culture naturally prevail, and in which the rule of acceptability reigns. Because they are all too "strange," Shakespeare, Dostoyevsky, and Kafka must be adapted to be accepted. Hence the second negative consequence: the question of truth reappears (it is impossible *not* to ask it), but in the following form: *the "true" translation is the translation that is adequate at a specific moment*, et cetera, adequate not in its relation to the source text (*source oriented* [in English in the text]), but in relation to the target culture (*target oriented* [in English in the text]). The "true" translation is the one that is acceptable, the one that transmits and integrates the foreign work into the receptor polysystem.

We can see the bewildering consequence of this line of reasoning: the translator's agency is now determined not by the desire to "reveal" in the full sense of the term the foreign work (an autonomous desire that only obeys, among many limitations, what du Bellay called "the law of translation" [211–12]), but by the (relative) state of openness or closure of the receptor culture. If this culture demands translations that are rather source oriented, there will be translations of this kind, and the translators will submit, consciously or not, to this injunction; if it demands target-oriented translations, the opposite will be true. There again, the schema seems self-evident, but it negates any autonomy of translation, and, in fact, it negates the whole history of translation in the West. If translators, from Saint Jerome on, had only worried about obeying norms, translation would never have been in the West this "primary" (not "secondary" or "peripheral") shaper of languages, literatures, and cultures that it has been and still is. It is quite true that translators have had to and still have to compromise with these norms (as can be seen in Luther or Amyot), or that they have even adopted some of them (Schlegel wanted a Shakespeare both faithful to the original and germanized, *integrated,* that is the word, into German literature, but for him this integration presupposed faithfulness). However, these translators never lost sight of the autonomous truth of their task.

Toury must have realized the unforeseen reactionary character of his initial theses (to justify the existing reductive modes of translation or even to encourage them), since he wrote an article, which I have not been able to read, titled "The Translator as a Nonconformist-to-be, or: How to Train Translators so as to Violate Translational Norms."[27] In reality, the Tel Aviv school fluctuates between two concepts of translation, the concepts that Toury describes when he speaks of an "initial norm." Toury cannot help but think that "true" translation is the first one, translation that is source oriented; but

---

27. Needless to say, many translators have never needed to be taught this. But it is true that many could really use it.

because the Tel Aviv theorists' field of study and of analysis is target-oriented translation, that is, literary *translatio* interpreted as a normed integration, they are led to give greater importance to "real" translation, the most common one statistically, that is, translation/adaptation, and to construct their analyses on this basis.

An important point remains. As we shall see, it is an essential one for the orientation of translation analyses: the place of the "translating subject" in this school of thought.

The dominance of functionalism, even in an enriched version, prevents, in my opinion, any reflection about the translating subject, which Brisset nonetheless keeps calling for (*Sociocritique* 251–57). This subject appears in her book only as a "relay of the norms of the social discourse and of the institution that establishes them and sanctions them" (199).

However, the very notion of subject, whatever interpretation we give to the word, supposes both the notion of *individuation* (every subject is this subject right here; it is unique), of *reflection* (every subject is a "oneself" [*soi*], a being that relates to "oneself" [*soi-même*]), and of *freedom* (every subject is responsible). This notion of subject also applies to the translating psyche. Admittedly, becoming a simple relay is one of its possible states. And if many translators are but "relay[s] of the norms of the social discourse," it is always a choice, even if this choice is not quite conscious. Because he is *responsible* for his work, the translator can and must be judged: a translation is always *individual*, always a translation by . . . , because it proceeds from an individuality, even one subjected to "norms." A translator who conforms completely to norms only proves that he *decided* to make them his own, admittedly most often in the barely conscious shadows of his psyche. The concept of internalization used by Toury and Brisset may have a socio-psychological value, but it does not have much to say about the subjectivity of the translating subject.

There is even more of a choice because any translator knows, a priori, so to speak, that there is—as du Bellay and Peletier called it in the sixteenth century—a "law of translation" (Jacques Peletier [du Mans], qtd. in Horguelin 64) that is entirely independent of "social discourses," a Law in the strongest sense of the word, which, in this case, the translator is not free to modify. He who submits to this Law is a translator. Perrot d'Ablancourt, who took many liberties with the originals and proclaimed that he did so loud and clear, wrote about his version of Lucian's works: "It is not translation strictly speaking; it is worth more than translation" (Horguelin 94).

There may be something "more" than translation, but there is "proper" translation, and Perrot knows it. Nonetheless, the content of the law of translation cannot be reduced to what du Bellay or anyone else says about it. It cannot be expressed in dogmatic and absolute terms because any formulation that we could give of it would remain marked by elements of our doxa, would remain relative. This relativity is why there is no definition of translation any more than there is one for poetry, theater, and so forth. And yet there is an "idea" of translation, of poetry, of theater that, albeit indefinable, is neither imaginary nor empty nor abstract but, on the contrary, quite rich in content: translation is always "more" than translation, ad infinitum. *The only way to gain access to this wealth of contents is through history.* Far from bringing the proof that translation is a changing, relative thing without identity or borders, history, from one period to the next, reveals to us the disconcerting richness of translation and of its Idea. The so-called variations of the very notion of translation at various times may thus be read as preferential manifestations of one of the contents of this Idea, or of several of them. Translation does not appear in the Middle Ages as it does during the Renaissance. *Translatio* is not *traductio*. But both are actualizations, manifestations of *La traduction*.[28]

For the translator, the history of translation is thus something that one must inevitably know, although not necessarily in the manner of a historian.[29] A translator without historical consciousness is a crippled translator, a prisoner of his representation of translation and of those carried by the social discourses of the moment. Similarly, a translator who retranslates a work already translated many times had better know the history of its translations,

---

28. The various essential words with which, in the West, linguistic and cultural spaces have "named" translation—*translation* in English; *traduction, traducción, tradução*, and *traduzione* in romance languages; *Übersetzen* in German (and *Übertragung*)—also constitute differential manifestations of the idea of translation. Each of these words, *translation, traduction*, and *Übersetzung*, has its own significance; even it is an equivalent in current exchanges or in dictionaries. Each is "untranslatable." Each actualizes specific contents of the Idea in a determined configuration. This is why there was a constitution of translation traditions specific to the affected linguistic and cultural spheres, which of course are not closed unto themselves but keep intersecting throughout history without losing their identities. See my article "De la translation à la traduction."

29. Valery Larbaud is the best example of a translator who never stopped "traveling in the history of translation" in a way that was characteristic of his own personality and of his figure as translator. One must reread *Sous l'invocation de saint Jérôme* to realize how well he knew this history and its most obscure figures.

either to fit into a tradition or to be inspired by one of the translations from this tradition[30] or to break away from it.

To summarize before moving on to my conception of translation analyses, let me say that, in spite of the strong criticisms I have just made of the functionalist school, I don't deny its great positive contribution. Between an analysis that is too militant in Meschonnic's style and an analysis that is too functionalist, too sociological in Toury's or Brisset's style, there is room for another discourse that, far from being opposed polemically to the first two, would be able to gain its autonomy while doing them justice. The critical analyses of Meschonnic (and of all those who produce analyses of the same kind, that is, evaluations of translations based on a detailed examination of the original and a source-oriented concept of translation[31]) seem to be the natural continuation of this suspicious attitude of the "simple" reader of translations, whom Masson describes so well ("Territoire de Babel" 157–60). Even when they are conceptually well equipped, these analyses question the translations and the translators—an essential characteristic.

Toury's and Brisset's analyses obviously *suspend* the natural attitude of the reader of translations, since they advocate a complete neutrality of judgment. But two consequences follow. First, the translated text is *objectified*, transformed into an object of knowledge; it is no longer something

---

30. In his introduction to his translation of Sappho, *Poèmes et fragments,* Philippe Brunet strikingly writes: "From the scanned translation of Catullus by André Markowicz... and toward the measured versions of Belleau and Baïf, which are rhythmic but meant to be sung, one could inscribe the project to retranslate the Sapphic poem, then the whole of Sappho according to the same principle. One wished one could have given the whole of these translations, be they old, modern, measured, rhymed, if only to give back to Sappho's book the movement that is its own and to reestablish every new phase of translation, a possible image of a possible image of the text, in its fragility" (23). This translator is a notable example of a historical consciousness and of a retranslation full of conviviality.

31. As Steiner does in *After Babel.* In chapter 5, which is not the most interesting, there are remarkable micro-analyses of translations of Shakespeare, Supervielle, and Hopkins, and they are "positive" analyses. Unfortunately, Steiner almost never lingers on a translation but always moves from one to the other, leaving the reader with a brilliant trail of remarks, often profound but never developed, never "exploited." Efim Etkind also offers extremely interesting analyses of poetic translations that are written (in the case of his critical stance) in a highly entertaining polemical style. Unlike Steiner's analyses, these are full analyses of poems and of their translations. One may not agree with many of Etkind's assertions; one may have a very different interpretation of the "crisis" of the poetic tradition. Nonetheless, in many places this book is quite stimulating and is an example of a translation evaluation that is expeditious but convincing in its form.

one questions in order to criticize or praise. Secondly, as we have seen, the translation is in all cases *justified* since the analysis itself shows that it could not be other than what it was. One supposes that the followers of this school realize, at least deep down, the properly untenable character, from every point of view, of such a neutrality. Even someone like Derrida, who refuses to choose between Broda and du Bouchet, knows on which side the most "faithful" translation is. He simply does not want to get involved in "Parisian" quarrels. He is certainly not neutral. In translation, one cannot, one should not, be neutral. Neutrality is not the corrective to dogmatism.

But if being neutral means being objective, and if being objective means being scientific, and if any true neutrality is impossible in translation, isn't the contemporary project of a science of translation called into question? There is here an ambiguity that must quickly be dispelled. "Science of translation" can mean a rigorous discursive and conceptual knowledge of translation and translations, which attempts to achieve its own scientificity. But it can also mean endeavoring to constitute a positivist and pseudo-scientific knowledge of translation, borrowing slavishly and uncritically from the procedures of the "exact" sciences. In the twentieth century, all the great names in the human sciences seem to have felt, at one point or another, this temptation (here again Barthes is typical, but we could mention at random Lévi-Strauss, Braudel, Lacan, etc.). Their works show that they have always been able to go beyond this temptation and found scientific discourses that are rigorous but specific to their disciplines, scientific discourses that are also *critical discourses,* and thus not neutral. History, sociology (see the work of Alain Touraine), and ethnology are not neutral. *These are non-ideological critical sciences.* Such must be "the science of translation," whatever its orientation, methodology, basic concepts, and so forth.

TOWARD A METHOD

I will now attempt to draw the architectonics of a translation analysis that will take into account the forms developed by Meschonnic and the Tel Aviv school, develop a methodology and concepts (at least partially original), and parallel the Benjaminian concept of translation criticism, which I mentioned above. I will present the most developed and the most exhaustive form of this architectonics, which, in fact, might prove to be a book rather than an article. However, of course, the maximal form presented here can be modulated according to the specific objectives of each analyst and adapted to all standardized text types (article, paper, essay, monograph, survey, dissertation, etc.). Actually, my purpose is not to present a model but a possible analytical path.

My analytical path will be divided into successive stages (a move that corresponds to the concept of method). The first steps relate to the preliminary work, in other words, the actual *reading* of the translation (or, as the case may be, of the translations) and of the original (not to mention the many parallel readings that come to support these two readings). The following steps involve the fundamental moments of the critical act itself as it will appear in written form. This second part will also present the basic categories that structure this criticism and that differ from both Meschonnic's categories and those of the functionalist school.

The form of this kind of analysis gradually took shape for me as I was "practicing" individual studies of translations, trying to specify (and systematize) their procedures. The first steps owe much to my work as a literary translator, in particular to the difficult translation of Roberto Arlt's *Los siete locos* into French (*Les sept fous*), which I coauthored with Isabelle Berman. It was while reading and rereading, together and on our own, the successive versions of this translation, and while going back and forth between these versions and the original in about the order that will be described below, that we learned something not at all obvious: *we learned how to read a translation.*[32]

Translation Reading and Rereading

To a distrustful and finicky eye, and to a purely neutral and objective approach, let us oppose a *receptive gaze* that places only limited trust in the translated text. Such is, and such will be, the fundamental gesture of the critical act: to suspend any hasty judgment, and to embark on a long, patient activity of reading and rereading the translation(s) *while completely setting aside the original text.* The first reading still remains, inevitably, that of a foreign work in French. The second reading reads the translation as a translation, which implies a *conversion* of perspective. For, as I have already stated, one is not born a reader of translations, but made one.

---

32. The proposed path is thus a generalization based on several personal paths. Its concrete forms will vary according to the analysts, the translations, the originals in question, and so forth.

To set the original aside, to resist the urge to compare, this is a point that cannot be emphasized enough. It is only through this reading of the translation that we can sense whether the translated text "stands." "To stand" has a double meaning: to stand as a written text in the receptor language, in other words, primarily, not to be outside the written norms of this language,[33] and to stand, beyond this basic requirement, as a real text (i.e., something that has a systematic, correlative, and organic character in all its constituent parts). What the reading or rereading may or may not reveal is the translation's degree of *immanent consistency* outside any relation to the original, as well as its degree of *immanent life:* there are translations—and the reviewers of literary magazine are quite aware of this but then leave it at that—that are "cold," "stiff," "spirited," "lively," and so forth.

This rereading also inevitably uncovers problematic "textual zones," zones in which defectiveness can be glimpsed: the translated text seems suddenly to weaken, to be discordant, to lose its rhythm; or, on the contrary, it seems too easy, too fluent, too impersonally "French"; or it even abruptly displays words, turns of phrase, collocations that clash; or, lastly, it is overrun by fashionable expressions, turns of phrase that echo the language of the original and that reveal the phenomenon of contamination (what is called "interference").

Inversely, the rereading also, but not always, brings to light textual zones I would describe as miraculous in that we find not only obviously accomplished passages but also writing that is *writing of translation,* writing that no French writer could have written, a foreigner's writing harmoniously moved into French without any friction (or if there is a friction, a beneficial one).[34] These textual zones, in which the translator has *foreign-written* in French and thus has produced a new French, are zones full of grace and rich-

---

33. That is, quite simply, to be "well written" in the most elementary sense. Many translations with a large distribution do not meet this criterion. For example, Hannah Arendt's essay *On Revolution,* published in French as *Essai sur la révolution* in the Gallimard paperback collection, is almost impossible to read because of its defective and floundering syntax, whereas Arendt is known for the clarity, fluidity, and evenness of her style. Here the translated text does not "stand" and the reader notices this right away. However, this translation of an important book is disseminated without ever having been criticized, and this is quite typical.

34. In his introduction to the anthology *49+1 nouveaux poètes américains,* Emmanuel Hocquart writes: "I sometimes read American poetry in English. But reading it in French is my true pleasure. That is when I really 'suddenly see something.' My satisfaction could then be expressed in the following terms: no French poet would have ever written this. . . . I value the idea that translation is the kind of representation I need to see better and understand better (in) my own language" (Hocquart and Royet-Journoud 10).

ness in translated text, full of *felicity*. For instance, when reading Hopkins's *Naufrage du Deutschland* (*The Wreck of the Deutschland*) or other poems by him translated by Michel Leyris, we feel both the long labor that translation has been and the felicity that it has finally become.

I must insist on the importance of these "impressions": they, and they alone, will orient my subsequent work, which, itself, will be analytical. To let oneself be overcome, shaped, by these impressions is to give a solid ground to the criticism to come. Of course, one must not leave it at that, for not only may impressions be false, but many translations are misleading and thus produce false impressions.[35]

We have read and reread the translation; we have formed an impression (or an impression has taken form in us). We must now turn or return to the original.

The Readings of the Original[36]

This reading and rereading of the original also sets aside the translation. But it does not forget these textual zones in which the translation sometimes seems to be problematic, sometimes felicitous. It reads and rereads them, underlines them, to prepare for the upcoming confrontation.

Moving from a simple cursory reading, the reading of the original quickly becomes a textual pre-analysis; that is, it locates all the stylistic characteristics, whatever they may be, that *individuate* the writing and the language of the original[37] and that constitute a network of systematic correlations. Here it is not necessary to try to be exhaustive; this reading is concerned with locating types of sentences; types of propositional sequencing; and types of usage of adjectives, adverbs, tense, prepositions, and so forth. This reading, of course,

---

35. But perhaps this occurs on a different level. When a reviewer in an article speaks about a translation that is brilliant, elegant, and so on, there is reason to be cautious: often these are translations that "seduce" to hide their defectivity or their ethnocentrism. But there are also translations that deserve these qualifiers, mostly because they are also true of the original.

36. These readings, like the previous reading, cannot be separate from parallel readings: the reading of an author's other works, the reading of the translator's other translations, critical readings, informative readings, and so forth. But it seems to me that these parallel readings must occur slightly after these first two essential readings. There must first be an *intimacy* with both the translated text and the original, without too much mediation.

37. See Ricœur: "Style is labor that individuates, that is that produces an individual [*de l'individuel*]" (*Du texte à l'action* 109). [From *Text to Action* (82). *De l'individuel* means "individual matter," "individuality." Trans. Note]

detects recurring words, key words (see Gresset).³⁸ On a more global scale, it seeks to identify the relation in the work that ties writing to language, the rhythmic patterns that carry the text in its totality. *Here the critic does the same work of reading that the translator did, or is supposed to have done, before and during the translation.*

It is the same work, and yet not quite the same, because the reading done by the translator is, as I stressed in *The Experience of the Foreign*,³⁹ already a pre-translation, a reading done within the horizon of translation, and all the individuating characteristics of the text that I have mentioned are discovered as much within the movement of the act of translation as *before*. It is in this movement that translation has its own autonomous *criticisme*. Most certainly, this *criticisme* cannot be simply based on the encounter between the translator and the text. It must turn to numerous parallel readings, other works by the same author, various studies about this author and about his times, and the like. Chateaubriand said that in order to retranslate *Paradise Lost*, he surrounded himself with "all the disquisitions of scholiasts" (120). When retranslating the *Odyssey* and underlining its often formulaic style, Jaccottet referred to studies by German specialists of Homer (postface 411). To translate Hopkins and to understand his notion of "inscape," Leyris read Gilson's book on Duns Scot. For his recent translation of Pindar, Savignac read the poet's French and German translations as well as the studies of major modern scholars of ancient Greek culture.

Generally speaking, translating requires numerous and various readings. An ignorant translator—that is, one who does not read in this way—is a deficient translator. One translates with books.⁴⁰ I call this necessary recourse to readings (and to other "tools" in the sense Illich gives to the term) the

---

38. Identifying these characteristics involves identifying all the metaphorical networks, which are often neglected by the translator. As Sylviane Garnerone, quoted in Gresset, states quite well, "If the translator doesn't 'go after' [Faulkner's] various metaphorical networks ... he cannot hope to communicate the symbolic structure of the whole which is buttressed by the metaphorical networks" (509). The metaphorical networks are not the only ones; there are networks of signifiers, terms, concepts, and Gresset adds to these various identifications intertextual elements (reference to another work by the same author) and hypertextual elements (reference to works by other authors). Of course.

39. In this note from *The Experience of the Foreign* (248–49), the concept of hermeneutic is understood in a sense that is too restrictive, too tied to romantic hermeneutics only (Schleiermacher).

40. And not only with dictionaries.

support of the act of translation. This notion is related to, but not identical to, that of supporting the translation itself.[41]

The fact that the act of translation must be supported in no way detracts from its fundamental autonomy. Here I mean, first, that the readings done by the translator are not restricted but free.[42] No textual analysis, in particular, not even the one done by a translator capable of conducting one, can constitute the *inevitable* basis of the work of translation—as it is sometimes thought, and as it was naively thought several years ago with Vinay and Darbelnet—that translation is an "applied linguistics." The most perceptive textual analysis, even the kind whose goal is to discover "translemes,"[43] is and can only be one among other supports of translation.

In general, we must categorically refuse, especially now that the teaching of literary translation has begun, any *infeudation* of translation to any conceptual discourse that would, directly or indirectly, tell translation "what to do." This applies to textual analysis, poetics, linguistics, but also (if not to say especially) to the various kinds of "traductologies." These traductologies should develop their discourse on translation without in any way claiming to regulate translation practice. It should be noted that these traductologies are intended (in principle) for non-translators as much as for translators.

---

41. The support of the translation includes all the paratexts that come to its support: introduction, preface, postface, notes, glossaries, and so forth. The translation cannot be "bare" or it runs the risk of not achieving the literary transfer. Today the translation supports proposed by the classical period, then by the philological period (the nineteenth century), are no longer sufficient. They must be rethought—and they are by some translators. The issue of these new supports, and of a new consensus about them, is extremely important.

42. "And now back to Yeats again, to 'The Sorrow of Love,' where he says of the girl with 'red mournful lips' that she is 'doomed like Odysseus and the labouring ships.'... I translated "labouring" with qui *boitent / au loin*.... For these words did not come to me by the short circuiting that people think of as running from text to translation by way of the translator. They came by a more roundabout route that took in my own past.... With Verlaine at the back of my mind, I sketched out a kind of poem... a poem I've never since completed—and which, twelve years later, on an impulse, I tore up to give life to my translation" (Bonnefoy, "Translating Poetry" 186–92).

43. See Annie Brisset: "I call *transleme* a translation unit with semiotic characteristics, because it is a *unit-system* composed of elements that are significantly interdependent.... A transleme is a *network of relations* that unites, in a semantic relationship, a set of elements belonging either to the level of form or of content" ("Poésie" 263). Brisset adds about the "overcoded" character of the poetic text: "The translation of a poetic text necessarily originates in a *hierarchization of the translemes* within a translating program." This hierarchization, in the concrete practice of the translator, is founded, as we shall see, on a translation project.

Consequently there should be a reciprocal relation of non-infeudation between one and the other (i.e., translation does not depend on traductology any more than traductology is simply an explication of the work of translation, but there is a reciprocal autonomy between the two).

I call *pre-analysis* the reading made by the translation critic because it is done only in order to prepare for the confrontation. Like the translator's reading, the critic's reading cannot avoid the cycle of readings already mentioned. These readings are more connected, more systematic, than those of the translator, but they are not subordinated to specific types of analyses either, except that, like Meschonnic, Toury, and Brisset, I consider what linguistics, poetics, structural analysis, and stylistics have revealed about language, literary works, and texts in the twentieth century an *unumgänglich* [*incontournable*][44] of the critical task. Not, let me repeat, in the sense that these sciences, these bodies of knowledge, would constitute constraining bases, but in the sense that our approach to language, to texts, to literary works is marked by what they teach us.[45] The translation critic is more bound to these "sciences" than the translator, since the critic must produce a rigorous conceptual discourse.

This pre-analysis and the readings that accompany it will lead to a patient labor consisting of selecting pertinent and significant stylistic examples (broadly speaking) in the original. The rigor of the confrontation—except in the case of a short text where "everything" is analyzed—must, of necessity, depend on examples. Their selection is a delicate and essential moment.

What is selected, extracted here from an interpretation of the literary work (which will vary depending upon the analyst), are those passages of the original that are, so to speak, the places where the work condenses, represents, signifies, or symbolizes itself. These passages are signifying zones where a literary work reaches its own purpose (not necessarily that of the author) and its own center of gravity. Writing here has a high degree of necessity. These passages are not

---

44. The word *incontournable*, which is quite fashionable in France at the moment and considered pedantic by some people, was used for the first time in a significant way some thirty years ago when André Préau translated Heidegger's term *unumgänglich* in his translation of *Vorträge und Aufsätze* [in French, *Essais et conférences*]. Heidegger used it to say that History was the *incontournable* [inevitability] of historical science, and Nature the *incontournable* of physics. That dimension is a given and, for those sciences, one that is by definition inexhaustible. Since that time, the word has slowly begun to be used among Heideggerians, of course, and lately, in all circles in France, political and media circles included. But it is an old word, one that came from translation and from a worthy translator.

45. Who would read a myth as it was read *before* Lévi-Strauss?

necessarily visible during a simple reading, and this is why, most often, they are revealed or their existence is confirmed through the interpretive work. In a poem, it may be one or a few lines; in a novel, selected passages; in a collection of short stories, the final sentence of the last story (as in James Joyce's *Dubliners*[46]); in a play, one or two lines that, all at once, give us the meaning of the whole work in a precise and dazzling way; in an essay, sentences that, all of a sudden, in their structure, attest most closely to the movement and struggle of the thought.[47] Unlike traditional "selected passages" in anthologies, these are not always the most beautiful, aesthetically speaking. But whether they are beautiful or not, they all reveal the signifiance in a writing that has, I must say it again, the highest possible degree of necessity. All the other parts of the work are marked, in various degrees, and whatever their formal perfection may be, by a *random quality*, in the sense that, because they do not possess this absolute scriptural necessity, they could always have been written differently. This applies even to the most outwardly perfect poem; witness the abundance of drafts, versions, states, variants of a text throughout literature. The final work is complete, definitive, but it always keeps a trace of this gestation, this experimentation phase from which it branched off toward its final shape. Thus, whatever the final degree of systematicity or unity displayed by a literary work, by essence it includes aleatory parts. If the proportion of aleatory elements is too great, or rather, if the weight of the aleatory overcomes that of the necessary, the literary work is affected by it; one sometimes feels this is the case with parts of Baudelaire's *Les fleurs du mal*. Inversely, if the proportion of the necessary (inasmuch as it can be intended) greatly prevails over what is aleatory, the work is threatened by a sort of monological formalism, as in the case of Flaubert or Valéry. The random has its own necessity in the economy of the literary work.

This "dialectic" of the necessary and the aleatory (which must not be confused with the distinction, itself necessary and aleatory, between the "marked" and the "unmarked") is crucial for the critic and the translator. As Gérard Genette has stated, "the intangibility of poetry is a 'modern idea' that it is time to shake up a bit" (*Palimpsests* 455).

---

46. "His soul swooned slowly as he heard the snow falling faintly through the universe and faintly falling, like the descent of their last end, upon all the living and the dead" (224).

47. See, for example, the first two paragraphs of the introduction in Gérard Granel, *L'équivoque ontologique*.

Genette mentions in a footnote on the same page that the idea of the intangibility of the poetic text or, by extension, of the literary text is linked to the notion of untranslatability, another dogma, not specifically modern, but constantly reaffirmed nowadays by poets and theorists like Jakobson. The coexistence of intangible and tangible elements in the literary work is of great importance for the translator; it specifies as much as, or even more than, the presence of "marked" and "unmarked" elements, the space of his possible freedom. Inversely, the confusion between the "marked" and the "unmarked," between the necessary and the aleatory, annihilates any freedom the translator may have and leads to a disastrous literalism (particularly syntactic literalism).

To summarize: before the concrete analysis of the translated text, the following must be done:

- A textual pre-analysis that identifies a number of fundamental stylistic traits of the original
- An interpretation of the work allowing the selection of its signifying passages

We have delved into the translated text; we have identified its weak and strong zones; we have analyzed and interpreted the original and gathered an exhaustive, reasoned, and representative corpus of examples. Are we ready for the confrontation? Absolutely not! We may know the stylistic system of the original, but we know nothing about the system of the translation. We have indeed felt that the translation has a system since it seems to stand (here obviously I am only speaking of this case), but we have no idea of the why, the how, or the logic of this system. If we initiate fleeting comparisons between the work and its translation, for instance in the case of a bilingual book of poems, we may see, right away, a global correspondence, but also choices, gaps, various changes that, without being shocking, do surprise us: one wonders why "this" was rendered by "that," whereas. . . .

The person who reads the version of Emily Dickinson published by Claire Malroux or the translation of Yeats by Jean-Yves Masson inevitably wonders about the reason behind various permutations, clarifications, deletions of a connector, and the like, without calling into question the obvious quality of these translations. The reader thinks about the "reasons" explaining thousands of small "divergences," which together seem to define the idiosyncrasy of the translation. This questioning gets a new impetus when the reader compares these translations of Yeats and Dickinson to, for example, those by Bonnefoy and Reumaun: there are even more divergences, but different ones! It is so because each translator has his own system, his own coherence, his way to "diverge," to "space" [*espacer*],[48] in Joachim du Bellay's words. In order to understand the logic of the translated text, we must go back to the *translating work* itself and, beyond that, to the *translator*.

In Search of the Translator

Going to the translator is an essential methodological turning point that is all the more essential, as we saw above, since one of the tasks of a hermeneutics of translation is to consider the translating subject. Thus, when dealing with a translation, we must firmly ask, "Who is the translator?" After all, when faced with a literary work, we relentlessly ask, "Who is the author?" But these two questions do not really have the same content. The question about the author concerns the biographical, psychological, existential elements meant to illuminate his work. Even if we wanted to limit the importance of these elements within the framework of a structural and immanent analysis, no one would deny that it is difficult to apprehend the work of authors like du Bellay, Rousseau, Hölderlin, Balzac, Proust, or Celan if we don't know anything about the lives of these authors. Work and life are linked.

The purpose of the question "Who is the translator?" is different. Apart from a few exceptions like Saint Jerome and Armand Robin,[49] the translator's life is not our concern, and neither are his moods. Nonetheless, it is becoming increasingly unthinkable for the translator to remain the total stranger he is most of the time. We need to know whether he is French or foreign, whether he is "only" a translator or if he has another significant professional activity, such as teaching (as is the case of many literary translators in France). In addition, we want to know whether he is also a writer and if he has produced literary works, from what languages he translates, what relationships he has

---

48. [This word has been translated as "to expatiate" or "to stray," but neither term actually renders the sense of *espacer* at the time du Bellay used it, that is, to order by leaving a specific space between things, or separate by means of a space, in particular letters, words, or lines. Trans. Note]

49. In addition to being the focus of the classic work by Valery Larbaud, Saint Jerome was the subject of a picturesque novel by Quebecois writer Jean Marcel, *Jérôme ou de la traduction*. [Armand Robin (1912–61) is a French poet and translator who translated from many (twenty-two) languages. Trans. Note]

with these works, if he is bilingual and of what kind, what types of works he usually translates and what other works he has translated, if he translates several authors (the most frequent case) or one author (like Claire Cayron). We want to know what his linguistic and literary domains are, whether he has produced a body of translation as defined earlier, and what his major translations are. We want to know if he has written articles, studies, dissertations, monographs about the works he has translated and, finally, if he has written about his own practice as a translator, about the principles that guide it, about his translations and translation in general.[50]

This is already quite a lot, but it may only be pure "information." We must go further and determine his translating stance, his translation project, and his translating horizon.

The Translating Position

Every translator has a specific relationship to his own activity, a certain conception or perception of translation, of its meaning, its purpose, its forms and modes. Conception and perception are not purely personal, since the translator is indeed marked by a whole historical, social, literary, and ideological discourse on translation (and on the writing of literature). The translating position is, so to speak, the compromise between the way in which the translator, as a subject caught by the *translation drive*,[51] perceives the task of translation, and the way in which he has internalized the surrounding discourse on translation (the norms). The translating position, as compromise, is the result of an *elaboration*: it is the self-positioning of the translator vis-à-vis translation, a self-positioning that, once chosen (for it is, in fact, a choice) *binds* the translator, in the sense given by the philosopher Alain when he said that character is an oath.

---

50. The list could go on: Has he also translated with other translators? How? and so forth.

51. In a letter to A. W. Schlegel, November 30, 1797, Novalis uses the expression *Übersetzungstrieb*, "translation drive" or "impulse to translate," about German. This is a striking expression, which we must read from the significations that Trieb has deployed throughout the history of German language, literature, and thought, but also—inevitably—from the meaning that Freud gave it, and then the Lacanian interpretation of Freud. It is the *drive to translate* that makes the translator a translator: what pushes him to translation, what pushes him in the space of translation. This drive may arise of its own or be awakened by another person. What is this drive? What is its specificity? We don't know yet, as we don't have yet a theory of the translating subject. We only know that it is at the base of every *destiny* of translation. [Novalis, *Briefe und Dokumente* (367). Trans. Note]

The translating position is not easy to express and doesn't need to be expressed, but it can be articulated, indicated, and transformed into *representations*. However, these representations do not always express the truth of the translation position, especially when they appear in strongly coded texts like prefaces or conventional speaking situations like interviews. Here the translator tends to give voice to the doxa and to impersonal topoi about translation.

It is through the elaboration of a translating position that the subjectivity of the translator is constituted and acquires its own signifying depth, which is always threatened by three major dangers: chameleon-like shapelessness, capricious freedom, and the temptation to be self-effacing. There is no translator without a translating position. But there are as many translating positions as there are translators. These positions can be reconstituted from the translations themselves, which express them implicitly, and from the various statements that the translator has made about his translations, about translating, or about any other themes. These positions are also linked to the *language position* of the translators: their relation to foreign languages and to the mother tongue, their being-in-languages (which takes on many different empirical forms but which is always a *specific being-in-languages,* distinct from other being-in-languages that are not concerned with translation), and they are linked to the translators' *scriptural position* (their relation to writing and to literary works). A theory of the translating subject will be possible only when we are able to consider together the translator's translating position, language position, and scriptural position.

The Translation Project

In a paper I presented during the day-long session dedicated to Freud at the ATLAS[52] in 1988, I attempted for the first time to define the concept of a translation project:[53]

> In a successful translation, the union of autonomy and heteronomy can only result from what could be called a translation project, a project that doesn't necessarily have to be theoretical.... The translator can determine a priori

---

52. Assises de la Traduction Littéraire en Arles. [Annual literary translators' conference in Arles, Provence. Trans. Note]

53. This term was initially borrowed from Daniel Gouadec, who uses it in the context of specialized translation.

what degree of autonomy or heteronomy he will give to his translation, and he can do so on the basis of a pre-analysis. I use the word pre-analysis because one has never really analyzed a text before translating it. ("Observations sur la traduction" 114)

Every consistent translation is carried by a project, or an articulated purpose. The project or aspiration is determined both by the translating position and the specific demands of each work to be translated. They don't need to be expressed discursively or, a fortiori, to be theorized. The project defines the way in which the translator is going to realize the literary transfer[54] and to take charge of the translation itself, to choose a "mode" of translation, a translation "style." Let us consider the case of the translators who decided to introduce the poetic works of Kathleen Raine in France. They could have chosen one of several options: to do an anthology of Raine's poems based on her different collections or to provide the collections themselves, in whole or in part. They chose to translate several of these collections in their entirety.[55] Then, they could have proposed a monolingual (French only) or bilingual edition. They chose the latter. Finally they could have presented a "bare" edition without paratextual matter (introduction, etc.) or one with paratexts. They chose the second option. This is their project of literary transfer. So our study of their translations—and only ours, since the translators don't mention their translation work in the paratexts—reveals their chosen mode of translation, their style of translating, which is the second aspect of their project.

The forms of a translation project when it is expressed by the translators are multiple. Let us consider the translation of Shakespeare's works over the last forty years; Michel Leyris's project is stated rather briefly,[56] while Yves Bonnefoy's is presented at length and linked to a "certain idea of translation" ("L'idée de la traduction"). Déprats' project is not only thoroughly and clearly described (as was his Freud translation for the Presses Universitaires de France), but also theorized as a global project that includes the mode of translation and a reflection on the translation of dramatic works, the transla-

---

54. [The author uses the French word *translation*, which means transfer, as opposed to the English meaning of translation. Trans. Note]
55. Kathleen Raine, *Sur un rivage désert, Isis errante*, and *Le premier jour*.
56. "Pourquoi retraduire Shakespeare," "Une posture," and "Confessions de traducteurs." Leyris's introduction to *Macbeth* does not mention translation.

tion of Shakespeare in particular, and the types of paratexts that will support the translated texts (140–44).

Here the critic sees an *absolute circle,* not a vicious one: he must read the translation on the basis of its project, but the truth of this project is, in the end, accessible only based on the translation itself and on the type of literary transfer that it achieves. For everything that a translator can say and write about his project becomes a reality only in the translation. And yet the translation is never more than the realization of the project: it goes *where* and *up to the limits* of where the project leads it. It tells us the truth of the project only by revealing to us *how* it was carried out (and not whether, in the end, it has been carried out) and what the *consequences* of the project in relation to the original were.

Thus it is impossible to say, "Project A seems good, but let's look at the results!"[57] because these results are only the outcome of the project. If the translation doesn't "stand," it is the fault of the project alone, or of a specific aspect of the project.

Under these conditions the critic must still enter the circle and go all the way around it.

These statements may only shock those who confuse *project* (and perhaps the term is misleading) with the notion of *theoretical project* or *a priori schema.* Quite obviously, a project that is completely laid out and fixed becomes, or runs the risk of becoming, rigid and dogmatic. Thus the increasingly accepted—and not without good reasons—"rule" according to which a *marked* word in the original must *always* be rendered by the same word in the translated text, whatever the context may be, a rule that tradition did not know, quite to the contrary (Aulotte, "Jacques Amyot"), such a rule can become rigid. Certainly, when Georg Trakl uses the adjective *leise* [softly] in his poems, it must always be translated with the same word, because, for him, it is a fundamental adjective. The same goes for *gerne* [willingly][58] in Hölderlin or *because* in Faulkner (Gresset, "Le 'parce que'"). A foreign translator would have the same imperative for the adjective *vaste* [vast] in Baudelaire. But this rule cannot be generalized. The rule, to my mind, ceases to be absolutely valid when, because of aleatory or stereotyped elements that

---

57. For Bernard Lortholary's response to my paper at the Freud session during the ATLAS meeting, see *Cinquièmes assises de la traduction littéraire.*

58. [Actually, German-English translation experts point out that *gerne* cannot be translated directly. Trans. Note]

are found in any text, a key word momentarily loses its *marked* character. Such is the case for the words *Wunsch* and *wünschen* in a text by Freud.

Consider the French version in the standard translation published by Presses Universitaires de France of the sentence "S'agissant de telles fructueuses difficultés, le cas de maladie à décrire ici ne laisse rien à souhaiter" (Freud, *Œuvres* 13:8).[59] The end of the French sentence "ne laisse rien à désirer" corresponds to the German "nichts *zu wünschen* [my emphasis] übrig." As *wünschen* [to wish], like *Wunsch* [wish], is a key term in Freud, the translators decided to translate it here as "ne laissait rien à souhaiter" [didn't leave anything to be wished for] instead of the French collocation "ne laissait rien à désirer" [didn't leave anything to be desired]. Not only is it jarring when you read it, but it seems to me that here *wünschen*, as taken in a collocation, has lost its significance and that it must thus be rendered by *désirer* [to be desired] even if, in the same text by Freud, there are many marked occurrences of *Wunsch* or *wünschen*.

Let me make a last comment about the translation project: its existence does not contradict the immediate, intuitive character of translation that is often mentioned. Indeed, the *intuitivity* of translation is steeped in reflexivity. What Hölderlin said about the poet also applies to the translator: his sensitivity must be entirely organized. The German translator of Latin American literature Meyer Clason once told me that he was a *Bauchübersetzer*, a translator who translates with his guts. That is what every translator must be if he wants his translation to wrench our guts.[60] But Meyer Clason, who had translated *Grande sertão: Veredes* by Guimarães Rosa, a work itself marked by a mix of popular orality and reflexivity, knew quite well that his work had required (from him) a great deal of reflection, which he presented in an article that was anything but naive.

The Horizon of the Translator

The translating position and the translation project are in turn caught in a *horizon*. I borrow the term and concept from modern hermeneutics. Devel-

---

59. ["With such fruitful difficulties, the case of the illness to be described here does not leave anything to be desired." Trans. Note]

60. George Belmont used to tell the story of a friend's cook, a peasant woman from the Savoy mountains. During a soirée given by his friend, an Irish poet read aloud his translation of one of Belmont's poems. After listening, the cook said: "I don't understand it, but it must be beautiful because it's making thunder in my guts" (183).

oped in philosophy by Husserl and Heidegger, this concept was developed more concretely and epistemologically by H. G. Gadamer and Paul Ricœur, then, for literary hermeneutics, in an extremely fruitful way by Hans Robert Jauss.[61] It is this form that proves particularly helpful for a hermeneutics of translation.

In a preliminary description, the horizon can be defined as the set of linguistic, literary, cultural, and historical parameters that "determine" the ways of feeling, acting, and thinking of the translator. I use "determine" in quotation marks because I am not speaking of simple determinations in the sense of conditionings, whether they are thought of in structural or causal terms. For example, when Philippe Brunet retranslated Sappho in 1991, the horizon of his retranslation, *the place from which* he retranslated Sappho, is specified in a plurality of horizons that are more or less co-articulated. First, there is the "state" of contemporary French lyric poetry. There is also the knowledge about Greek lyric poetry and, more generally, about Greek culture that is accumulating today, particularly in France, and that is quite different from the knowledge of previous centuries. This knowledge itself testifies to a different relation to ancient Greece and to ancient Greco-Roman civilization in general. It is impossible not to notice that this retranslation takes place at a time when, in France, the number of historical studies about Greek and Roman poets is increasing; when there is also an increase in translations and retranslations of Greek and Roman poets; when the texts of the great "classics" of antiquity (Seneca, Cicero, Plini, Ovid, Plutarch, etc.) are appearing in a special edition.[62] All this taken together shows a deepening movement of our culture toward ancient Greece and Rome—the meaning of which we do not yet know—and thus, to use Jauss's expression (see *Pour une herméneutique littéraire* 366), testifies to the existence of a certain "horizon of expectations" by a certain French public turning/returning to the Greek and Roman "thing."

There is also the relation of contemporary French lyric poetry (with all the "matrices" or patterns it offers the translator) to its own tradition (rejection, distance, integration, continuity, break, etc.). This relation alone allows, or does not allow, the translator to possibly turn to former forms of lyric poetry in order to retranslate Sappho.

61. In particular, in *Pour une herméneutique littéraire*, see 25–26. Jauss even described the history of the concept of horizon. [This edition is composed of selections from Jauss, *Ästhetische Erfahrung* (1:660–71). Trans. Note]
62. Albeit with questionable presuppositions and processes.

Then, there are all the existing translations of Sappho in France since the sixteenth century. Whether or not the translator chooses to read them, he belongs to a tradition, which makes him a retranslator, with everything that this position implies.

Finally (but is this list really exhaustive?), there is the state of current discussions in France and even elsewhere in the West about the translation of poetry and of translation in general.

It is easy to see that all these parameters constitute the necessary horizon of the translator of Sappho and that this horizon is itself plural.

The notion of horizon has a double nature. On one hand, referring to the place from which the action of the translator has meaning and can unfold, it points to the open space of this action. On the other hand, it refers to what closes, what encloses, the translator in a circle of limited possibilities.[63] In French, common usage confirms this, when people speak, in the first sense, of a life "with no horizon" (without opening, without perspective), and in the second sense, of someone with a "limited horizon."

With the concept of horizon, I want to move away from the reduction of the translator to the role of a "relay" in functionalism and structuralism, which are completely determined socio-ideologically and which, moreover, reduce the real to an interlocking sequence of laws and systems.[64] Here, following Ricœur and Jauss, I am speaking of *horizon*, of *experience*, of *world*, of *action*, of *de-contextualization* and *re-contextualization*, all fundamental concepts of modern hermeneutics that are closely correlated and that, at least for the first four, have the same duality: these concepts are both objective and subjective, positive and negative, and they point toward a finitude and an infinitude. These are obviously not "functional" concepts, in the sense that they don't lend themselves well to the construction of formal models or analysis, but in my opinion, they enable us to better grasp the translative dimension in its immanent life and its various dialectics.

---

63. Here theater plays its role and stirs up noteworthy retranslations; for example, Bruno Bayen, a director, writer, and translator, translated *Oedipus at Colonus* and directed *Euripidis* at Ariane Mnouchkine's Théâtre du Soleil in a very thoughtful translation by Mayotte and Jean Bollack. See Bayen, *Œdipe à Colone*. In this sense, J.-C. Bailly is right to say: "The horizon is the closure" (*Le paradis du sens* 79).

64. However, I don't deny the existence of these determinations and the value of the analyses that examine them. More generally, I don't dispute what Michel Foucault once said: "Everything may be thought of within the order of the system, the rule, and the norm" [*The Order of Things* 360. Trans. Note].

This admitted recourse to modern hermeneutics, which is simultaneously a reflection on poetics, ethics, history, and politics,[65] seems justified to me insofar as the fundamental lines of our theory of translation are poetics, ethics, and history; that is, at a specific point of its trajectory, the autonomous development of our translation research meets hermeneutics, which has not concerned itself specifically with questions of translation—except, to a limited extent, with Gadamer (Berman, "La traduction et ses discours" 16).

When relying on this approach, we must avoid doing "philosophy" of translation and being wholly limited by its problematics. No more than literary hermeneutics, translation hermeneutics is not a subcategory of philosophical hermeneutics, which in turn is only an intellectual trend in the modern philosophical Babel. There are other philosophical trends concerned with translation: I mention in no particular order Benjamin, Heidegger, Derrida, Serres, Quine, Wittgenstein (in fact, no modern philosophy can really escape the encounter with translation). Moreover, there is the reflection of psychoanalysis on translation and the being-in-languages, which has been constant since Freud himself.[66] Then, there is the considerable work of linguistics[67] on translation and, although less developed, that of ethnology (Malinowski, Clastres, and many others).

---

65. This is not the place to discuss in detail the link (itself historical) between translation and politics in the broad sense of the term: in the Arabic and Christian Middle Ages and during the Renaissance, the constitution of nation-states was supported by real "translation policies." Such is the case today, although in a different way. For a discussion of these policies in Europe and their possible development, see my article "Les systèmes d'aide publique à la traduction en Europe."

66. Here we can mention the studies or comments of Lacan, Laplanche, Bettelheim, Granoff, Allouch and the journal *Littoral*, Bernard Thys, German García, and so forth. Psychoanalytic writings on translation range from reflections on the "problems" linked to the translation of Freud (and more recently to the translation of Lacan) to more radical questioning about the translating act itself and the human being-in-languages. This psychoanalytic *thought* about translation is not *transferable*, in that it can only be the work of psychoanalysts. I must mention in passing that my *Experience of the Foreign* has found attentive readers among psychoanalysts.

67. In my article "La traduction et ses discours," I underestimated the contribution of linguistics to traductological reflection (83–95). The article displays a certain "anti-linguistic" prejudice, perhaps caused by the fame (excessive fame, in my mind) of Georges Mounin's *Les problèmes théoriques de la traduction*, a work that is certainly worthy but not central (even in Mounin's corpus). I now think that when rightly interrogated, linguistics can give us invaluable elements for a rigorous reflection on translation, as in Benveniste, for example. More generally, I hold that translation hermeneutics is not the only discourse on translation that would hold its truth, and also that the translation dimension concerns all the bodies of knowledge and disciplines, and that they have the right to deal with it. It is thus important to study, listen to, and accept

The third phase of our trajectory is now defined and is articulated in three stages:

- Study of the translating position
- Study of the translation project
- Study of the translation horizon

These three stages do not follow each other in a linear way. If the analysis of the horizon is generally preliminary, that of the translating position and of the project cannot be easily separated. And the analysis of the project, by virtue of the circle mentioned earlier, consists of two phases:

- A first analysis based both on the reading of the translation(s), which provides an X-ray of the project, and on everything the translator may have said in various texts (prefaces, afterwords, articles, and interviews, about translation or not, for everything here is a clue), when they exist. Actually, if you look closely, you find that the translator expresses himself on translation, but sometimes his words must be interpreted. Complete silence is rare.
- The comparative work itself, which is by definition an analysis of the translation, of the original, and of the modes of implementation of the project. The truth (and the validity) of the project is thus measured both *in itself and in its result*.

THE ANALYSIS OF THE TRANSLATION

We have undoubtedly arrived at the concrete and critical phase in the criticism of translations: the well-founded confrontation (well founded in the sense that we have secured a series of *bases* for the confrontation) between the original and its translation.

---

what these bodies of knowledge and disciplines tell us about translation. I would even say that it is indispensable. Also traductology, be it hermeneutic, functionalist, and so forth, is the only discourse to speak *solely* about the translation dimension. Thus, on one side, we have various non-traductological discourses dealing with translation from their vantage points, and, on the other, a set of discourses, called *traductology, translatology, science of translation* [in English in the text], *Übersetzungswissenschaft*, often heterogeneous, but that only deal with translation.

Forms of the Analysis

The form of the analysis may vary according to whether we are dealing with *one* translation (*a* poem, *a* short story) or the translation of a *group* of works (a collection of poems, etc.) or the *entire production* of a translator. In all cases, *whole bodies of works*—not isolated, limited excerpts—are analyzed. In fact, the three possibilities cannot easily be distinguished, since the analysis of *a* single translation by *a* translator can hardly be achieved without an examination of his other translations. What happens is that in each case it is the center of gravity of criticism that shifts.

The form of the analysis varies also depending on whether the analysis focuses on one translation by a translator (according to the three modes already mentioned) or involves comparative studies of other translations of the same work. For instance, there are studies of the German translations of Baudelaire's *Les fleurs du mal* (George, Benjamin, etc.). The basic methodology may remain the same, but the final form of the analysis changes. But this is only a hypothetical case. More importantly, even if one essentially considers only a single translation of a work, it is always fruitful also to compare it to other translations when they exist. The translation analysis then becomes an analysis of a retranslation, and it is almost always the case. At least it constitutes its most productive form by virtue of the fact that the analysis of a "first" translation is only, and can only be, a limited analysis. Why? Because every first translation, as Derrida suggests in the note mentioned above, is imperfect and, so to speak, impure. It is imperfect because translation defectiveness and the impact of "norms" appear often heavily, and it is impure because it is both an introduction and a translation. This is why every "first" translation calls for a retranslation (which does not always come to be). It is in retranslation, better yet, in successive or simultaneous retranslations, that translation is played out, not only within the space of the receptor language and culture, but in other languages and cultures. In other words, the horizon of a French retranslation has three dimensions:

- Previous translations into French
- French contemporary translations
- Foreign translations

It is not unusual for a translator to consult foreign translations in order to translate a work, even for the first time, in his own language. It is even enough for him to know, even by hearsay, that the work has already been translated somewhere, for the nature of his work to change. He is not the first one. I have encountered these two situations: when translating *Yo el supremo* by Roa Bastos, I consulted the (preceding) German translation, while for the translation of Schleiermacher's "Methoden des Übersetzens"[68] ("Des différentes méthodes du traduire"), V. García Yebra's Spanish version proved quite useful. As for the *Sept fous* by Roberto Arlt, I knew of Italian and German versions done well before ours. I came "after." *Actually, one may consider every translation that comes after another, even if it is a foreign one, to be ipso facto a retranslation, which means that there are many more retranslations than first translations!*

It follows that an analysis of translation is almost always an analysis of retranslation, which, while focusing on a specific work of translation, also "summons" other translations and often *must* even do so: it is hard to imagine that a study of Kafka's *Trial* by Goldschmidt could be accomplished without any reference to the previous translation by Alexandre Vialatte.

The appearance of other translations in the analysis of a translation also has a pedagogical value. The "solutions" brought by each translator to the translation of a work (which depend on their respective projects) are so varied, so unexpected, that they introduce us, during the analysis, and almost without any other comment, to a dual *plural* dimension: that of translation, which is always that of translation*s* in the plural, and that of the work itself, which also exists in the mode of an infinite plurality. Through the work of analysis, the reader or listener is thus freed from any naïveté or dogmatism. Pedagogically speaking, this plurality of translations of the same text is stimulating: in spite of the numerous versions of Shakespeare's *Sonnets*, I too can (re)translate them. Many retranslations appear suddenly after a translator reads a translation, particularly in poetry.

Finally, the specific form of the criticism will vary depending on the types of works translated, on the specific works in question, and so forth.

The Confrontation

In principle, the confrontation takes place in a four-fold mode. First, there is a confrontation between the selected elements and passages in the original and the rendering of the elements and corresponding passages in the translation.

---

68. [In English, "On the Different Methods of Translation." Trans. Note]

Secondly, there is an inverse confrontation between the textual zones of the translation found to be problematic or accomplished and the corresponding textual zones of the original. Obviously these two confrontations should not be juxtaposed mechanically like the pieces of a puzzle.

Third, there is a confrontation—within the first two—with other translations (in most cases). Fourth, there is also the confrontation between the translation and its project, which reveals the ultimate "how" of its realization, linked, in the final analysis, to the translator's subjectivity and his innermost choices: almost identical projects will always lead to different translations. This confrontation also reveals, as I said earlier, the consequences of the project: what it has "yielded."

This last confrontation cannot point out any discordance between the project and its realization, or, if a discordance is noticed, the confrontation must determine its nature, its forms, and its cause. Most often, when one thinks one has discovered such a discordance, it is because one has not completely analyzed the project and its consequences, which can easily happen when the project has to be reconstituted hypothetically.

But what can appear as discordant, a gap between the project and the translation, is the defectiveness inherent in the act of translation. Whatever the logic and coherence of a project may be, whatever the project is, there is, there will always be, some defectiveness in a translation. The absence of a translation project may unleash all the forms of defectiveness, but the existence of a project is no guarantee against defectiveness.

What may also appear discordant is the coexistence of contradictory parts in a project. However, these can only be latent or local contradictions; otherwise, there is incoherence and thus an absence of project; by definition, a project implies coherence.

Since *defectiveness operates* at the ultimate level of specific *choices* and more generally at the level of a local contact with the original (hence there are always a few questionable final choices, errors, mistranslations, omissions, slips of the pen, etc.), there is never any reason to relate discordances to the project, but to the subjectivity of the translator.

Other (minor) discordances may result from translation choices that momentarily violate the project because they follow different laws. This case is not rare and often involves the interference of the discourse of the doxa, from which no translator can totally escape, for instance, when the translator starts to clarify, explain, gallicize unnecessarily. In short, it is the *finitude* of the translator that explains the discordances in relation to the project. But it can only be a matter of limited discordances, although they may be numerous.

The Style of the Confrontation

As a labor of writing, the confrontation must face the problem of its communicability, that is, of its readability. Reading a number of translation analyses reveals that the confrontation is fraught with numerous perils:

- High reliance on technical terminology (use of non-explicated terms from linguistics, semiotics, etc.)
- Intrusion of the original text language or that of a foreign translation alluded to
- Dense, fastidious, thus potentially stifling analysis
- Specialized, isolated analysis that seems to be limited to a comparison without opening onto larger questions

The terminological technicality, which may be found in Meschonnic as well as in Toury and Brisset, implies a reduction of communicability while guaranteeing, in those specific cases, a greater rigor in the discourse. The "technicality" of a critical text is not a negative trait, with its apparatus of concepts and often of terms that are new or drawn from a great variety of disciplines. It has its justification, but it nonetheless threatens the fundamental purpose of criticism, which is to open a text to multiple audiences who cannot be assumed to be either too broad or reduced to a handful of *the happy few* [in English in the text]. It is logical that the gesture of opening should be also open. The translation analyst will therefore have to *explicitate* in one way or another, and as much as possible, his terminology and his concepts to de-hermetize his discourse (except when the context and circumstances would suggest otherwise). But, after all, this is only a detail.

The second danger faced by translation analysis at this stage is more serious: it is *the danger of the irruption, both massive and fragmented, of the original language into its discourse.* This language cannot be assumed to be known by the reader or by all the readers. The critic must assume, even if this is not empirically true, that his first reader is the reader of the translation, the very person who, in most cases, reads the translation because he could not read the original in the source language. For the analysis to be both open and fruitful for the reader, the introduction of fragments from the original must therefore be accompanied by a number of explicitating procedures. Here, the purpose of "retranslations," if they exist, would not be so much to correct (i.e., to provide a better "solution," as Meschonnic does), but to make the foreign text resonate *prosaically*.[69] "Key" foreign terms, which are often untranslatable, like the English term *self*,[70] the Spanish *goce* [joy], or the German *Sehnsucht* [longing], must be explicated, and explicating a fundamental word from another language (that is, deploying all its signifiance) in one's own language is always possible (see Goldschmidt), even if this word has no *equivalent* (thus, no preestablished translation) in one's language.

The third peril that the analyst may encounter is that of his text's character— it may be dense, meticulous, both massive and fragmented, loose and tight—all things that may render it off-putting and, one could say, static, whereas the critic aims at leading the reader into a *constant and exciting* opening movement.[71] Not only must the reader be taken into the movement of the comparative analysis, but this movement must be for him transparent, rich, and always opened into the plurality of perspectives and horizons that constitutes the translating dimension itself. The dense, micro-level confrontation between fragments of the original and of the translation, as Meschonnic practices it, is indeed guided by a project and is in no way an arbitrary alignment of inconsequential remarks. Moreover, one could say that the denseness of this confrontation is counterbalanced by the frequent violence of the tone, which, if not amusing, as in Etkind's writings, at least shakes the reader up; but as soon as the confrontation becomes lengthy, as in the otherwise remarkable analysis of Humboldt's translation (Meschonnic, "Poétique d'un texte"), because of its inevitable heaviness, it creates a certain weariness in the reader. That weariness would not be that important if it did not often prevent rereading, the very act (Meschonnic says so in *La rime et la vie*[72]) through which we truly appropriate

---

69. That is what Etkind did.

70. In this regard, Ricœur notes that "French does not have any accurate term to translate the word 'self'" (*Le temps raconté* 234). I will go back to the term "self" in the second part of the chapter when discussing John Donne.

71. It may be the accumulation of quotes, foreign or not, that creates the impression of a mosaic that is both *dispersed and condensed at the same time*.

72. "Reading only starts with rereading. . . . As soon as one rereads, and as a possible difference steals into the first and second time, and into each of the other times a new difference, then reading itself begins to seem, through reading itself, like an act that has its own historicity, its own status distinct from that of its object" (Meschonnic, *La rime et al vie* 113).

a text. You must always try to write in such a way as to elicit in the reader the desire to reread your text.

In order for the movement of the analysis to be transparent, rich, and open to the plurality of questions[73] posed by the translating dimension, let me suggest three procedures that make the analysis an authentic labor of writing.

The first is clarity of presentation, to use Hölderlin's expression,[74] a clarity that does not imply any classicism but involves, for the critic, a certain number of concrete stylistic requirements and self-imposed interdictions (avoiding excessive use of jargon, of inflated syntactic forms, of ellipses—up to a point, or more precisely, up to the point at which these self-imposed interdictions do not damage the movement of the thought, its rigor, etc.).

The second procedure is the unceasing *reflexivity* of the discourse that "loosens" the encounter between original and translation and is realized foremost in the form of *digressivity*. To say that the analysis, when moving through specific examples, is reflexive means that it goes further than sticking the confronted texts side by side (in the sense of sticking close *to them* and sticking *them* together), and also that it always moves away from them to shed light at the proper distance, to look back on its own discourse and statements.

Third, the analysis takes the form of digressivity. This consists of unfolding—every time it proves necessary—from the consideration of a specific example a series of questions, perspectives, insights, and of thinking them through for some time, a time that must be measured.[75] To take an example that will be examined in the second part of this book, when French translators of John Donne translate the lines:

---

73. The translating dimension gives rise to a plurality of questions/answers dialectics that the analysis must take up, every time in a unique way. For the dialectic of questions and answers in literary space, see Jauss, *Pour une herméneutique littéraire* (39–101).

74. "Nous n'apprenons rien plus difficilement que le libre usage du rationnel. Et, je le crois, c'est justement la clarté de la présentation qui nous est originellement aussi naturelle qu'aux Grecs le feu du ciel" (Hölderlin, *Œuvres* 640). ["We learn nothing with more difficulty than to freely use the national. And, I believe that it is precisely the clarity of the presentation that is so natural to us as is the Greeks the fire from heaven" (letter to Casimir Ulrich Böhlendorff, December 4, 1804. *Sämtliche Werke* 425–26; *Essays and Letters on Theory* 149). The French text contains a typographical error (the "use of the rational" instead of "national" [from the German *Nationelle*]), but Berman meant to use "national" as he did in *L'épreuve de l'étranger*, where the quote is accurate. Actually, Berman uses the neologism "libre usage du nationel" to indicate that the word has a greater import than the standard "national" (86). Trans. Note]

75. Literature experiences forms of unmeasured digressivity that are sometimes intentional, sometimes nearly pathological, sometimes both at once, which make reading both captivating and stifling. Thomas de Quincey is an obvious example. See Éric Dayre, "Thomas de Quincey" (14–36).

> As souls unbodied, bodies uncloth'd must be,
> To taste whole joyes

as

> Il n'est qu'âmes sans chair et que chairs dévêtues
> Pour jouir pleinement

at least three questions arise about specific translation choices: rendering "body" as "chair" [flesh] when elsewhere Donne thematizes the difference between "body" and "flesh"; then rendering "to taste whole joyes" as "jouir pleinement" [to delight fully] when "joy" is a fundamental word in Donne's poetry, and even in Western poetry; and last, less visibly, rendering the negative words "unbodied"/"uncloth'd," which Donne uses in parallel, first with a weak privative expression like "sans" [without], then with a negative word, "dévêtues" [unclothed], without restituting the parallelism "unbodied"/"uncloth'd," and without thinking about the presence of this parallelism, about the frequency of negative terms in Donne (five in this poem), in English poetry, and in poetry in general, not to mention its importance in colloquial speech, in mysticism, and in philosophy, three domains to which Donne's poetry is tied. This reflection, in which the translators did not engage any more than they thought about "body" or "joy," must be the task of analysis if light is to be shed on the original passage for the reader: to make him appreciate the poetic "stakes" present in what may seem just a detail; to criticize in all fairness the translators' choices; and, as we shall see later, to open the horizon for other choices, other solutions, other translation projects.

At the same time, digressions allow the analysis to avoid being an *explication de texte*. Digressions ensure the analysis's *scriptural autonomy* (Abdelkebir Khatibi) and give it the character of a commentary, or what I will call *commentativity* (see Berman, "Critique, commentaire et traduction").

Along with reflexivity, digressivity, and commentativity, subjectivity plays a role in the analyst's transparent discourse. For he alone *decides* to leap into an excursus, certainly not without good reason, but also swept along by the digressive and commentative demon that dwells in every critic. Choosing concision or length is the prerogative of each critic, as is the decision of whether to use footnotes or not.

The Foundation of the Evaluation

The last problem facing the translation analyst is considerable, and it may seem surprising that I mention it only now. If, in order to be a real "criticism," the analysis must necessarily lead to an evaluation of the translator's work, following in this the readers' expectations and the nature of any reading of translation, will this evaluation, even if it is accompanied by all possible supporting examples, not simply reflect the ideas, the theories, or whatever one may call it, that the critic has about literature and translation? If this analysis is not to be neutral, how can it avoid being dogmatic, or at least avoid favoring a specific conception of translation?

I think that it is possible to base any evaluation on a *double criterion* that escapes this danger; that is, one that involves no other conception of translation than the one that today, and even in earlier times, is the subject of a fundamental, fairly widespread *consensus*—although never perfect and all too implicit—both among translators and among all people interested in translation. These criteria are of an *ethical* and *poetic* nature (poetic in the largest sense of the term).

The *poeticality* of a translation lies in the fact that the translator achieved a real textual work, that he *created a text* in a more or less close correspondence with the textuality of the original. That the translator must *always* create a text does not prejudge at all the *mode* or the *purpose* of the translation:[76] among the translation of Lucian by Perrot d'Ablancourt, a typical *Belle infidèle* translation, the translation of *Arabian Nights* by Galland, Baudelaire's Poe, Chateaubriand's translation of *Paradise Lost*, Leyris's Hopkins, Jaccottet's *Odyssey*, Klossowski's *Aeneid*, Robin's non-translated poetry, there is no common ground, apart from the fact that in all cases there is textual work (poetic work in the largest sense) and production of a true *creative work*. Even if the translator thinks that his work is but a pale reflection, an echo of the "real" work, he must always want to *create a text [faire œuvre]*.

Ethics lies in the respect, or rather, *in a certain respect for the original*. Jean-Yves Masson was able to define this ethics in a few convincing and compact lines, which are worth quoting: "The concepts resulting from a reflection on ethics can be applied to translation precisely because of a meditation on the

---

76. Here *purpose* refers to the global objective of the translation, for instance to appropriate, to gallicize, or to integrate Plutarch into French culture. The *mode* is the set of translation strategies deployed to obtain this result.

notion of *respect*. If the translation *respects* the original, it can and it even *must* enter into dialogue with the original, it must face it, and *stand up to* it. The dimension of respect does not include the self-abasement of the one who respects his own respect. The translated text is first of all an offering made to the original text" ("Territoire de Babel" 158; emphasis added).

In all the translations mentioned, the respect that can "face" the original text, that can "stand up to it" and thus be situated as an offering, is present, even in Perrot. But we know that for the translator, such respect is the most difficult thing to achieve. Masson points out the "prejudice" that consists in believing that to translate is "simply" to respect the alterity of the text, and that consequently implies both the "annihilation" of the translator and the "servile" attachment to the letter of the text.[77] But the ethics of translation is threatened by an inverse danger and a more widespread one at that: *non-truthfulness, deception*. These include all the forms of manipulation of the original that Meschonnic points out (but there are others), which all express the translator's deeply disrespectful attitude toward the original, and in the end also toward the readers. However, there is untruthfulness *only* insofar as the manipulations are silent, *unacknowledged*. Not saying what one is going to do, for instance, to adapt rather than to translate, or doing something other than what one has announced, is what caused the profession to be associated with the Italian saying *Traddutore traditore,* and that the critic must forcefully denounce. The translator has every right as soon as he is open. When Garneau says in his *Macbeth*, "J'saute du vers 38 au vers 47 parc'c'est mêlé mêlant"

---

77. Like the whole tradition, Dolet denounces this servility: "I want to mention the folly of other translators who, instead of freedom, subject themselves to servitude. They are so foolish that they attempt to render line by line or verse by verse. Through this mistake they often distort the meaning of the author whom they are translating and do not express the grace and perfection of either language. You will carefully avoid this vice, which demonstrates no other thing but the ignorance of the translator" (54).

The exacerbated literalism of some translations, like François Fédier's translation, shows how current this prejudice is, especially if it is confused with the defenses of "decentering," of translation as "relation," or as "experience of the foreign." The great merit of Jean-Yves Masson is that he describes in a few words the thin dividing line, an ethical line, not a poetic one. I can say so, as I have worked on the problem of literality and I have given up this term because of the insurmountable ambiguity it contains: whether we want it or not, "literality" means *word for word,* sentence for sentence, and implies a destructive attachment to this word for word, sentence for sentence. But at the same time, literality means an attachment to the letter, to the exact words, and a respect for the work's letter. Is it possible to completely give up a word that means both the most naive relation to a text and the most intimate one?

["I'm jumping from line 38 to 47 'cause it's so confusing"] (qtd. in Brisset, *Sociocritique* 207), there is no reason to consider the omission unacceptable; it is acknowledged and pulls his translation, in part, toward adaptation. When Yves Bonnefoy translates Yeats's "Sailing to Byzantium" as "Byzance, l'autre rive" ["Byzantium, the Other Shore"], for lack of something better, it sounds very much like . . . Bonnefoy. But there is no reason to say that he imposes his poetics on Yeats, since he has explained himself at length both about this (particular) point and about the translator's freedom (*Quarante-cinq poèmes* 7–31). Perrot d'Ablancourt did not hide at all his omissions, additions, embellishments, and the like: he frankly discussed them in his prefaces and his notes. When translating Novalis's *Fragments* in an explicating and gallicizing manner (in passing, let me mention that I find it unacceptable because of the translator's disrespect for the stylistics, conciseness, and mystical terminology of the poet), Armel Guerne at least openly mentioned this ("Introduction").

Consequently I have tried to specify the basis of a translation evaluation that is the widest, fairest, and the most consensual possible. The proposed criteria are valid for a traditional translation as well as for a modern one, and they imply no bias regarding the purpose or the modes of translation. Ethics and poeticality guarantee, first, that in one way or another, there is a correspondence to the original and to one's language. I use the word "correspondence" purposefully because of its rich polysemy and its indeterminacy as well. It is a fundamental existential and ontological signifier (see Baudelaire's "Correspondances"). It is also a concrete signifier: in French, when describing travel by train or metro, we speak of catching or missing the *correspondance* [connection]; in epistolary vocabulary, of "keeping up a correspondence"; and so forth. Translation must always "correspond" in the plurality of all these meanings.

Ethics and poeticality also guarantee that there is a creation in the translating language that broadens it, amplifies it, and enriches it, to assume the vocabulary of translation, at all levels, where need be. When saying this, I am not saying anything new (and I definitely don't want to): this *creation in correspondence* has always been considered the highest task of translation. Discussions about literalism or freedom, *source-oriented* or *target-oriented* [in English in the text] translation and translators, without being meaningless, remind me of what Foucault said about Marxism (something that seemed shocking at the time) in *The Order of Things*: "Their controversies may have stirred up a few waves and created a few surface ripples, but they are no more than storms in a children's wading pool" (262).

What is certain in any case is that these discussions can take place *only* on the ground of this consensual idea of translation. That is why there is no need to present a new conception of translation, not only because the "Idea" of translation was "bequeathed" to us in some way "once and for all," but because during each historical period, this "Idea" is embodied in a particular figure, which in turn determines entirely, or predominantly, our personal idea of translation. Today, this figure is the one shaped by German romanticism (Goethe, Humboldt, and Hölderlin), but it lost its external "romantic" characteristics long ago, and it has become the modern figure of translation. The translator of today can only situate himself in relation to this figure. He can reject it, that is, he can translate according to a previous figure, one from the classical period, for instance, Marguerite Yourcenar translating from ancient Greek (*La couronne et la lyre*), or even a figure from the Middle Ages (i.e., limiting oneself to the translation of meanings and terms, as is done in specialized translation). In all cases, consciously or not, the translator acts in relation to the modern figure of translation. He can do so: this freedom is also his right.

THE RECEPTION OF TRANSLATION

I will not dwell on this stage of criticism, which can be autonomous or integrated into other stages, depending on the situation. As with any study of the reception of a work, it is quite important, but not always possible in the case of translated works. For there is more of a reception of "foreign works" in printed media, that is, in the literary sections of daily newspapers, weeklies, literary journals and magazines, critical works about foreign authors, and so forth, than a reception of translations as such. One must first know if the translation has been noticed (concretely, if the fact that it is a translation, done by translator X, has been mentioned). If it has been noticed, one must know whether it was evaluated, analyzed; that is, one must see how it has appeared to critics and reviewers and, depending on this appearance, how it was judged and presented to the public. On the whole, translations are not a topic over which much ink is spilled, even if, in regard to the French press, things have somewhat improved over the last few years or, in any case, are evolving. Reviewers rarely venture to speak seriously about the work of translators. When they do speak about it, it is often to denounce them. Compliments, somewhat less frequent, are generally as poorly grounded, which means as little justified by reasons, as blame. When I analyzed Klossowski's *Énéide*, I met with one exception: the files of the publisher Gallimard consisted of more than forty articles and studies published in newspapers and magazines all over the Francophone world and even in Spain the very year the translation came out. There were as many substantive articles (Deguy, Leyris, Brion, Picon, etc.) as newspaper articles. Here, the study of reception was possible and fruitful. But since 1964, no French translation has given rise to such echoes.

PRODUCTIVE CRITICISM

This sixth and last stage of our journey is warranted in principle only when the analysis has dealt with a translation that imperatively calls for a retranslation, either because it is too defective or unsatisfactory, or because it has become obsolete. In this case, the analysis must become a positive criticism, a "productive" criticism in the sense Friedrich Schlegel spoke of "a criticism that would not be so much the commentary of an already existing, finished and withered literature, as the organon of a literature still to be achieved, to be formed, and even to be begun. An organon of literature, therefore a criticism that would not only explain and conserve, but that would be productive itself, at least indirectly" (*Kritische Schriften* 424–25, qtd. in Berman, *The Experience of the Foreign* 123).

Applied to translated literature, this productive criticism will thus articulate, or attempt to articulate, the principles of a retranslation of the work in question, and thus of new projects of translation. It is not a question of proposing a new project (this is the work of the translators themselves) nor of playing the role of advice giver, but of preparing a space for retranslation in the most rigorous way possible. The exposition of the retranslation's principles must be neither too general nor too narrow and exclusive, since the very life of the translation lies in the unpredictable plurality of the simultaneous or successive versions of the same work. It is a positive thing that two translations of Yeats (one by Yves Bonnefoy in 1989, and the other by

Jean-Yves Masson in 1990) came out almost at the same time, with related but different translation projects. It is translation *copia*.[78]

With this last stage, translation analysis becomes, as the reference to Schlegel shows, criticism in the highest sense; that is, it attempts to realize itself as a productive, life-giving, critical act. In the case of the analysis of a "successful" translation, the analysis's goal, as Schlegel also said in the text quoted by Benjamin, is to "present the representation anew, [to] once again form what is already formed. . . . It will complement, rejuvenate, newly fashion the work."[79] That is to say that it will demonstrate [*de-monstrare*] the excellence and the reasons for the excellence of the translation. The enriching power of the analysis lies then in the (de)monstration to the reader of the positive *creative act* [*faire-œuvre*] of the *translator,* and in the exemplary character of the translation itself.[80]

---

78. [*Copia verborum*, abundance of words. Trans. Note]
79. ["The Concept of Criticism" 154. Trans. Note]
80. That a translation is *exemplary* does not mean that it is a *model*.

PART II

John Donne, Translations, and Retranslations

ELEGY XIX: GOING TO BED

1   Come, Madam, come, all rest my powers defie,
2   Until I labour, I in labour lie.
3   The foe oft-times having the foe in sight,
4   Is tir'd with standing though he never fight.
5   Off with that girdle, like heavens Zone glittering,
6   But a far fairier world incompassing.
7   Unpin that spangled breastplate which you wear,
8   That th'eyes of busie fooles may be stopt there.
9   Unlace your self, for that harmonious chyme,
10   Tells me from you, that now it is bed time.
11   Off with that happy busk, which I envie,
12   That still can be, and still can stand so nigh.
13   Your gown going off, such beauteous state reveals,
14   As when from flowry meads th'hills shadow steales.
15   Off with that wyerie Coronet and shew
16   The haiery Diademe which on you doth grow:
17   Now off with those shooes, and then safely tread
18   In this loves hallow'd temple, this soft bed.
19   In such white robes, heaven's Angels us'd to be

20   Receavd by men; Thou Angel bringst with thee
21   A heaven like Mahomets Paradise; and though
22   Ill spirits walk in white, we easly know,
23   By this these Angels from an evil sprite,
24   Those set our hairs, but these our flesh upright
25   Licence my roaving hands, and let them go,
26   Before, behind, between, above, below.
27   O my America! my new-found-land,
28   My kingdome, safeliest when with one man man'd
29   My Myne of precious stones, My Emperie,
30   How blest am I in this discovering thee!
31   To enter in these bonds, is to be free;
32   Then where my hand is set, my seal shall be.
33   Full nakedness! All joyes are due to thee,
34   As souls unbodied, bodies uncloth'd must be,
35   To taste whole joyes. Gems which you women use
36   Are like Atlanta's balls, cast in mens views,
37   That when a folls eye lighteth on a Gem,
38   His earthly soul may covet theirs, not them.
39   Like pictures, or like books gay coverings made
40   For lay-men, are all women thus array'd;
41   Themselves are mystic books, which only wee
42   (Whom their imputed grace will dignifie)
43   Must see reveal'd. Then since that I may know;
44   As liberally, as to a Midwife, shew
45   Thy self: cast all, yea, this white lynnen hence,
46   Here is no penance, much less innocence.
47   To teach thee, I am naked first; why than
48   What needst thou have more covering then a man.

Translation by Yves Denis
ÉLÉGIE XIX: LE COUCHER DE SA MAÎTRESSE

1   Madame, allons! la fièvre du labeur m'empoigne,
2   Et je meurs de besoin si je ne m'embesoigne!
3   L'ennemi qui souvent aperçoit l'ennemi

4   Sans jamais l'engager n'est plus tant affermi.
5   Ôtez cette ceinture, heureuse galaxie
6   De l'astre le plus beau de la cosmographie;
7   Dégrafez maintenant l'éclatant corselet
8   Où s'arrête des sots le regard indiscret;
9   Délacez-vous: cette musique ensorceleuse
10 M'annonce du coucher l'heure délicieuse.
11 Ôtez ce busc heureux que toujours j'envierai
12 De demeurer si calme en demeurant si près.
13 Votre robe enlevée évoque la féerie
14 De l'ombre abandonnant la campagne fleurie.
15 Ôtez ce tortil roide, et que brille à mes yeux
16 Le diadème seul de vos souples cheveux.
17 Et maintenant, pieds nus, et d'un pas peu farouche,
18 Pénétrez dans le temple, en cette molle couche.
19 C'est dans ce blanc linon que les Anges, jadis,
20 Aux hommes paraissaient. Le divin Paradis
21 Qui partout t'accompagne est celui du Prophète;
22 S'il arrive qu'un Noir Esprit de blanc se vête,
23 Il n'est point malaisé de percer son faux air:
24 Il peut bien faire arcer le poil, mais pas la chair.
25 Laisse, laisse quêter ma main buissonnière
26 Par-dessus, par-dessous, entre, devant, derrière!
27 Terre-Neuve! Amérique! ô ma possession,
28 Qu'un seul homme garnit mieux qu'une garnison!
29 Ma mine de pierres précieuses! mon Empire,
30 Dont l'exploration m'est bienheureux délire!
31 À qui entre en ces nœuds liberté point ne faut:
32 Donc, où j'ai mis la main j'apposerai mon sceau.
33 Total nudité, toutes joies te sont dues!
34 Il n'est qu'âmes sans chair et que chairs dévêtues
35 Pour jouir pleinement. Femmes, vos affiquets
36 Sont pommes d'Atalante, offertes aux benêts,
37 Dont les yeux allumés de terrestre appétence,
38 Convoitant l'attribut, négligent la substance.
39 Tableau, livre profane et richement relié.
40 De la Femme tel est l'aspect séculier.

41 Mais en Livre Mystique elle ne doit paraître,
42 Faire honneur de la grâce imputée à son être,
43 Qu'à nous seuls. Aussi bien, pour mon enseignement,
44 Comme à la sage-femme, offre-toi largement.
45 Ôte, ôte ce lin candide! La pénitence
46 Ici n'est pas de mise, encore moins l'innocence.
47 Regarde, je suis nu. Je ne vois pas pourquoi
48 Tu te voudrais couvrir d'autre chose que moi.

Translation by Philippe de Rothschild
ÉLÉGIE XIX: LE COUCHER DE SA MAÎTRESSE

1 Viens, dame, viens, mes forces repos défient,
2 Près d'œuvrer, déjà j'œuvre et veille d'envie
3 Comme ennemi face à l'ennemi trop vu,
4 Au guet s'agace de ne s'être battu.
5 Ta ceinture ôte, pan de ciel tout lumière,
6 Mais plus beau le bel univers qu'elle enserre.
7 Du buste, bannis ces boucles en diamants
8 Pour capter les yeux des fols exécutants.
9 Délace-toi, ce carillon rythmé donne,
10 Qui me dit le lit est prêt, son heure sonne.
11 Cet heureux corset ôte, j'en suis jaloux,
12 Raide à te toucher, raide et si près de tout.
13 Robe ôtée, ô découvre les places belles,
14 Prés en fleurs que monts hors de l'ombre révèlent.
15 Ta tiare attardée ôte, lors je vois
16 Ta couronne, tes cheveux à flots sur toi.
17 Souliers ôtés, marche sans peur, va t'étendre
18 Au temple béni d'amour, le lit si tendre.
19 Sous tels voiles blancs, du ciel, Anges allaient
20 Voir les mortels. Tu, mon ange, un ciel nous fais,
21 Le paradis de Mahomet. Si s'avance
22 En blanc quelque esprit mauvais, la différence
23 D'ange à démon est telle, à nos yeux c'est clair,
24 L'un nous dresse les cheveux, l'autre la chair.

25 Licence veut ma main rôdeuse, qu'elle erre
26 En haut, en bas, entre deux, devant, derrière,
27 Mes Amériques, ma Neuve Terre, ô toi,
28 Royaume que manie un homme, homme-roi.
29 Mine à pierres précieuses, mon Empire,
30 Te découvrir, moi, béni je dois me dire.
31 Sitôt dans cet enclos entré, libre on est.
32 Où ma main se meut, sur toi le sceau je mets.
33 Nu! Nudité due! À toi ta joie est due.
34 Sans chair va l'âme, le corps veut chair non vêtue
35 À suivre son plaisir. Femme, tes bijoux,
36 Les fruits d'Atalante aux yeux d'homme si fou
37 Qu'à leurs reflets l'œil imbécile étincelle,
38 Âme basse, il brûle pour eux, non pour elle.
39 Tels tableaux et livres reliés gaiement,
40 Telle pour l'homme, femme a son vêtement.
41 C'est pour nous seul qu'elle est livre mystique,
42 —Nous digne d'elle de par sa grâce unique—
43 À révéler. Puisque admis là je me sais,
44 Comme à sage-femme ouvre-toi, donne accès
45 De toi. Ce linge si blanc au loin rejette,
46 De tout pénitence innocence est nette.
47 Pour t'enseigner, le premier, nu je suis. Quoi,
48 Pour te couvrir est-il mieux qu'homme sur toi?

Translation by Auguste Morel (1925)
DE SA MAISTRESSE ALLANT AU LICT

1 Ça Madame venez, tout repos mes ardeurs défient;
2 Jusqu'à ce que travaille, en travail je demeure.
3 L'ennemy parfois, ayant son ennemy en veue,
4 Est fourbu de l'attente et n'a point combatu.
5 Ceste ceinture ostez, comme arc du ciel gemmée,
6 Encores qu'encernant un monde tant plus beau.
7 Détachez ce plastron scintillant que posez
8 Comme bornes aux yeux fureteurs des galands.

9   Vous délacez, que cet enchanteur tintement
10   M'apprenne enfin de vous qu'il est l'heure du lict.
11   A bas ce busc heureux que je jalouse
12   De pouvoir rester coy, et toutefois si proche.
13   Vostre robe en tombant suavité révèle
14   Autant qu'ombre des monts quittant la prée en fleur
15   Ostez ceste couronne aprestée, et monstrez
16   Le diadème de cheveulx qui sur vous croist.
17   Ostez souliers et bas; lors doulcement foulez
18   Ce temple consacré d'amour, ce lit moëlleux.
19   C'est en tels blancs habits que les anges souloient
20   Aux hommes se montrer; toi mon ange m'apportes
21   Un ineffable paradis de Mahomet; et nonobstant
22   Qu'esprits malins cheminent blancs, nous distinguons
23   Aisément par ceci les bons esprits des maléfiques:
24   Les uns font poil dresser, aultres font chair roidir.
25   Donne à mes mains errantes congé, qu'elles aillent
26   Devant, derrière, entre, dessus, dessoubs.
27   Ha, mon Amérique, mon Nouveau-Monde,
28   Mon royaume, plus seur quand peuplé d'un seul homme,
29   Ma mine de pierreries, o mon empyre,
30   Quel heur est donc le mien quand je t'explore ainsi!
31   S'avanturer en ces liens c'est estre libre;
32   Lors où ma main se pose, y restera mon ame.
33   Nudité grande! à toy toutes joyes sont deues;
34   Ainsi qu'ames ont faict, les corps se doivent dépouiller
35   Pour gouster pleine joye. Ces joyaux femmes qu'arborez
36   Sont balle d'Atalante occupant l'œil des hommes;
37   Que si regarde d'un fol à ces brillans s'allume,
38   Son cœur grossier les va convoitant, non point vous.
39   Comme pourtraicts, ou gays dessus des livres faicts
40   Pour le siècle, sont les femmes ainsi parées.
41   Elles qui sont en soy mystiques livres, que nous,
42   —si voulons exalter leur grâce dispensée—
43   Devons voir révéler. Lors que savoir je puys,
44   Avec mesme largesse qu'à ta chambrière te monstre
45   Toute; et ce blanc linge ici rejette;

46   Innocence n'encourt aulcune pénitence:
47   Pour t'enseigner ne suy-je nud; adoncques
48   Qu'as-tu besoin de plus que le couvert d'un homme.

Translation by Octavio Paz
ELEGÍA: ANTES DE ACOSTARSE

1   Ven, ven, todo reposo mi fuerza desafía.
2   Reposar es mi fuerza pues tendido me esfuerzo:
3   No es enemigo el enemigo
4   Hasta que no lo ciñe nuestro mortal abrazo.
5   Tu ceñidor desciñe, meridiano
6   Que un mundo más hermoso que el del cielo
7   Aprisiona en su luz; desprende
8   El prendedor de estrellas que llevas en el pecho
9   Por detener ojos entrometidos;
10 Desenlaza tu ser, campanas armoniosas
11 Nos dicen, sin decirlo, que es hora de acostarse.
12 Ese feliz corpiño que yo envidio,
13 Pegado a ti como si fuese vivo:
14 ¡Fuera! Fuera el vestido, surjan valles salvajes
15 Entre las sombras de tus montes, fuera el tocado,
16 Caiga tu pelo, tu diadema,
17 Descálzate y camina sin miedo hasta la cama.
18 También de blancas ropas revestidos los ángeles
19 El cielo al hombre muestran, más tú, blanca, contigo
20 A un cielo mahometano me conduces.
21 Verdad que los espectros van de blanco
22 Pero por ti distingo al buen del mal espíritu:
23 Uno hiela la sangre, tú la enciendes.
24 Deja correr mis manos vagabundas
25 Atrás, arriba, enfrente, abajo y entre,
26 Mi América encontrada: Terranova,
27 Reino sólo por mi poblado,
28 Mi venero precioso, mi dominio.
29 Goces, descubrimientos,

30 Mi libertad alcanzo entre tus lazos:
31 Lo que toco, mis manos lo han sellado.
32 La plena desnudez es goce entero:
33 Para gozar la gloria las almas desencarnan,
34 Los cuerpos se desvisten.
35 Las joyas que te cubren
36 Son como las pelotas de Atalanta:
37 Brillan, roban la vista de los tontos.
38 La mujer es secreta:
39   Apariencia pintada,
40 Como libro de estampas para indoctos
41 Que esconde un texto místico, tan sólo
42 Revelado a los ojos que traspasan
43 Adornos y atavíos.
44 Quiero saber quién eres tú: descúbrete,
45 Sé natural como en el parto,
46 Más allá de la pena y la innocencia
47 Deja caer esa camisa blanca,
48 Mírame, ven, ¿qué mejor manta
49 Para tu desnudez, que yo, desnudo?

NETWORK OF POEMS RELATED TO "GOING TO BED"

Epithalamion made at Lincolnes Inne (l. 73–85)	Loves Progress	Sapho to Philaenis
Epithalamion on the Lady Elizabeth	GOING TO BED	The Extasie
On the progresse of the soule (essentiall and accidental joyes)	Hymne to God, my God in my sicknesse	

I shall now turn to the analysis of the *Poèmes de John Donne* published in 1962 by Jean Fuzier and Yves Denis and compare it briefly with translations by Philippe de Rothschild, Pierre Legouis, Yves Bonnefoy, Octavio Paz, Auguste Morel, and Robert Ellrodt. The book by Fuzier and Denis is a bilingual edition, which has been out of print or impossible to find for a long time. This is admittedly almost a historical constant of Donne's *translatio* in France. Léon-Gabriel Gros reports that his first book, published by Éditions Charlot in 1946, came out at the same time that the publisher closed down and that he never saw a single copy of his book. The second book, by Pierre Legouis, was published in 1955 by Aubier and has been out of print for a long time, as is Léon-Gabriel Gros' book, published in 1964 by Seghers.

There are only three possibilities for the French reader who today[1] wants to acquire Donne in translation: to go to the Compagnie bookstore in Paris in order to purchase one of the few remaining issues of the *Dossier John Donne*, published in 1983 by the Swiss publisher L'Âge d'Homme, which, in addition to a wealth of scholarly articles, provides a few translations of poems by Fuzier and Denis and by Philippe de Rothschild; to buy issue 2 of the journal *Palimpsestes* (1990), which includes two translations of Donne by Yves Bonnefoy; or to buy the volume *Poèmes élisabéthains* by Philippe de Rothschild, which includes three poems by Donne—not very representative ones—translated into French. It is true that the reader who loves John Donne's works can find (but for how long?) Robert Ellrodt's wonderful book about the English metaphysical poets, the first volume of which is devoted to Donne.[2] This book is all the more useful because all the quotes from Donne (poems, letters, sermons, and other writings) are remarkably well translated. One chapter of the equally wonderful study by John Carey, *John Donne: Life, Mind and Art* (1981), has been translated by Claude Minière and published in the poetry journal *Po&sie* under the title "Au sujet de John Donne" ["About John Donne"].

The real literary transfer of John Donne has obviously not taken place yet, whereas the transfer of William Blake and Gerard Manley Hopkins is well under way. Why is this so?

This question must remain all the more open, as in French poetic circles and among those interested in poetry, the name of Donne is often mentioned and held in reverence. The name circulates, but the work does not, and its breadth and extent (I shall come back to this point) are completely unknown.

In keeping with its origin—a seminar given in 1989—my analysis will mostly focus on one poem by Donne, Elegy XIX, later titled "Going to Bed," but without being limited to it. It is the reading of this particular poem, rather than of all of Donne's works, that initially provided the impetus for a commentary and then for a comparative analysis of its translations (Fuzier/Denis, Rothschild, and Paz). It is worth briefly retracing the circumstances in which I literally fell upon this poem and its Mexican translation. In 1988,

---

1. This was written in November 1991.—French editor's note
2. The last volume, which also deals with Donne, is out of print.

during a mission in Argentina, I happened to find in a library an old copy of the magazine *Sur,* founded by Victoria Ocampo, in which I saw several translations: the first was a translation of Paul Valéry's poem "La dormeuse" by Jorge Guillén, a superb translation, and the other of Donne's "Going to Bed" by Octavio Paz, a more superb translation yet, if quite free. When reading "Going to Bed" and its Mexican counterpart "Antes de acostarse," I had the very strong impression of being in the presence of a *unique* love poem. I thought it was unique in the works of Donne (whom I didn't know well), but also unique in Western lyric love poetry.

This poem of nudity, of joy, of love between man and woman, obviously had analogues in Western poetry, was indeed linked to other poems by Donne (as I was to learn later), but it was nonetheless unique, and the telling fact that it had not been included in the first (posthumous) edition of Donne's poems bore witness to this uniqueness.

Paz's free translation did correspond, in its undeniable preeminence, in the soundness of its fidelities as well as of its omissions, to the uniqueness of this poem. Thus, facing each other in *Sur,* the poems reflected and enriched each other, revealing the secret relations that Donne, by his own admission, had always had with the poetry of the Spanish Golden Age.[3]

Back home, I looked for a French translation and encountered the situation I have previously described. Information I received from an English literature scholar at the University of Paris III confirmed the deplorable state of Donne's *translatio* in France: even in public libraries, some books were missing. However, chance led me to the Compagnie bookstore, where I happened to find (at the time, I was looking for another book) the large Donne volume published by L'Âge d'Homme. In its pages, I discovered two French translations of "Going to Bed": one by Rothschild, the other by Fuzier and Denis. It was a true shock and a deep disappointment. Why? What in Donne and in Paz was both complex and simple, reflexive and immediate, with rhetoric, lyricism, and thought intertwined, was, in the French translations, fused in a compact mass, the language of which—archaic, more than archaizing—made it difficult to read. It was clear that the authors had

---

3. In 1623, Donne wrote to Buckingham: "I can thus make myself believe that I am where your Lordship is, in Spain, that in my poor library, where indeed I am, I can turn mine eye towards no shelf, in any profession, from the mistress of my youth, Poetry, to the wife of mine age, Divinity, but that I meet more authors of that nation than of any other" (qtd. in Paz, *Traducción* 27).

meant to produce a poetic work; had worked with rhyme, prosody, and so forth; and even that they had succeeded in producing, in a certain way, a poem. But this poem full of old and obscure words (*affiquets, arcer, tortil*),[4] about which it was difficult to know whether it was written in sixteenth- or seventeenth-century French, did not correspond to Donne's poem. Many images, many expressions, that I had thought both quite moving and essential to the poem had been replaced. Both translations revealed meticulous care and produced a "precious" poem, whereas Donne's poem, although flowery on occasion, existed on the mode of an almost brutal intertwining of lived and reflexive matter that was its own. Does this mean that these translations were "bad," that they were "failures," and that one should ignore them? My reaction was different. My deep disappointment led me to wonder why these translators, who, according to the information contained in the special issue of L'Âge d'Homme, were specialists on Donne and Elizabethan poetry (Fuzier, in particular, had translated Shakespeare's poetry), had come to a result that was so disappointing to me, not to say traumatizing. *Where* did these men, who were obviously scrupulous and who cared about Donne, find these choices? Where did this translation system (undoubtedly *there was a system*) come from, a system that—it was also obvious to me—did not render Donne's poem and, instead of corresponding to it, made it distant, opaque, and turned it into a curiosity worthy of an antique dealer's shop?

Such was the experience that led me to give a seminar on "Going to Bed" in 1989 and, on that occasion, to refine further notions that I thought essential for the analysis of translations (horizon, project, signifying and aleatory parts of the poem, etc.). This book is the developed, radicalized, and systematized revision of that seminar. Both my past seminar and the present analysis *rest* on the experience that I have related, and that, for this reason, is not anecdotal at all; rather, it is the *threshold and the ground of the work of criticism.*

---

4. [Although rarely used, *affiquets* (brooch) can be found in the Larousse dictionary; *tortil* (heraldry mantling or ribbon around a crown) is found only in the *Dictionnaire des mots rares et précieux,* while *arcer* (to have an erection) is not found. Trans. Note]

THE TRANSLATORS

As the translation of Donne is the work of two individuals, it is important to first know who these people are and how they shared the work, the translation process.

It has not been easy to obtain accurate and direct information about Yves Denis. Now deceased, he was a high school English teacher who, before the publication of *Poèmes de John Donne* by Gallimard, had published in the *Nouvelle revue française* a translation of "The Extasie," with a mention of the forthcoming publication of the book. This mention indicated that the translation had only one author. Later, Yves Denis prepared a collection of translations of English poetry, which did not come out but which his colleagues and friends hope to publish someday.

We know a lot more about Jean Fuzier, first because he did the translation of Shakespeare's poems in the Pléiade edition in 1959, that is, before the co-translation of Donne. In the introduction, Fuzier lays out the principles of his translation of Shakespeare. It is worth quoting him because what he says applies—in part—to the translation of Donne:

> It is ... out of concern for fidelity that verse was chosen as a tool for this translation. In the *Sonnets,* and even more so in the two little epics in the Italian style, "Venus and Adonis" and "Lucrezia," rhetoric often overcomes lyricism and stylistic exercise overcomes inspiration; the *concetti* that are plentiful in both genres are sometimes tolerable only thanks to the play of rhythms and rhymes: the best written prose dulls its piquancy when it doesn't emphasize its poverty. It thus seemed natural to keep the framework Shakespeare chose for his thought, and to serve this thought through approximate, if not identical, means. Nonetheless, literal accuracy was not sacrificed.... Interpretation was most often avoided; the density, even the obscurity of some passages was respected; finally archaism, while not systematically sought after, was chosen every time its use allowed us to approximate as closely as possible the structure of a sentence, or to transcribe it in the original tone. (*Poèmes* 25)

But Jean Fuzier was not *only* a translator. He was a professor at the prestigious École Normale Supérieure, then at the University of Montpellier, where he directed the Center of Elizabethan Studies, which publishes, or used to publish in 1989, a journal titled *Cahiers élisabéthains*. We find one of his articles, entitled "John Donne et la formalité de l'essence—essai d'interprétation prosodique et rhétorique du Sonnet sacré XIV" ["John Donne and the Formality of Essence: Toward a Prosodic and Rhetorical Interpretation of Holy Sonnet XIV"], in the special issue by L'Âge d'Homme. His analysis is clear and measured; its goal is to show that the sonnet discussed "reflects in its prosody the microcosmic upheaval that it describes" and does so in conformity with "the principle, dear to the Elizabethans, of correspondences between the different levels of the universal scale" (45) and, with regard to Donne in general, to show "the informative value of the prosodic and rhetorical elements (which classical usage does not separate much) of Donne's poetry, and . . . confirm that form is indeed the 'formality of essence'" (48).[5]

Although here Fuzier is not speaking at all about issues of translation, we shall see that these statements about the formality of essence weigh heavily on the translation work that he did alone (his translation of Shakespeare) and with Denis.

With regard to the collaboration of the two translators and the sharing of tasks, the table of contents informs us that Yves Denis translated most of the holy sonnets, while Jean Fuzier did most of the elegies, songs, and sonnets. Overall, Fuzier did the greater part of the work. About Holy Sonnet XIV, he evokes the "unequaled version by Yves Denis from *Poèmes de John Donne*" (42), but as we read these poems, and even if we know the other translations by Fuzier, there is nothing that allows us to see any difference between the two translators. This pair—we don't know much about the way the translators worked together for the shared tasks—has a third party, Jean-Robert Poisson, who wrote the foreword to the book.[6] As the author of the foreword, Poisson's task was to present Donne to the French public and to describe the labor involved in translating his works. However, in reality, his function is more important: he was in charge of rereading, correcting, and even reorienting the work of his "friends," particularly when he felt it was going somewhat in the wrong direction.[7] Finally, he produced the first

---

5. The expression "formality of essence" is borrowed from Rémy de Gourmont.

6. The foreword is the only paratext of the book, along with the back cover and the table of contents. There are no notes.

7. "In one [translator], he went after the redundancies, the 'padding' as Malherbe would say. . . . The other was too fond of precious niceties, and was constantly reminded that Donne's spoken style is jaw-breaking [in English in the text] and tense, precisely like Mallarmé's style." (Poisson 22).

evaluation of these translations: "They are beautiful and faithful" (22). As we can see, the role of Jean-Roger Poisson is quite important.

The Book and Its Translation Horizon

I shall not spend much time on this point, since I shall return to it in detail when I study the reception of the Fuzier and Denis translation. Let me simply and briefly say that the horizon of this translation is the 1960s, with its major translations: *Les prophètes* by Jean Grosjean (1955), *Hamlet* by Bonnefoy (1957), the Hopkins by Leyris (1957), *L'Enéide* by Klossowski (1964), the *Poèmes élisabéthains* by Philippe de Rothschild (1969), the *Chant des chants* [*Song of Songs*] by Meschonnic (1970), *L'homme sans qualités* [*The Man without Qualities*] by Jaccottet (1956), and the Parmenides edited by Jean Beaufret and translated by J. J. Rivière (1957). This list, which is both incomplete and personal, nonetheless includes translations that at the time were noticed in the press and elsewhere. But in no way do they form a "whole." Then, there are the discussions and reflections on poetry and its translation as they can be found in *La revue de poésie*[8] and *Change* ("La traduction en jeu") or in Michel Deguy's *Actes* (1966).

These translations do not form a "whole," nor a fortiori, as I thought at the time, a homogeneous movement (for some of the translations), because apparently there is not enough circulation of translations and of discussions surrounding them from one domain to the next. Moreover, at the time there clearly were positions that were irreconcilable from several points of view, in particular about poetic translation. I shall return to this point later in further detail.

What I can say now is that the 1960s were rich in translations, and the ununified diversity I just mentioned bears witness to this richness, and also to the great gaps between practices and theories. Some very specific projects, like the Dante by Pézard, give rise to attempts at retranslations of Dante (*La revue de poésie*) that are all different (although not in competition with one another). The translations sometimes echo each other, and sometimes they do not.

With regard to the near horizon of Donne translations, I have already mentioned previous translations. I presume that Fuzier and Denis must have been aware of them and that their work is a conscious attempt to go *further*— further than Legouis and, for "Going to Bed," further than Auguste Morel.

---

8. The first issues are impossible to find. See further p. xx.

In his introduction, Legouis had clearly and modestly defined the scope of his translation project, quite in keeping with the Aubier series[9] in which he was publishing it, and with the intended audience of his book, to whom it is dedicated: "my students at Besançon and Lyon, who helped me discover all the possible meanings of these texts" (*Poèmes choisis* 5). "We have constantly resisted the temptation to elevate Donne's vocabulary, everywhere he preferred the most simple, the most common term. . . . However, our punctuation, which is purposefully modern and grammatical, may guide the beginning reader, who is confused by the punctuation of the original which, following Elizabethan usage, indicates not so much the syntactical relations between words as the way to say the lines" (49).

Fuzier and Denis' desire to go further, to produce a true *poetic translation* of Donne, is already evident in the fact that their collection was published with Gallimard, the greatest French publisher of great poetry, such as the translations of Grosjean and Klossowski. Clearly Fuzier and Denis intend—their choice of publisher and series shows this in and of itself—to go beyond the stage of an introduction. The fact that the volume was announced through a prepublication a year before in the *NRF* shows that its publication was considered a literary event. The fact that Gallimard and the journal *NRF* accepted the translation of Fuzier and Denis shows that they shared, beyond any empirical contingencies, their conviction that it was necessary to have a retranslation of Donne that was "at last poetical," and that they agreed with the authors' translation project, as well as with its result. Thus there was *a horizon of editorial expectancy* for Donne that reflected both the poetic policy of Gallimard and, we can surmise, a horizon of expectancy from the public. It is certain that the public interested in poetry, in foreign poetry, in English poetry, and in metaphysical English poetry was waiting for Donne (as it is still waiting for him), and it is no less certain that the translation by Fuzier and Denis was indeed read, at the time. In 1980, it went the way of the preceding translation and was out of print (although the special issue in the L'Âge d'Homme series mentions a reedition from 1980 as impossible to find and mentioned nowhere else). We do not know why there was no reedition.[10]

As for the field of English poetic translations (in the largest sense, which

---

9. [A social science research series published by Flammarion. Trans. Note]

10. Klossowski's *Enéide* was also out of print, but it was reedited in 1980 and was never as impossible to locate as the translation of Donne by Fuzier and Denis.

includes theater and poetry, great literature), it is not homogeneous. Leyris's work [*œuvre*] of translation began during the 1930s and follows its own logic, hardly influenced by Klossowski's work in 1964. It continues still, a long river, a unique monument of prose and poetry transfer. Bonnefoy's translation *œuvre* has just started. It can be considered in its uniqueness, and also in its general traits, as characteristic of the translation ambitions of the times, with Jaccottet's translation *œuvre*, which then took on, after more "radical" beginnings (translations of Góngora and of the *Odyssey*), its quasi-definitive aspect. Fuzier and Denis' work, like that of Philippe de Rothschild at the end of this period, is of a quite different ilk, even if Leyris and Bonnefoy pay attention to prosody and versification. The projects are quite different. *The field of English poetic translations is thus divided.*

THE TRANSLATION PROJECT

Let us now turn to Fuzier and Denis' translation project, as it appears when we read the introduction by Poisson, the back cover, the article by Fuzier in the L'Âge d'Homme volume, and his prologue on the translation of Shakespeare's *Sonnets*.

A Very Selective Anthology

As any translation project is also a project of literary transfer, I must say immediately that the collection by Fuzier and Denis is limited to Donne's poetry. Of course, this would seem natural for a poet's anthology. But Donne wrote works, sermons, letters, which also constitute an *œuvre*. Of course, these works would not be part of an *œuvre* if the poems did not exist. And it is possible to limit an anthology to poems, quite legitimately, in an anthology precisely aiming to be a true poetic labor. However, my comment is not totally out of place since, almost at the same time, Leyris chose to present Hopkins with his prose writings and his drawings, in addition to the poems. For each project a different selection.

Denis and Fuzier's collection is thus based exclusively on Donne's poetic works: a first selection, a first choice. Within this first choice comes a second one, as stated by Poisson:

We hope to keep the best of Donne: excluding the official poems,[11] we translated roughly half of the elegies, songs and sonnets, and sacred sonnets, ordering the texts in the sense of a spiritual ascent, from the "darkest" poems about failed loves, an ascent where bodies have a part, "progress of the soul" to borrow a title from Donne. (22)

Now we know: half of the "non-official" poems were selected and ordered according to—according to what? To a certain interpretation of Donne's poetic trajectory, which would be symbolized by the title of one of his poems, "Of the Progresse of the Soule" (which, by the way, is not included in the anthology). For the moment, let me simply observe that the selection is reasoned (quantitatively) and well founded (on a specific reading of Donne). I shall see when I evaluate the project about this foundation. In any case, Fuzier and Denis (and Poisson) mean to propose *a certain vision of Donne* to the reader. It is their right; it is even inevitable.

A Poetic Anthology

Then, the authors propose a *poetic* version of the poet, as the back cover rather naively indicates:

To faithfully serve their author, the translators were naturally led to use verse, as they did not find any other instrument that would give full justice to Donne's poetry, the varied meter and supple and nervous prosody of which could not but be disfigured by the best of prose.

But today translating Donne "in verse" may mean *two things*. Basically, it means to produce a poem that corresponds to his poetry, something in verse, indeed. But *how* this is achieved remains uncertain. As is well known, many modern translators of poetry do not force themselves to reproduce the original's traditional versification forms, nor even to find traditional French formal "equivalents." Others, to the contrary, consider translating traditional poetry without its form a betrayal. Between these two opposite

---

11. Poisson had already stated in the foreword that "if we disregard the arid terrain of official poetry" (14), that is, the epithalamions, which Legouis had partially translated, and the verse letters. In short, they exclude the so-called occasional poetry, which is here openly undervalued.

positions there is room for various intermediary positions. Clearly, as their translation shows, Fuzier and Denis belong to the second camp. It is not only their translation that shows it, but also Fuzier's text on the "formality of essence," which found its application well before in his translation of Shakespeare, since, as Fuzier says, it contains an "exact" reproduction of its "poetic forms." With regard to Donne, nowhere do the translators say that there is an exact reproduction of his "poetic forms," but this is not the most important thing; what matters is the choice of a traditional versification with which to translate the poet. It is even one of the *fundamental* choices, heavy with consequences, of this translation project.

A "French Donne"

As Poisson tells us, this traditional poetic version must produce "authentic French poems, those that Donne might have written had he been bilingual like Rilke" (22).

The purpose of this version is thus to create a *French* Donne, which, once again, may mean two things: a Donne *in French,* which can stand on its own poetically (as Leyris's Hopkins stands without there being the ambition to produce a "French Hopkins"), or a Donne who would seem to have risen out of the French poetic *terroir,* such as it was configured at the end of the sixteenth century. This is not the same thing. Not insignificantly, Poisson had earlier wondered in his introduction, "Was there a French Donne?" (19). After going through several sixteenth- and seventeenth-century French poets, he admits "that we had to scour through a century of poetry, from Délie (1544) to Polyeucte (1643) in order to find, terribly distorted and diluted, a [French] Donne" (20–21).

But, according to Poisson, if there was really no French Donne, *there could be one after the fact* (as there could be a French Dante, a French Shakespeare, afterwards, even much later), thanks to a poetic translation that would be able to mobilize the prosodic, rhythmic, syntactical, lexical, and rhetorical resources of the "'grotesque,' 'baroque,' 'précieux' poetry of the sixteenth and seventeenth centuries" (22), that of authors like Scève, Ronsard, Sponde, and Saint-Amand (19–20). As this French Donne would still be the real Donne (that is, an English poet), we would finally have a "Franco-English metaphysical poet" (22), whose work, being authentically French, would no longer be accessible only to "English speakers" (22) as the original was (by definition), or Legouis' version, which was explicitly intended for English literature students.

Let me note here that the French Donne to be constituted is placed within the tradition of "grotesque," "baroque," and "precious" French poets of the sixteenth and seventeenth centuries. That Donne is *like* the poets of this tradition is the second immanent interpretation of the Fuzier and Denis project.

An Archaizing Version

As I mentioned earlier, in his introduction to his translation of Shakespeare's poem, Fuzier wrote: "Finally archaism, while not systematically sought after, was chosen every time its use allowed us to approximate as closely as possible the structure of a sentence, or to transcribe it in the original tone" (*Poèmes* 25).

The writing of the *Sonnets* demonstrates that Fuzier took his statement seriously. It is the same situation with Donne: on the whole, the translation is archaizing. It is so at all levels, and quite openly. Let us take two examples at random in Elegy X, "The Dreame":

When you are gone, and Reason *gone with you,*
Then Fantasie *is Queene and Soule, and all* (l. 9–10)

is rendered as:

Avec toi partira ma raison; fantaisie
Ores sera ma reine et mon âme et mon tout (53),[12]

which, with the *ores* so dear to Joachim du Bellay, sounds to the ear of any French reader like an imitation of a line from the sixteenth century. It is the same thing for line 22:

Alas, true joyes at best are dreame enough

which becomes:

---

12. [Literally,
   With you shall go my reson; fantasie
   Now will be my queene and my soul
   And my all.
Ores (now) is archaic and not used alone in French. Trans. Note]

Las! Le plus vrai plaisir n'est jà que trop rêvé. (52–53)[13]

It is clear that the translators wanted a French Donne from the French sixteenth and seventeenth centuries, which would resemble most what a Donne *translated in his time* in France would have been, with this difference that they see this Donne *in the image of* the "grotesque," "baroque," "precious" poets of the French sixteenth and seventeenth centuries. The translation will thus become precious, rhetorical, complex, intricate, as are the poets quoted by Poisson and, still according to Poisson, as Donne himself is.

The similarity with Pézard's own project is obvious, except that Pézard's goal—to translate *all of Dante* in a fictive Old French contemporary with the language of the Italian poet—is more impressive and more authoritative, both through its totalizing aspect and its return to a state of language still further away from us. Fuzier and Denis' translation remains a retranslation (it comes after Morel, Legouis, and even Gros) and a partial translation (thus selective, interpretative, and so forth).

The four "facets" of the project, which range from the general to the particular, to what defines most closely its specificity, seem coherent. The basic choice (a translation in verse, poetic, that is inevitably selective inasmuch as it is not complete) is followed by specific choices (a translation using traditional versification, with the goal of creating a Donne in the likeness of French poets who are—partially—equivalent, and thus a translation called to rely on archaism for the most part). This seems coherent.

If the translators, no more than Poisson, whom we have read between the lines, did not choose to *present their project,* it is because in fact the translation *itself presents* the project and *the volume is bilingual.* In this way, if he so desires, the reader may compare the texts. It is as if the translators were telling us, "It is up to you to see if our overall choice and our specific choices were good, if our 'liberties' were good, if we reached our goal," et cetera.

I thus argue that the translation by Fuzier and Denis lives within the "ethical dimension" mentioned by Masson. Their translation has the *courage* to show itself, and it shows itself only by being placed *facing the original.*

13. [Literally,
   Alas! The most true pleasure
   Is only all too much dreamt.

Las is an archaic form of *hélas* also favored by du Bellay, and *jà* is not used. Trans. Note]

CRITICAL EXAMINATION OF THE PROJECT

It now seems possible and legitimate to examine the project that I have just reconstituted, because it clearly determines the translations from beginning to end, and because its critical examination alone will allow us to shed light—to begin to shed light—on the reasons for the obvious limitations of these translations. I will then have all the time necessary to examine "Going to Bed" and its versions, and thus to go the full length of my analytic circle. Moreover, Fuzier and Denis' project, which is far from being theirs alone—it is also, in part, that of Efim Etkind and of all his collaborators—raises fundamental questions for the translation of poetry that it is best to deal with *before* the linear confrontation.

I shall leave aside the first facet of the project—the fact that it is a doubly selective anthology that eliminates the prose pieces and orders the selected poems according to a specific "trajectory"—while reserving the right to go back to it at the end of my analysis, when proposing other principles for another project of translation (in its usual sense) and of a literary *transfer* of Donne.

The Poetic Version

The discussion of the Fuzier and Denis project must begin—without coming to an end right away—with the second facet: to offer a version *that is not a prose version* (be it disguised in verse), to produce "real" poems, and to offer a version in verse that obeys the rules of traditional versification, following the fact that Donne did write according to traditional rules (even if he somewhat upset them, as he was criticized for doing). It is a priori possible to raise questions about these two points.

That Donne's poems must be translated in verse, not in prose, seems evident. But we shall see that this "evidence" is not quite obvious, unless one proposes a totally flat and empty concept of the *prosaic* in general. For the moment, it suffices to ask two simple questions: What can a translation that is labeled "Mallarmean" and "Valéryan" (according to Léon-Gabriel Gros)—thus supposedly 100 percent poetic—do with the prosaic elements of Donne's poetry, such as colloquialisms (Poisson reminds the translators about the "spoken style" of Donne, but "spoken style" is prose, is *within the medium of prose*), and with the terminological networks (alchemy, medicine, astronomy, etc.) that are so numerous in Donne (and that also belong to the domain of prose)?[14] We shall see how the translation handles this. Then, how do we explain that a translation "without rhythm," like that of Legouis, a translation therefore that is "not really poetic," can give the impression, modestly but efficiently, of opening unto the poetic world of Donne more than the obfuscating—because archaizing—translation by Fuzier and Denis? I do not deny that their translation is more poetically "wrought," but that Legouis' more prosaic translation leads us more directly into the world of Donne cannot be denied either. So is it really evident that here prose has no role to play? Two great poets thought about prose and its powers quite differently from its detractors, about whom one wonders if they thought ever so briefly about what it is. Goethe says:

> I honor both rhythm and rhyme, by which means alone poetry becomes poetry; but what has a really deep and essential efficacy, what truly educates and cultivates is what remains of the poet when he is translated into prose. What is left is the absolutely pure substance whose dazzling appearance often succeeds in creating the illusion it exists when it is absent, and which it hides when it is present. (*Poésie et vérité* 316–17)[15]

And Pasternak: "We drag the everyday into prose for the sake of the poetry of it. We draw prose into poetry for the sake of the music of it" (*Sauf-conduit*, qtd. in Robin, *Écrits oubliés* 67).[16]

That said, it would be absurd to argue that a "prose" translation of Donne's poems is conceivable. I am saying first that neither prose nor prosifying translation can be reduced to the tattered representations that people all too often have of it, and that a *certain "prosaic work" within poetic translation must be conceived*. I will return to this point at the end of the analysis. I am also saying not only that the question of prose or verse should not be

---

14. Ellrodt implicitly points out this essential prosaic style in Donne when he says that his poems "refuse to sustain a lyrical flight for long," adding in a note, meaningfully, "It is not certain that a poem must be poetic in its entirety" (see *L'inspiration personnelle* 198).

15. [The published English translation is as follows: "I honour both the rhythm and the rhyme, by which poetry first becomes poetry; but what is really deeply and fundamentally effective—what is truly educative and inspiring, is what remains of the poet when he is translated into prose. What is left is the pure and perfect essence, which beauties of form may strive to simulate when absent, and when present serve only to conceal" (*Autobiography* 2:41). Trans. Note]

16. Also qtd. in Robin, *Poésie sans passeport* (135). [Pasternak, *Safe Conduct* (181). Trans. Note]

generalized, but also that *it can be clarified only in light of the crisis of modern poetic translation, at least in France.*

For Fuzier it is *evident* that, when dealing with poetry that is written in traditional verse, one must translate it, if not with the same versification, at least with the *same type of traditional formal resources.* Even today such is the position of Efim Etkind (ix–xix), who criticizes most French poetry translators for this, except—of course—Fuzier, in spite of a few minor objections (216–17). One may think first that Efim Etkind points to the existence of such a crisis, and he is right in that, and secondly that he judges it too lightly, as if it were something that could be changed at will, and on top of that from the horizon of Russian poetic culture, in which there is no crisis (or so it seems) of poetic translation (a crisis that is inevitably that of poetry itself).[17] Etkind *does recognize* the existence of a crisis of this kind (in France) while *underestimating* its range, depth, and nature, but Fuzier himself does not seem to know there is a crisis, and so, what crisis are we speaking about? Like any crisis, it is manifested through symptoms, and these symptoms are the problems posed to the modern translator by poetic translation, whatever its "domain." No one has been able to evoke better than Jacques Roubaud the nature, the range, and the multiplicity of these problems, and he is also the one who has dared speak again, after Mallarmé, about the deep crisis of "traditional versification" in France. He writes about the translation of the troubadours:

> Translating is never simple; but what we have just said about the art of the troubadours brings to the fore some of the specific difficulties in translating them. First, it is a counted and rhymed poetry, which is very difficult to handle in the current state of French poetry, a poetry characterized by a still unresolved crisis of traditional versification. Second, translating with nineteenth-century verse was not possible for me; neither was it in ordinary free verse. Nor did I want to produce only a paraphrase in prose. To look for the conditions of a rhythmic restitution that would take into account

---

17. "Among the French translators of Russian poetry a debate has pitted the advocates of a translation in non-rhymed free verse against those who attempt to use the resources of French traditional versification. The first group has solid arguments. First, they invoke the relative poverty of the French meter repertoire ... and of French rhyme dictionaries compared to the extraordinary wealth of an inflexed language like Russian. Secondly, they mention ... the aging of regular French verse, which today is experienced like an archaism, against the youth of Russian verse" (Aucouturier 1571).

the whole of the formal architecture and of the modes of adaptation of this architecture to the current conditions of language and poetry would have been a long and exacting undertaking, well beyond my capacities, but I hope to be able someday to carry out a few experiments in this direction. Last, the very nature of the troubadours' language, the fact that it is a medieval language that is a close cousin of French, adds another quite particular hurdle: to mark chronological distance through the systematic borrowing of an archaizing vocabulary and syntax keeps placing the translator on the edge of an unsatisfactory dialect, a dialect one could call a linguistic version of "pseudo-medieval Normandy inns with real fake beams." However, at the same time, the complete acclimatization to contemporary expression erases in great part the irreducible flavor of the original. The terms are present in our current language but they are veiled and weakened; they seem "childish" and naive, which is of course but the reflection of our desire to forget our poetic origins. (*Les troubadours* 57)

The crisis about which Roubaud is speaking, and whose paralyzing surface effects he describes—what to do?—is a crisis of "the formality of essence." Indeed, the forms of "traditional versification" were the very embodiment of this formality, as Fuzier says, with the difference still that this formality, like all formalities, had always been technical, manipulative, and artificial. This technicality of formality does indeed belong to poetry. But it is inherent to poetry that its technicality and formality both belong to its "essence" and do not belong to it; that technicality and formality sometimes break away from this "essence"; that the identity of formality and essence—of which rhyme may be the symbol—breaks down. And what Rilke called "a great goddess, the divinity of the most secret and most ancient coincidences... a perpetually affirmative 'yes,' which the gods condescend to appose to our most innocent emotions" (*Lettres françaises* 122–23),[18] becomes "pure rhymstery by rhymesters." The crisis of traditional versification does not mean that it has become an old rag fit for the dumpster, but that it has lost its authority, its supremacy, its naturalness, its self-evidence, and that there is an insistent *fracture* between essence and formality. Again, Roubaud says:

---

18. [The English published version mistakenly reads "oppose" instead of "appose" (*Letters to Merline* 99–100). Trans. Note]

The successive storms experienced by verse traditions ... created among poets an increasingly acute sense of a difficulty; the difficulty of what Jacques Réda calls "la tourne" [the turn]. The act, which used to seem so natural, of stopping the plow of the line after "an average length of words," to turn back (jumping!) and start a new furrow ... suddenly seems strange, makes you unsure. The self-evidence of the number, of the measure, the evidence of the "naturalness" of the caesuras, of the pauses, no longer garners support. (*La vieillesse d'Alexandre* 196)

Hence an immediate consequence: it is impossible for the poet as well as for the translator of poetry—even traditional poetry—to *simply* turn to old versification. For the translator of poetry, this is running the risk (of course, everything depends on the individual case and on the domain) of poetic failure, of pastiche, of "vulgar doggerel."[19] It is not being dogmatic to say that a translator who is not aware of this crisis—when it directly affects his practice—hasn't thought through what his translation position should be: as translator of poetry, he must, albeit uneasily, live in the crisis.

But there is more, with regard to the translation of old traditional poetry (as is the case with Donne). At the same time that a crisis of "verse" broke out in the nineteenth century, so did a crisis of *rhetoric*.[20] This crisis is truly of such magnitude that it is shaking the whole edifice of Western culture because, from the Greeks to the nineteenth century, the *paideia*[21] of rhetoric has been formative at all levels.

This crisis hits hard the translators who work with poems from the tradition since, as Fuzier states, "classical usage" hardly makes the distinction between "prosodic and rhetorical elements," whereas the translator

---

19. The attempts at traditional meter translation of Rilke praised by Etkind in opposition to free verse translations of prose in disguise are a sad example of this. See Etkind's book *Un art en crise* (56–57).

20. The link between the two crises is all the closer since, as Joseph Venturini states, "rhetoric, ... in antiquity, found in prose its best ground to develop—whereas versified writing preferred lyricism and elegy—now enters directly, as if it were breaking in, into modern rhymed poetry" (114).

21. [*Paideia* refers to the Athenian concept of education and upbringing "designed to give pupils a rounded cultural education, especially with a view to public life. Hence: the sum of physical and intellectual achievement to which an individual or (collectively) a society can aspire; a society's culture." The principal subjects of the classical *paideia* were rhetoric, grammar, mathematics, music, philosophy, geography, natural history, and gymnastics ("Paideia"). Trans. Note]

must work within a horizon in which the practice and the experience of rhetoric have become problematic. It is true that poeticians, semiologists, psychoanalysts, philosophers, linguists, historians, and many others attempt to "go back to" rhetoric, to "seek rejuvenation" in it. True, rhetoric hasn't disappeared. There is a plethora of rhetorical devices used in literature, in politics, in advertising, and so forth. But there is no longer any *paideia,* and thus no rhetorical *culture.*

What is the translator of "eloquent" poetry to do? He can become a rhetorician, like the Shakespeare of the *Sonnets,* and, good imitator (or pasticheur) that he is, he can produce a French sonnet that is (formally) "equivalent" to the English sonnet. This can be quite successful, but with two conditions, which have a rather high cost.

The first condition is, necessarily, that one immerse oneself in total archaism, with all the risk of *artificiality* and *obscurity* that this implies. Even if this condition is met, even if archaism seems natural and clear, the fact remains that, because of the crisis of our relation to rhetoric, *the rhetoric of the translated poem will collide with its poeticality for us,* the recipients of the translation; one does not translate for Mademoiselle de Gournay.[22] We shall see how this works in the case of Donne.

What then? Then, one must admit with Roubaud that there cannot be any general solution or general way. There are only specific ways, specific solutions to be found. Donne, Shakespeare, Milton, Goethe, Rilke—each author poses his own set of problems on this matter—but each from the vantage of a certain number of reflections about what is *still* possible and what is *no longer* possible. In fact, the crisis is perverse: it puts all the traditional translating paths off limits without quite forbidding them. Hence, at the beginning of each path, we must stop and think, depending on the work to translate and on the problems that Roubaud mentions. And it is especially necessary, perhaps, not to open up *new* paths, but at least to *reopen all the paths.* But how can this be done? The end of this analysis will consider a few examples of *poetic translation reopening* that, in light of our considerations, seem convincing.

The "French Donne"

Here too, there are questions to be asked. When translating Donne, does one have to use the resources of the French poetic language of the time and,

---

22. [The adopted daughter of Montaigne. Trans. Note]

preferably, the resources of the works that, at least partially, "resemble" that of Donne in order to produce a "French Donne"? It is certain that avoiding "pseudo-medieval Normandy inns with real fake beams" is not the same as avoiding archaism and, in particular (although not exclusively), poetic language resources of the "contemporary" period of Donne. I shall come back in due time to this question of the recourse to archaism, to *archaic elements*. In any case, it needs to be clearly distinguished from the (quasi) *systematic practice* of archaism, which is the practice of Pézard and Fuzier and Denis. *It is one thing to use archaisms, and another to be archaic.*

However, the appeal to poets who "resemble" Donne, and thus the reconstitution of a French Donne who is "equivalent" to the English one—as Poisson says, a "Franco-English" one—seems to me quite questionable. Why? Quite simply because there is no French poet contemporary of Donne who is like him (he is hardly like any of *his* English contemporaries, as no Donne scholar fails to mention!). Not only is there no French poet who resembles him in reality (and Poisson recognizes this indirectly), but *imagining* a French Donne is impossible: it would require ignoring the radical difference between English and French poetry of the late sixteenth century. These two poetry domains are not even *contemporary,* in the sense that they are not situated in the same poetic, theatrical, cultural, and linguistic time. There is good reason for the fact that neither Donne nor Shakespeare (not to mention the other Elizabethans, it seems) was translated into French at the time or during the seventeenth century, when books by all kinds of writers could circulate throughout Europe. This is not to say that nothing passed from one culture to the other. For instance, Florio was translating Montaigne, and North translated Amyot's Plutarch (*Les vies des hommes illustres*). But nothing in the *innermost nature* of French literature and poetry moved to Great Britain, and vice versa. The time had not come. Only the passage through literary *transfer* and the translation of the innermost nature [*intime*] of a culture can guarantee that someday, in an unpredictable form, there will arise the *twin* figure of one of our most French poets or writers in England, Hungary, or Spain. The real literary transfer has its own time, its *kairos.* We can only work toward it. In the absence of such a mutual passage of the innermost, that is, of a proximity-in-distance (Chateaubriand translating Milton; Baudelaire, Edgar Allan Poe; Stefan George, Baudelaire; and so forth), there cannot be anything like a "French Donne." Donne remains English, and he has almost remained so until today, as we shall see. This does not mean that he won't ever be able *to pass* into France, or that he must "become" French! We do not wish for the London writer to become Parisian. Rather, we need a Donne who is quite Londonian, but in French. Besides, why force this Englishman, who did not have much of a liking for these "Men of France, changeable Camelions" (Fuzier and Denis, "On his Mistris") to become French?

Donne and the English Poetic Domain

We are here coming to two (hidden) flaws in Fuzier and Denis' project: first, an insufficient reflection—surprising for specialists on Donne—about the specificity of the English poetic field, not only the Elizabethan field but the field in general—and thus about the current problems presented by its translation and its literary transfer. The word "insufficient" may not be the right one; it would be better to say "unilateral." The same observation applies to the second flaw: an inadequate reflection on the form and the content of Donne's poetry, to use this rather dull expression. This work of reflection had already been done, two years before the publication of the Denis and Fuzier translation, by Robert Ellrodt, who published his work in 1960. And so, at the same time that the two translators were "chiseling" their Donne, Ellrodt was analyzing and thinking through his work with impressive insight. It is surprising to read the following passage, in which Ellrodt rejects any approach to Donne's poetry that is solely (or preferentially) based on the "formality of essence"—what applies to the critic also applies to the translator:

> We have shown that the modulations of the line follow the very inflections of feeling and the meanderings of thought.... But is the felicitous harmony of rhythm and sense a characteristic that allows us to see the originality of Donne? Is there a great poet who does not have it? ... In fact, the study of versification cannot give us the criterion for poetic originality.... Prosodic analysis alone cannot reveal the total effect that is perceived on the only level that is common to the ear and the mind: tone. (*L'inspiration personnelle* 196–97)[23]

Even if one does not agree with these statements and if, for instance, one finds them subjective and powerless compared to the precision of prosodic and rhetorical analysis, the fact remains, and it is more formidable, that a

---

23. Obviously it would be better to read both quotes in their entirety and in context, that is, in chapter 7, "De l'ambiguïté à la dissonance."

unilateral involvement in this type of analysis leads to the loss—both for the critic and the translator—of an entire aspect of Donne's poetry (and of English poetry, and poetry in general) that is no less real and "objective" than the other. This dimension in Donne has been admirably described by Ellrodt and Carey. We shall thus refer the readers to their fascinating studies.

With regard to the English poetic field, we can say the following: every translator and critic of English poetry knows that, throughout history, and in part because of a specific relationship to its language, English poetry has developed specific characteristics, *specific individuating* traits that cannot be found in French, Italian, or Spanish poetry, even if there are mutual resemblances or apparent similarities. In his introduction to his translation of "Going to Bed," Octavio Paz opposes the linguistic traits of Golden Age poetry to those of the English metaphysical poets:

> All the great poets of that period tend to create a learned language, an accomplished one among some, a refined language among most. At the same time they write poems in colloquial language, but both currents, the popular and the learned one, flow in parallel in their works without ever mixing. However, among the English metaphysical poets, there is often a clash between literary and colloquial language, the abstract and the concrete, the old and the new. (*Traducción* 28)[24]

This "colloquialism," which is integrated (intertwined) with other elements that are not so, such as rhetoric and abstraction, can be found in Donne and in many English poets (and today in American poets). It is allied, in a disconcerting way for us French readers, with a *compactness* of writing without any equivalent in our poetic history. De Quincey thus describes Donne:

> Massy diamonds compose the very substance of his poem on the Metempsychosis, thoughts and descriptions which have the fervent and gloomy sublimity of Ezekiel or Aeschylus, whilst a diamond dust of rhetorical brilliancies is strewed over the whole of his occasional verse and his prose. (Qtd. by Poisson 17)[25]

---

24. Similarly, Ellrodt says (Paz may have read his works): "The poetic world of Donne ... leaves the impression of an obscure world, criss-crossed with flashes of lightning" (*L'inspiration personnelle* 98).

25. [De Quincey, "Rhetoric" (101). Trans. Note]

These comments, which may be applied in fact to all or almost all of Donne's poetry (at least before the holy sonnets) may find an unexpected echo in a remark by the essayist Alain that should give food for thought to any translator of English poetry and to any translator in this field who claims Mallarmé's influence and who perhaps confuses him with Valéry (they are both translators of English poetry, but quite different, with a different relation both to language and to English poetry):

> If someone attempts to translate a poem by Shelley into French, he will first introduce spaces, as is the custom among our poets who are almost all a little too fond of oration. Thus measuring according to the rules of public declamation, the translator will place his *whos* and his *whichs*, these syntactic posts that provide support and, if I may say so, that prevent substantial words from cutting into each other. I do not scorn this art of articulation; in fact I rather like it; a sort of friendship of reason issues forth. But in the end it is no longer the English art of speaking, so condensed, so compact, brilliant, precious and strongly enigmatic.
>
> I have the idea that one can always translate a poet, be it an English, Latin, or Greek poet, exactly word for word, without adding anything, and even keeping the order of the words, so that finally one will find the meter and even the rhyme. I have rarely pushed the experiment that far; it takes time, I would say months, and a rare patience. At first one arrives at a sort of barbaric mosaic; the pieces are poorly joined; the cement glues them together but does not bring them together. There remains the power, the sparkle, even a certain violence, and perhaps more than it should. It is more English than English, more Greek than Greek, more Latin than Latin.
>
> ... As we know, Mallarmé was an English teacher by trade. His job was to translate poets who cannot be translated. I can easily guess how he learned how to translate by gritting his teeth; whence it happened that French appeared to him with a new face, all syntax diminished, and words directly joined, the chisel ruling the drawing. Here is a new logic, and I hold its thread. Here are juxtaposed substances, like precious stones joined solely through the force of metal. Pure relations of existence, as nature shows them, without any why nor how. Play of substantives and of verbs. Put your mind to this work; it will think all anew. It will see all anew. *(Propos de littérature 56–57)*

Thus the translation of English poetry, or of a very important line of English poets (there is no need, evidently, to postulate a total homogeneity in this poetry), has posed specific problems in France, and it has done so for a long time. Alain points out the obstacle of the "eloquence" of our poetry. Bonnefoy mentioned the obstacle of "essentialism"; Déprats, that of its lack of "orality." That said, they do not use any of these obstacles as a pretext for a decree of untranslatability.[26] But obstacle there is, and one caused by important specificities. In spite of Poisson's comment, there is no trace in Denis and Fuzier of a reflection on these questions. The immediate consequence of this lack of reflection is that Donne is not translated in his *Englishness;* for instance, colloquialism (which is certainly not characteristic of his work alone) completely disappears from the translation, since the project is not concerned with it. What is much more serious is that the interweaving of colloquialism, rhetoric, logic, and poeticality that is characteristic of Donne disappears in favor of a formal uniformity that would be that of a "precious" French poet for whom precisely only what is "formal" would count, be it verse related, rhetorical, or intellectual: a *conceit* reduced to a play of witty language. We are far from Ellrodt, who states when attempting—and it is difficult, quite difficult—to define what is *distinctive* in Donne:

> He is concerned with exploring an experience, with defining a living reality by way of concepts. In his works, thought is the language of emotion.... Every experience is both lived and thought. (*L'inspiration personnelle* 120)

The unfaithfulness is in fact twofold: the interweaving of linguistic elements aiming simultaneously at maintaining the experience as "lived" and at "thinking" it, which is specific to Donne, is replaced by a French *abstract* articulation (which belongs to no specific poet, to no poetic horizon) that is purely rhetorico-intellectual. As a result, when reading the translations, a reader who did not know anything about Donne would not even *guess* that he is an *English* poet. He could be a Golden Age Spaniard, a German baroque

---

26. Speaking about Hopkins, Leyris said the most beautiful act of faith: we must find the moment when "French, after appearing for a long time like a smooth defensive wall against which the battering ram of the poem struggled in vain, allowed us to suddenly glimpse a secret passageway" (*Poèmes* 16).

writer, or an Italian mannerist. This translation mostly projects the profile of a typical French poet of the time, which is another consequence of Denis and Fuzier's project.

Let us now move more decisively from the misunderstanding of Donne's *Englishness* to that of his most characteristic *poeticality*. The rhetorical formal and precious vision that Denis and Fuzier have of Donne (and of all the poetry of the period, one can surmise) prevents them from taking into consideration the poet's colloquialism, in spite of Poisson's warning. But evidently Donne is not only colloquial. He is a poet in whom speculativeness, rhetoric, sensitivity, colloquialism are united in a unique way—unique in all of English poetry, unique in Western poetry. This *extreme* uniqueness is obviously difficult to capture, even if it can easily be perceived. Ellrodt attempted to do it, and I quoted him briefly. Rather than attempting to merely detect the work of reflection in Donne—a work that leads to the formal intertwining to which I am referring and that, for Ellrodt, rests on a certain "identity of aspiration," giving a unity to Donne's poetry as well as his life[27]—Carey attempts to define the *work of the imaginary* in the poet and speaks of "a connecting and compacting tendency which spreads through all his thought and poetry" (275; Minière 115). And then: "Donne's vision was conjunctive only because it was disjunctive, and he synthesized only because he was by nature analytic" (266).

This last remark allows me to say that, in Donne, the work of the imaginary, the work of reflection, the play of mind and lyrical spirit intermingle, and, as we can guess, not without violent clashes. But, fundamentally, I agree with Ellrodt that Donne is a poet who "thinks." Naturally this thought follows existing forms of thought, and the most varied ones, from Thomist or Scotist scholastics to the new modern modes of thought, from alchemy to the various discourses of emerging sciences and technologies. His originality is twofold: Donne moves *naturally* (so to speak) within "metaphysical" thought and no less naturally anchors this thought in "singular experience" (his own) (Ellrodt, *L'inspiration personnelle* 211). If metaphysics, in the strict sense of the term, is the thought that thinks the world, the soul and the body, the here and now and the beyond, time and eternity, love, God, and death, in a figure each time unique to each thinker since Plato and Aristotle, Donne—without being at all a "philosopher"—naturally thinks all this in the language and the multiple terminologies historically invented by meta-

---

27. See note 44, where the quotation is amplified.

physics and theology, but always in reference, as Ellrodt states, to *experience* (in this, he is English again): first, the experience of the love of women and of the multiple situations in which this experience holds sway (Donne's love poems, as we shall see, are occasional poems); religious experience, to which the sonnets correspond; and the monumental mass of the sermons, as metaphysical as the love poems (when they are so). It is this familiarity with metaphysics and this ability to constantly link it to his experience and beyond it to the *experience of Everyman* that makes Donne what he is, that makes him a great thinking poet and a great metaphysical sermon writer. And of course, in spite of his uniqueness, I think that Donne belongs to the great English tradition (without ignoring individual differences): Milton, Blake, Coleridge, and Hopkins, to mention the greatest poets.

But "thought" implies "concept." In order to define the specificity of terms and of concepts in Donne, Ellrodt speaks of "concrete concept" (*L'inspiration personnelle* 256), "most often a heavy, dense, concept that is substantial in some way" (254). But the whole of Donne's "concrete concepts" forms a network, as does the whole of the instrumental, technical, and scientific terms and concepts. All the poems are thus "innervated"[28] conceptually and metaphorically (it is the same thing), and this innervation is also what ensures the deep unity of all of Donne's poetry, to which I shall return when discussing "Going to Bed." Here, Jean-Marie Benoist said the essential: "Donne's poetry is ... an extraordinary topology, the richness of which consists of an endless referral of one poem to the other in a network of mutual *translation*" (12; emphasis mine).[29]

Fuzier and Denis' project totally "forgets" this experiential/reflexive dimension of Donne and this metaphorical and conceptual innervation of all his poetry.[30] It thus treats the poems as rhetorico-prosodic totalities where the words (be they terms or other words) are basically aleatory—the only necessity

---

28. [Carey's text says "run through," and the French translation "innervé" (innervated). Trans. Note]

29. Similarly Carey states, "It is as if Donne had thought out these poems as variant formulations of a persistent and ultimately insoluble problem never solved, which involved the simultaneous possession of contraries" (269).

30. This omission is all the more surprising that it is not complete. Both the analysis and the translation of Sonnet XIV show an awareness of Donne's precise vocabulary. See Fuzier, "La formalité de l'essence" (44). But this attention to terminology is far from systematic and is totally absent when it comes to the "profane" poems.

being "versification" in the large sense of the word. Thus, for the needs of the cause, of *this particular* cause, when Donne says, "The Women," if "poetic transposition" demands it, Fuzier and Denis will put "La femme" ["Woman" or "The woman"]. The translators treat each poem both as a particular poem (this totality right here) and as a poem like the others (that will have to be subjected to the same archaizing and rhetorical treatment). However, as I said, being "situational," each poem is *singular* and at the same time, as Benoist points out, linked to the others "in a network of mutual translation."[31] To speak of a "translation network" is already to state a principle or one of the fundamental principles of translation as well as of the literary *transfer* of Donne. This principle is founded on his work's dialectic between the uniqueness of every poem and the fact that the poem is in a network (terminological, thematic, metaphoric, reflexive, rhetorical networks, and so forth) with all the others, often through sub-networks. To translate Donne is first to carry across the totality of the concrete forms of the topology that intertwine each poetic unit with the other. To translate Donne is "simply" *to be in harmony with the translating structure of his poems.*

I have finished, for the moment, the critical examination of Fuzier and Denis' project. My criticisms are harsh, but the stakes raised by their project—as much for the translation of Donne as for poetic translation in general—require that fundamental questions be addressed (if only partially) and that equally fundamental objections be raised. To raise careful objections to the work of these translators is to *respect* it. To reject their work without explanation or to mention such-and-such isolated overwhelming "weakness" would be a sign of disdain. Before moving on to "Going to Bed" and as a transition, I will discuss "Sapho to Philaenis,"[32] which is part of a sub-network with "Going to Bed." The analysis of this poem and of its translation will demonstrate more concretely the consequences of Fuzier and Denis' project.

---

31. This network is particularly visible at the level of what Carey calls "Donne's favourite subjects," which are all "meeting places for opposites... problematic or technically complicated, surrounded by an outwork of theory" (261): angels, mummies, mandrakes, moneys, shadows, geographical atlases, coins, all have the same formal structure—and they all refer to each other in an endless network; they are all permutable, "translatable." For Donne, women are "like maps"; they have the same function of concentration, compacting, meeting of opposites. All these "favourite subjects" are—in accordance with their nature, with their concreteness and their formal structure—expressed in a *most precise* vocabulary that is not aleatory in the least.

32. [The title quoted in the original French is "Heroicall Epistle: Sapho to Philaenis" from *Poèmes de John Donne,* but the standard English editions of Donne's poetry list the poem under "Elegies." Trans. Note]

"SAPHO TO PHILAENIS"

The "heroic epistle" "Sapho to Philaenis," one of Donne's most beautiful love poems, is also one of the first *English* lesbian love poems. In modern editions, it almost met the same fate as "Going to Bed" in the first edition—it almost disappeared (see Carey 271–72). This "incursion" of the poet of the love of Woman has nothing to do with an erotic or libertine curiosity. It obeys the need to explore and to think through the *internal logic* of the love of woman for woman, of the same for the same. Here Carey imagines Donne "wishing to depict a union of lovers so complete that the two identities, being identical, sink into one" (271). The basis of this interest, unique in Donne's poetry, is a "situation revealing itself as a site of reciprocities and interactions" (Minière 111)[33] in a radical way. One may say that "Sapho to Philaenis" is indeed a situation: Sappho, alone, speaks to the absent Philaenis in front of her mirror, while touching her body. This call to Philaenis is also a paean to lesbian love as opposed to the love of men. Not only is love of woman for a woman a reflected love, but this reflected love also has for its foundation, according to Donne's subtle mind, the fact that the feminine body is itself a mirror of itself. Thus Sappho says to her absent woman friend:

> Thou art not soft, and cleare, and strait, and faire,
> As *Down,* as *Starts, Cedars,* and *Lillies* are,
> But thy right hand, and cheek, and eye, only
> Are like thy other hand, and cheek, and eye.[34]

---

33. [The original quote in Carey reads as follows: "simple situations which, when examined, split in half, revealing themselves as entailing reciprocity or interaction" (271). Trans. Note] Carey stresses Donne's attraction for verbs constructed with the prefix "inter-": to intertouch, intercharge, interaccuse, interassure, interinanimate, interwish, and interbring. The list itself bears witness to the importance of words for Donne—and of the deep-rooted need that leads the poet to create words.

34. Tu n'es pas douce et claire et nette et dessinée
  Comme le sont Dunes, Etoiles, Cèdres et Lys
  Mais ta main droite, la joue, l'œil, seuls
  Sont comme ton autre main, joue, œil. (Minière 111)

  [You are not soft and clear and straight and drawn
  As are Dunes, Stars, Cedars and Lilies
  But your right hand, cheek, eye, only
  Are like your other hand, cheek, eye. (Trans. Note)]

Philaenis is not "like" the stars and the cedars; she is not comparable to anything but to herself: *she is like herself* [*elle est comme elle*]. Donne says that this being like herself is "*naturall* Paradise" (l. 35), which has no need for "*perfection*" (l. 37).

From that, Sappho deduces that the love of men, compared to this perfection, is "too much" in that it brings the alterity of its sex as well as the trace of its passage like "Theeves trac'd, which rob when it snows" (l. 40).[35]

In contrast, love between women introduces neither alterity nor "more" in the snowy body of the loved one. And the following lines develop, with a rigorous logic, the truth of Sapphic love, the experience of the intertwining of the same with the same, of the confusion of Sappho's *self* [in English in the text] with Philaenis's *self*:

> My two lips, eyes, thighs, differ from thy two,
> But so, as thine from one another doe;
> And, oh, no more; the likenesse being such,
> Why should they not alike in all parts touch?
> Hand to strange hand, lippe to lippe none denies;
> Why should they brest to brest, or thighs to thighs? (l. 45–50)

Can we say that this dialectic is also pure rhetoric as, it is claimed, in Shakespeare? We can if we add that this rhetorical dialectic is also a poetic dialectic and a philosophical dialectic that comes directly from the great dialogues of the tradition, from *The Banquet* to Marsilio Ficino.[36] It is not that Donne plays rhetorically with the paradoxes of post- or neo-Platonic thought: situationally, he deploys the dialectic of the *self* embracing itself imaginarily with another *self* [in English in the text] that is and that is not itself:

> Likenesse begets such strange selfe flatterie
> That touching my selfe, all seems done to thee.
> My selfe I embrace, and mine owne hands I kisse,
> And amorously thanke my selfe for this. (l. 51–54)

---

35. "Comme on suit dans la neige un voleur à sa trace" (Fuzier and Denis 85). ["As one follows in the snow a thief's track." Trans. Note]

36. [Italian poet, philosopher, and translator of Plato. A major figure of the early Italian Renaissance. Trans. Note]

I shall come back to these *selves* when speaking about "Going to Bed." What happens to this *poetic logic* in the Fuzier and Denis version? Let us take lines 23–24, which seem in English to be most simple and colloquial:

> But thy right hand, and cheek, and eye, only
> Are like thy other hand, and cheek, and eye.

The translators propose:

> Mais ta joue and ta main, ta lèvre et ton oreille
> N'ont d'égales qu'en toi, où elles s'appareillent.[37]

The reader can only be *confused* by the liberties taken with details (no more right hand or eye, but a lip and an ear), as much as by the obfuscation of Donne's poetic logic—only because, it seems, of the rhyme "oreille"/ "s'appareillent." The same disdain for the factuality of individual words and the colloquialism of some lines can be found later, always for the benefit of versification and an undue intensification of the erotic and passional tone of the poem, as if the translators were attempting to present a yet more daring and fiery Donne, even in this poem. Such a movement of intensification of formal features at the service of the passionate leaves behind the more measured tone of the original and the factual precision of the lines. When Sappho says:

> Thy body is a naturall Paradise,
> In whose selfe, unmanur'd, all pleasure lies (l. 35–36)[38]

the lines are "polished" into:

---

37. [But your cheek and your hand, your lip and your ear,
    Have no equal but in you, where they pair.
Oreille (ear) rhymes with *appareillent* (pair). Trans. Note]
38. In his rendition Rothschild attempts to be both more literal and more precious:

> Paradis naturel ton corps est une terre
> Du plaisir sans fumure.
> [Natural Paradise your body is an earth
> Of pleasure without manure. (Trans. Note)]

He tries not to shy away too much from "unmanur'd."

Ton corps est paradis où croissent sans culture
Toutes les voluptés à l'état de nature.³⁹

The rhyme is kept, but Donne's colloquialism has been replaced with two "noble" classical lines: the coarse "unmanur'd" disappears, the deep "selfe" too; the very simple "pleasure," quite common in Donne, becomes the noun *voluptés;* "naturall" becomes *sans culture* [without culture]. How far removed this seems!

The idea, an essential one in Donne, that the body exists on the mode of the *self,* of the "it-self" (an idea that goes so far for him that, throughout his work, it provides the underlying structure for his conception of the relations of soul and of the self, each existing of the mode of the self, of the *thought* self, and thus unable to be totally foreign to the other), is erased by the translators.

Lines 51–52,

Likenesse begets such strange selfe flatterie,
That touching my selfe, all seems done to thee,

become in the Fuzier and Denis translation:

La ressemblance engendre une erreur si traîtresse
Que, caressant mon corps, c'est toi que je caresse.⁴⁰

Not only does the play of selves disappear, but the dialectic of touching oneself, which is equally a touch-the-self-of-the-other, a dialectic presented in this *abstract* form by Donne, is replaced by an intensified erotic gesture: "*Caressant* mon *corps,* c'est toi que je caresse" [Caressing my body, it is you who I caress].

But there is no caress here (no body either). Is this a detail? Absolutely not. I am concretely showing what I said earlier about the uniqueness of Donne's poems and, at the same time, their being-in-network. For "to touch" is an

---

39. [Your body is paradise where grow without culture
All the voluptuous pleasure in the state of nature. (Trans. Note)]
40. [Resemblance engenders such treacherous error
That, caressing my body, it is you whom I caress. (Trans. Note)]

essential signifier of his poetry. In "Of the Progresse of the Soule," Donne had invented the verb "to intertouch." Touch, contact, is not caress. We "are touching" here, let me repeat, on a general tendency of the translation by Fuzier and Denis to *intensify, for Donne's love poems (thus, in the majority of the poems), an erotic and passionate element* supposedly underlying the rhetoric and "pseudo philosophy" of the poet. It is a hypothesis, but the translation's liberties, which are rather disconcerting at first, may be thus explained. And it is again a consequence of the project, since this passionate and erotizing lyrical version, tightly laced up in its versification, is more in keeping with French poetry of the time, out of which they want to construct the French Donne.

When Sappho says:

My selfe I embrace, and mine owne hands I kisse,
And amorously thanke my selfe for this (l. 53–54)[41]

the lines become:

Je me baise les mains et m'étreins *follement*
Pour m'en remercier *très* amoureusement.[42]

We note two intensifiers: *follement* [wildly], an addition (for the rhyme), and *très* [very] (perhaps for the number of feet). Unfortunately, it would be easy to show that this frenzy, this unbridled passion, excitation of the senses, and ecstasy of the body do not belong to the poetry of Donne.

---

41. Je m'étreins et baise mes propres mains,
    Et me fête moi-même amoureusement. (Minière 112)

   [I embrace myself and kiss my own hands
   And congratulate myself amorously. (Trans. Note)]
42. [I kiss my own hands and embrace myself *wildly*,
    To thank myself *very* amorously. (Trans. Note)]

"GOING TO BED"

At last we are coming to "Going to Bed" and its translation (translations). The partial analysis of Fuzier and Denis will show the serious consequences of their project; it will also show, indirectly, what the foundations of another translation, and of a reflexive translation of lyric poetry, must be. This analysis presupposes an analysis of the original: simultaneously of its status, its structure, and its content. I said earlier that "Going to Bed" seemed to me to be a unique poem in Donne and in Western poetry. The reason for this remains to be shown. At the same time, this uniqueness does not isolate it, neither within Donne's works nor within the Western lyrical tradition. To explain its uniqueness is also to explain its links with other poems, other poetic traditions, and its being-in-constellation.

Paz tells us that the poem "may" have been written after Donne's marriage to Anne More, and thus for her. I tend to agree with him, unlike Fuzier and Denis, and unlike Rothschild, who translate the simple "Going to Bed" as "Le coucher de sa maîtresse" ["Going to Bed with One's Mistress"] and transform the poem into an erotic poem in the sense of French erotic poetry. But it will not be impossible to prove that this poem, although daring, even the most daring that I know, is at its core a poem of conjugal love, of *spousal love,* as Hopkins would say ("Epithalame," in *Grandeur de Dieu* 90).[43]

The uniqueness of the poem lies first in the love situation that is evoked. Any poem of Donne is anchored in a specific context and thus often in the present tense. Here, it is the present, as indicated by the present participle of the title, "Going to Bed,"[44] the moment when the man and his wife go to bed. I do not know of any poem that deals in such a prolix way—in fact from beginning to end—with this moment of mutual discovery, of the entry into nudity, which precedes caresses and embraces, and all the "carnal" texture of love. This is why one cannot say that this poem is "erotic" unless this word is used to mean anything. The poem may *appear erotic* because it seems to us that it constantly anticipates what "comes after." Rothschild comically falls for this illusion when he interprets the (obviously suggestive) lines 25–26:

---

43. ["Epithalamion" 171–73. Trans. Note]
44. Ellrodt has said everything that needs to be said on the importance of the present in Donne, who stated in a sermon: "Now, there is no vaster or all encompassing word" (*Sermons* 2:250, qtd. in Ellrodt, *L'inspiration personnelle* 89).

> Licence my roaving hands, and let them go,
> Before, behind, between, above, below

as the "approach of the body of the naked woman" ("Traduire 'Donne'" 78). But Donne has just said that his wife is wearing a white robe as angels do, and it is only at the end of the poem's line 45 that he asks her to completely undress.

This is all the more reason to keep the thematic uniqueness of the poem from translators who are too hurried. The sequence and the structure of the poem are simple.

Lines 1–4: Opening of the scene and request by the man.

Line 5–18: In this sequence, punctuated by five vigorous "off's," the woman is invited to remove, one by one, precisely, her adornments and clothes, except for a *white robe,* and to adjourn to bed. What is removed is named quite precisely, but it comes with a splendid cascade of images and praises. One can consider this part of the poem its rhetorical part—an elevated poetic rhetoric, but still a rhetoric:

> *Off with that happy busk, which I envie,*
> *That still can be, and still can stand so nigh.* (l. 11–12)

These lines, especially the second one, display a skillful (and successful) rhetoric.

Lines 19–24: There is an almost digressive and ratiocinating pause, but one that is used to introduce *significant religious* images in the poem, images directly linked to sensuality, as can be seen in line 24, the most daring one in the poem, since it evokes erection:

> Those set our hairs, but these our flesh upright.

I also use the word "pause" because, as Ellrodt argues, it is as if here the poem "refuses to support ... the lyrical flight." Ellrodt adds, "Isn't this faithfulness to lived experience?" (*L'inspiration personnelle* 198). It is absolutely true: after the abrupt succession of the "off," one must stop.

Line 25–34: There is a wonderful progression, the center of gravity of the poem, what makes its most unique uniqueness and, at the same time, places it in a whole constellation of Western lyric poetry.

This center is itself a rapid movement that goes from the discovery (not the caress) of the feminine body (under the robe), "Licence my roaving hands," to the discovery of the body as country, continent, kingdom, and other splendid metaphors. Thus, there is a rapid movement from sense perception, from physical contact to the metaphorical perception particular to Donne (in another elegy, he says that women are "all States—Americas, Newfoundland, Indias of spice and mine, world maps with meridians and creeks and fair Atlantic navels" [Carey 265]); then from this perception to "abstract" philosophical perception (l. 31, "to enter in these bonds, is to be free; Then ..."); then from this abstract reflection, in an ultimate movement both lyrical and metaphysical, the whole *essence* of the experience of "Going to Bed" is expressed:

> Full nakedness! All joyes are due to thee,
> As souls unbodied, bodies uncloth'd must be,
> To taste whole joyes. (l. 33–35)

These are unique lines, I think, where Ellrodt's statement that in Donne "every experience is both lived and thought" really finds its best illustration. Let me add, the experience is thought *poetically*. These lines can be called *poetic enunciations with truth as their purpose.*
Lines 35–43: Here the poem slows down again, almost digressively, on the theme of the double aspect, profane and sacred, of women, where, through rhetoric, *Donne's always religious* mode of thought is also affirmed.[45] It is also the pause before the "end."
Lines 44–48: The man asks the woman to undress as in front of a midwife

---

45. I can only mention it in passing here, but Donne has *always* been, all his life, both *religious* and *Christian*. The "religious" element in him is deeper than the "Christian" one; it is the "identity of aspiration" to which Ellrodt refers: "Thus, from the profane to the sacred, an essential identity of aspiration, an essential continuity of aspiration are affirmed in Donne's life and works.... The same search for reality, for substance: the man who claimed to draw 'full joyes' from the nakedness of a body is the same man who was looking for a 'substantial love' in passion and tenderness, the same man who must have aspired to the 'essential joy' promised in the beyond" (*L'inspiration personnelle* 152). But Donne is also a "true" Christian, which can be seen in his relation to the *body*. There again, Ellrodt is stunningly insightful: "That the body must be *both* scorned and honored, this apparent contradiction reflects a complexity of feeling that is hardly found outside of the Christian vision. Donne fully accepts the paradoxes of Christian doctrine ... which reveals to us both the decay of the body and its irreplaceable role, irreplaceable also for the life of the spirit" (230).

and to "shew / Thy self" (l. 44–45). It is the entry into the space of embrace where "Here is no penance, much less innocence" (l. 46).

Earlier too, on line 9, he has asked her to "Unlace your self."

Earlier too, it is the man who first undresses, "to touch thee," to cover with his naked body the naked body of his wife. Nakedness on nakedness, *self* on *self* [in English in the text].

The poem ends, almost quietly, with these lines, both simple and mysterious (why is the man naked first, why must the man "teach" the naked-being to the woman?).

It is the following part that could be, if you will, "erotic." But Donne's poetry, as far as I know, always *stops* at this threshold.

The uniqueness of this poem can now be better understood, especially if "Going to Bed" is momentarily placed in its network. We find the *thematic core* of this poem in two epithalamions, in particular in the poem "Lincolnes Inne":

Thy virgins girdle now untie,
And in thy nuptiall bed (loves altar) lye
A pleasing sacrifice; now dispossesse
Thee of these chaines and robes which were put on
T'adorne the day, not thee; for thou, alone,
Like vertue'and truth, art best in nakednesse.

Dénoue maintenant ta ceinture virginale
et dans ton lit nuptial (autel de l'amour), gis
agréable victime; défais-toi maintenant
de ces chaînes et de ces robes qui furent mises
pour orner le jour, et non point toi; car à toi, seule en cela
avec la vertu et la vérité, c'est la nudité qui va le mieux. (Legouis, *Poèmes choisis* 130)[46]

---

46. The epithalamion "On the Lady Elizabeth" is more risqué but directly linked to the theme of the soul that strips itself of the body, characteristic of "Going to Bed":

> A Bride, before a good night could be said,
> Should vanish from her cloathes into her bed,
> As Soules from bodies steale, and are not spy'd.

The French translation by Ellrodt is:

The tone is that of an epithalamion and is already close to that of "Going to Bed." (There are reasons to think that these two poems are from approximately the same period.)

"Loves Progress" (Fuzier and Denis 70–75) is the cartographic exploration—but here a rather libertine one—of the female body. The "progress" here is that of the hand that *uncovers* (when they let themselves be discovered)[47] seas, islands, continents, promontories, breathtaking heights of the reclining body of the lover. Thus, this is the same religious "situation" as "Going to Bed," but without the conjugal aura. Carey would call it a variant in a minor key.

"Sapho to Philaenis" presents the same situation, but without Philaenis. It is a space of touch, always, not of caresses, a space where two selves [in English in the text] mingle, whereas in "Going to Bed" they reveal each other and "cover" each other. It is also a variant, with the presentation of an extreme example.

The unfinished poem "Of the Progresse of the Soule" "touches" "Going to Bed" because it deals with *joys,* scholastically divided into "essential" and "accidental" joys (both categories are found on earth as well as in heaven).

"The Extasie" is linked to "Going to Bed" in that it treats—almost methodically—the relations of soul and body in love, and the necessity of the "incarnation" of the soul.

As for the late "Hymne to God my God, in my Sicknesse," one of the unique truly poetic poems of Donne after 1614, Benoist has pointed out its relation to "Going to Bed": "There is no break from the remarkable erotic vein of 'Going to Bed' and the ardent expectation of the meeting with God in 'Hymne to God my God, in my Sicknesse'" (12).

Not only is there no break, but we find the same images (body/map, which is here explored by doctors), and the same occurrence of *joy.* I must quote the first stanzas, as this poem is not a simple "variant" of "Going to Bed," but a poem in its own right, although not "unique" (except, perhaps, among Donne's religious poems):

Une épousée, avant qu'on ait le temps de souhaiter bonne nuit,
Devrait avoir déjà, hors de ses vêtements, disparu dans son lit
Comme l'âme hors du corps s'enfuit, inaperçue. (*L'inspiration personnelle* 215)

47. [In French *découvrir* means both "to uncover" and "to discover." Trans. Note]

HYMNE TO GOD MY GOD, IN MY SICKNESSE

1 Since I am comming to that Holy roome,
2   Where, with thy Quire of Saints for evermore,
3 I shall be made thy Musique; As I come
4   I tune the Instrument here at the dore,
5   And what I must doe then, thinke here before.

6 Whilst my Physitians by their love are growne
7   Cosmographers, and I their Mapp, who lie
8 Flat on this bed, that by them may be showne
9   That this is my South-west discoverie
10   *Per fretum febris,* by these streights to die,

11 I joy, that in these straits, I see my West;
12   For, though theire currants yeeld returne to none,
13 What shall my West hurt me? As West and East
14   In all flatt Maps (and I am one) are one,
15   So death doth touch the Resurrection.

16 Is the Pacifique Sea my home? Or are
17   The Easterne riches? Is *Jerusalem*?
18 *Anyan,* and *Magellan,* and *Gibraltare,*
19   All streights, and none but streights, are wayes to them,
20   Whether where *Japhet* dwelt, or *Cham,* or *Sem.*

21 We thinke that *Paradise* and *Calvarie,*
22   *Christs* Crosse, and *Adams* tree, stood in one place;
23 Looke Lord, and finde both *Adams* met in me;
24   As the first *Adams* sweat surrounds my face,
25   May the last *Adams* blood my soule embrace.

26 So, in his purple wrapp'd receive mee Lord,
27   By these his thornes give me his other Crowne;
28 And as to others soules I preach'd thy word,
29   Be this my Text, my Sermon to mine owne,
30   Therefore that he may raise the Lord throws down.

Translation by Yves Bonnefoy
À DIEU, MON DIEU, DANS MA MALADIE

1   Puisque j'accède à cette chambre sainte
2   Où, à jamais, dans le chœur des élus,
3   Je serai ta musique: en route encore
4   J'accorde l'instrument, près de la porte,
5   Et réfléchis à la tâche prochaine.

6   Mes médecins par amour se sont faits
7   Géographes, et moi leur mappemonde
8   Qui s'étale sur cette couche, pour qu'ils montrent
9   Que là, au bout, c'est mon passage du Sud-Ouest
10   Que je trouve, *per fretum febris*, en ces détroits où mourir.

11   Mais moi je me fais joie que ce soit l'Ouest
12   Qu'en ces resserrements je voie paraître
13   Car bien que ces courants soient sans retour
14   Quel mal me ferait l'Ouest? Couchant, levant
15   Sur toute carte plane se rejoignent,
16   Et j'en suis une, où Mort, c'est déjà renaître.

17   Est-ce le Pacifique ma demeure? Ou est-ce
18   L'inépuisable Orient? Ou *Jérusalem*?
19   *Anyan*, et *Magellan*, et *Gibraltar*
20   Sont des détroits: rien que d'étroit ne mène
21   Où soit vécut *Japhet*, soit *Cham*, soit *Sem*.

22   Nous pensons, ce fut même lieu, *Paradis*, *Calvaire*,
23   L'arbre d'*Adam*, la croix de *Jésus-Christ*.
24   Vois, Seigneur, vois qu'en moi se rencontrèrent
25   Les deux *Adams*: et à l'heure où ruisselle
26   La sueur du premier *Adam* sur mon visage,
27   Puisse le sang de l'Autre baigner mon âme!

28   Oh, drapé dans sa pourpre, accueille-moi,
29   Mon Dieu, et donne-moi à travers ses épines

30   Sa seconde couronne! À toutes âmes
31   J'ai prêché ta parole; pour la mienne
32   Que mon sermon ce soit, mon texte: mon Dieu
33   N'abat que pour dresser d'entre ceux qui tombent.

We can see here—as do those who read closely all the poems mentioned—how "Going to Bed" belongs to a whole network, a network with a *definite structure* (every other poem does not have the same "position"; some serve as a "core," others as "variants"—which are of various types—others still serve as "partial development," and the last one takes up the same theme in another situation, the man who is going to die facing his God and with his doctors, not the man facing his wife before the embrace—joy in both cases), but at the same time, this poem is unique, central within this network.

Empirically this uniqueness is found in the fact that the love situation itself is sustained from beginning to end, without being described.[48] However, it would be ridiculous to claim that "Going to Bed" is unique because it alone deals with this scene. Its real uniqueness lies elsewhere: it lies in the suspense of a few lines where, beyond any rhetoric, beyond even any ordinary lyricism, the poem enters a "metaphysical lyricism" where it joins, as we shall see, Pindar, the troubadours, Blake, Novalis, Hölderlin, and Hopkins, all "poets of joy."

In order to feel this progression near the last three lines, it is enough to reread the whole block of lines, which—in spite of its movements from level to level—is *one*:

> Licence my roaving hands, and let them go,
> Before, behind, between, above, below.
> O my America! my new-found-land,
> My kingdome, safeliest when with one man man'd
> My Myne of precious stones, My Emperie,
> How blest am I in this discovering thee!
> To enter in these bonds, is to be free;
> Then where my hand is set, my seal shall be.

---

48. According to Ellrodt, "Whatever the situation, even if he often speaks to the woman he loves, Donne never evokes her, unless it is metaphorically.... He does not describe her, does not compose any blazon. What he wants to communicate is the feeling to which she gives rise in us" ("Présence et permanence" 23–24).

Full nakedness! All joyes are due to thee,
As souls unbodied, bodies uncloth'd must be,
To taste whole joyes. (l. 25–34)

Joy and nakedness, these words are key words in Donne's poetry. I shall have the opportunity later to speak of *nakedness* in Donne. As we saw, joy is found in the poem addressed to God, Elegy III, "Change";[49] in Elegy X, "The Dreame";[50] in "Of the Progresse of the Soule," where part of the poem is devoted to the "essentiall joy in this life and in the next," and another to "accidentall joyes in both places." For Donne, the highest joy, the joy that never ceases to intensify and to grow, is that which rises among the chosen as the Resurrection draws near:

When earthly bodies more celestiall
Shall be, then Angels were, for they could fall;
This kindle of joy doth every day admit
Degrees of growth, but none of losing it. (l. 493–96)[51]

As Ellrodt points out, Donne rarely links joy and rest—the word "rest" appears only three times in his works (150). Joy is active. It is linked neither to rest nor to pleasure (not directly in any case), nor to enjoyment [*jouissance*]. Joy is joy: the poetic feeling or feelings above all else. The word often appears in the plural, as in "Going to Bed": "joyes," in accordance with the fact that the essence of joy is plural (unlike perhaps the other poetic feelings of sadness and melancholy, unless one thinks of du Bellay's "Les regrets" . . .).

There are also the verbs "to joy," found in "Hymne to God my God":

---

49. In Legouis, *Poèmes Choisis*,

   "Change" is the nursery
   Of musicke, joy, life, and eternity.

   Le changement est la pépinière
   de la musique, de la joie, de la vie et de l'éternité. (116–18)

50. "Alas, true joyes at best are dreame enough" (Fuzier and Denis 52–53).
51. Temps où les corps terrestres seront plus célestes
    que ne l'étaient les anges, car ceux-ci pouvaient déchoir,
    cette sorte de joie admet chaque jour
    des degrés de croissance, mais aucun de déperdition. (Legouis, *Poèmes choisis* 175)

I joy, that in these straits, I see my West

and "to rejoyce," in Elegy XVII, "Variety":

The heavens rejoice in motion. (Fuzier and Denis 64)

Telling us of joy (joys) as a feeling (an active one) of man in some "strong" moments, thus as something subjective but also like a feeling-of-the-heavens, thus of the "world,"[52] Donne, as we shall see, fits into a long poetic tradition, and even (incidentally) a philosophic one, since the sense of joy in "Of the Progresse of the Soule" is rather like Spinoza's joy: "Joy is man's passage from a lesser perfection to a greater one" (*Ethique* 26).[53]

Following Savignac, Pindar's French translator, I assume that Pindar was the first to say that joy is the poetic sentiment par excellence—the feeling that carries the poem as well as what the poem projects forward and illuminates in itself—"N'obscurcis pas la joie dans la vie: de beaucoup le plus important pour l'homme, un âge joyeux" (26).[54] Here I must quote the translator:

> In Pindar, there is a will to overcome sorrow and to have joy prevail above all else. If suffering, as his contemporary Aeschylus teaches us, may be a means of knowledge and salvation, for Pindar, it is joy that takes on this function. . . . Joy is the best way to know oneself; it teaches through the blossoming of the senses the virtualities of the self, like love; intensified by Pindar's words, joy make man "equal to kings." . . . Indeed, Pindar develops what was nascent in the Greek salutation "Rejoice." (Savignac 26–27)

Closer, and surprisingly close to Donne, we have the troubadours' *le joi* (not yet the feminine noun *la joie*), without there being, of course, any influence, any filiation. For them, *le joi* is expressly linked to *woman, nakedness, love, the world,* and *God,* thus to the same themes as Donne.

Thus Guillem Ademar writes, "Mais tant me tient dénudé de joie celle que

---

52. As Ellrodt points out, "the word 'world' comes back again and again in Donne's work" (*L'inspiration personnelle* 100).

53. [Part III, proposition 11, reads, "By Joy, therefore, I shall understand . . . that passion by which the Mind passes to a greater perfection" (Spinoza, *Collected Works* 500–1). Trans. Note]

54. ["Don't darken joy in life: the most important of all for man, a joyous age." Trans. Note]

Dieu me donne de tenir nue" (Roubaud, *Les troubadours* 16).⁵⁵ And Arnaut Daniel, in his splendid "Doux bruits et cris" ["Sweet Cries and Noises"]:

> God gracious . . . if he pleases, watches over my lady and me lying in the bedroom where we both decided a precious rendezvous of which so much joy I expect that her beautiful body, I kiss laughing, discover and admire against the light of the lamp. (Roubaud, *Les troubadours* 233–35)⁵⁶

Roubaud has shown that *le joi* is an essential word in the poetry of the troubadours. *Le joi* is linked to the love of the Lady and to her nakedness. What distinguishes it is that it also springs from the heart and, from there, irradiates onto the world—"my heart is so full of joy that everything changes nature" (*Les troubadours* 16)—and from the world as well. Thus for William IX, "all the joy of the world is our lady if we both love each another" (16).

We just saw in Donne this essence of joy, both *subjective* and *cosmic*, and the reader can also find it in two great "poems of joy," one "Heimkunft" ("Return") by Hölderlin (*Œuvres* 815–19) and the other "Epithalamion" by Hopkins (*Grandeur de Dieu* 87–91), which are too long to be quoted and commented on here.

We are far from any "sensualist" interpretation of joy or joys. What is common to *all* joys and makes their *poeticality* is both their tone of openness, of clarity, and the feeling of growth and intensity that they convey. Every joy is *luminous, ephiphanic, and intensifying*. Every joy is an experience of the revelation of a living essence. In "Going to Bed," the experience of amorous nakedness is a source of joy because it is the discovery not only of the "beautiful body" of the loved one, but of her *being*. This is why, as I said, Donne requests:

> Unlace your self (l. 9)
> . . . shew
> Thy self. (l. 44–45)

---

55. ["But she holds me so stripped of joy the woman whom God grants me to hold naked." Trans. Note]

56. [The original reads: "Dieu le grâcieux . . . veille s'il lui plaît ma dame et moi couchés en la chambre où tous deux nous décidâmes une précieuse entrevue dont tant de joie j'attends que son beau corps j'embrasse riant découvre et regarde contre la lumière de la lampe." Trans. Note]

Nakedness is the epiphany of the self (albeit a corporal self), not of the flesh, which, in the embrace, has its opacity, its obscurity. *Before* the embrace, there is that moment of pure joy—the facing of nakednesses. Joy is always pure.

It is worth noting that in "Going to Bed," however closely and concretely Donne follows the unfolding of the situation (he does not follow it; he orders it), he does not fail perhaps not to idealize it, but at least to *give it the purest course:* no incident, no haste, nothing unpleasantly empirical that would "disturb things."

When Blake writes: "The nakedness of woman is the work of God" (*Œuvres* 164–65)[57] or when Novalis says in his *New Fragments*, "There is but one Temple in the World; and that is the Body of Man. . . . We touch Heaven, when we lay our hand on a human body" (Guerne, *Les romantiques allemands* 233),[58] the two poets move within the same epiphanic and "religious" experience of the body and nakedness. For them, as for Donne, a single knot ties love, nakedness, woman, world, and joy. At its core, this knot is "religious" in the sense that joy, love, woman, and world are deeply connected to the "divine" and to God. But this is obviously not the place to speak about this depth, this innermost poetic joy.

We have thus placed, straight off, the poet of joy Donne in a vast constellation of poets in the hope of illuminating "Going to Bed," of giving it twin figures, while keeping the uniqueness of the elegy. But this placing in constellation will also allow us to reread the poet's lines more closely and to measure all their *rigor:*

Full nakedness! All joyes are due to thee. (l. 33)

Only the "full nakedness" [in English in the text] is source of joy(s). It is in love—human or divine love—that nakedness becomes "full," that is, infinite. This means that nakedness, the experience of nakedness, cannot be summarized in the "naked" fact of being naked. A passage from *The Guiltless* by Hermann Broch evokes this (potential) infinity of nakedness in human love. Thus speaks the servant Zerline: "I was naked, and he made

---

57. [*Marriage of Heaven and Hell* 151. Trans. Note]

58. ["Sophie, Oder über die Frauen" 292. Trans. Note] In his aphorisms Wallace Stevens also takes this position: "A poet looks at the world, somewhat as a man looks at a woman" (192). "The body is the great poem" (194).

me more naked, as if even nakedness had clothes that could be taken off" (*Les irresponsables* 110).[59]

The full "nakedness" is that of bodies as well as of souls. Souls experience nakedness, in turn, in a plurality of experiences—mystical ones (which was not possible for Donne, as we know), religious ones in the broad sense of the term, intellectual ones, and so forth. The whole "range" of joys corresponds to *full* nakedness and to the plurality of its forms, be they of the body[60] or of the soul. This is why Donne says, "All *joyes are due to thee.*"

Ellrodt, who notices everything, emphasizes the importance of the word "all" in Donne and even strives to define the specific use he makes of it. He asks: "Isn't it remarkable that the poet uses the word '*all*' to express intensity rather than scale?" (136–37).[61]

Here, the "all" is both extensive and intensive.

As souls unbodied, bodies uncloth'd must be,
To taste whole joyes. (l. 34–35)[62]

To "full nakedness" correspond "whole joyes." But as joys can become *full* through the full experience of nakedness (there is, so to speak, a point of saturation; once "full" like for the day of Resurrection, joy remains, although active, in its integrity), likewise nakedness remains infinite, as Zerline knows. It can only become yet fuller. The soul is never "naked" enough. And neither is the body.

We can see the *precision* of Donne's words, especially with seemingly worn-out words such as "whole," "full," and "all." For him, these are words of intensity, as when Sappho tells Philaenis, "*Thee,* my halfe, *my* all, *my* more" (l. 58).[63]

That Philaenis is the "half," the "all," and the "more" of Sappho is probably the terminologized expression of their relations. When Fuzier and Denis translate:

Toi qui es ma moitié, mon tout, mon plus que moi[64]

---

59. [*The Guiltless* 105. Trans. Note]
60. There are joyful experiences of corporal nakedness other than love.
61. The whole passage is worth reading.
62. In Ellrodt's translation: "Comme l'âme doit dépouiller son corps, le corps doit être dévêtu pour goûter des joies pleines." (*L'inspiration personnelle* 136–37).
63. Emphasis Donne's in Fuzier and Denis (84).
64. ["You who are my half, my all, my more than me." Trans. Note]

this "plus que moi" (used because of the rhyme with the preceding line?) destroys the intensive intransitivity of the "more." The intensive Sappho knows it well, she who only says to her lover: "Thee ... my *more* ... ," especially since the "bad" *more* constituted by man has been rejected.

But the rigor of these central lines of "Going to Bed" is also marked by the use of two *negative words:*

As souls *unbodied,* bodies *uncloth'd* must be.

Before coming to what these verbal forms express (as much as one can), I must linger—here we are at the point of a commentative digression—on the fact that Donne doesn't say something like "without body, without clothes," but that he chooses privative constructions. Privative constructions are not rare in his works. He has even applied one to his own destiny: ruined by his love match, he became, from Donne, *undone.* Without looking too hard, I found in "A nocturnall upon S. Lucies day":

'Tis the yeares midnight, and it is the dayes,
Lucies, who scarce seaven houres herself unmaskes.[65]

And in the already cited "Heroicall Epistle":

Thy body is a naturall Paradise,
In whose selfe, unmanur'd, all pleasure lies.[66]

It is interesting to note that in both cases the negative words are linked to the *self*. It is the same for *undone*: the one who has undone his life (by marrying) is him, *himself,* Donne. Similarly—I shall return to this—to *unbody* and to *unclothe* are active movements, movements of the self: to undress (oneself),

---

65. C'est le minuit de l'année, et c'est celui du jour,
De la Sainte-Lucie, qui se démasque à peine sept heures. (Legouis, *Poèmes choisis* 92)

[It is the year's midnight, and it is the day's,
Lucie's, who herself unmasks scarcely seven hours. (Trans. Note)]

66. In Legouis, *Poèmes choisis:*

Ton corps est un naturel Paradis
Dans l'être duquel, *unmanu'd,* sont tous plaisirs. (92; retranslation)

"Unmanur'd" means without manure or fertilizer (i.e., sperm).

to disincarnate (oneself), to unbody (oneself), to excarnate⁶⁷ (oneself). The same pattern can also be found in "Going to Bed," for *to unpin* (l. 7) and *to unlace your self* (l. 9). This poem alone has four negative words. The poet uses privative words—here verbs—not privative *turns of phrase*. It is worth asking the meaning of this choice. What are negative words? How important are they for language and for poetry? Without claiming to answer all these questions, we must (or we can) begin thinking about it.

In his dialogue "On the Origin of Beauty," Hopkins says, "You know how much use poetry makes of negative words and just for the reason that they express an antithesis" (*De l'origine* 51).⁶⁸ Hopkins gives the lines from Hamlet as an example: "Unhouseled, disappointed, unanneled" (1.5.77).⁶⁹

It is a fact that negative words often have a certain *poeticality*. Why is Gide's *s'impréciser* [to imprecise] more poetic than *devenir imprécis* [to become imprecise] or *s'estomper* [to become blurred]? Why is Chateaubriand's *inadorée* [unadored] more poetic than *non inadorée*? Why is it that in general the negative word seems to us full of force, of *signifiance*?

First, the negative word has the characteristic of coming from a positive word without automatically forming a necessary pair with it. Whereas the positive word exists in and of itself, the negative word, which expresses the lack or the absence of what is designated by the positive word ("appetence"/"inappetence," "observance"/"inobservance"), may not exist: one can always say the same thing with an expression like "lack of appetence," "without appetence," or even "non-appetence," a formation that, as we shall see, is more a term (a syntagm) than a "real" word. Is it "the same thing"? It is really not, indeed, but current usage can make do with words or turns of phrase like those quoted, or with positive words that have an equivalent privative or negative meaning.

Then, what are the necessity (I am not speaking here of practical necessity) and the significance of the negative word? *They are to allow language to say— inscribed in the flesh of the very word, riveted negative prefix, now married to the positive word and negativizing it (disobedience, inobservance)—the multiple forms of what Meister Eckhart calls the "not."*⁷⁰ No expression like

---

67. Yves Bonnefoy uses the neologism *s'excarner*.
68. [*The Journals and Papers* 114. Trans. Note]
69. Yves Bonnefoy translates the line as "Sans communion, viatique ni onction," and J.-M. Déprats as "Sans communion, viatique, ni onction."
70. "This *not* from which we must free ourselves: . . . you must become free of the 'Not.'

"lack of obedience" or "without appetite" has this power, even though "lack" and "without" are *specific, limited* interpretations of the "not," of active negation. "Disobedience" and "inobedience" express active negation and also loss, or lack. "Non-obedience" also expresses it, but it doesn't exist as a word. It does not negativize the positive word. It can always let it survive. Moreover, the sphere of functioning of its compounds is the sphere of fossilized speech, such as "non-assistance" to a person or persons in danger.⁷¹ Thus we can see the very significance of the true negative word: to capture in a word the "not" of Eckhart, or what Hegel calls the *work of the negative*. Forming an *immediate unity* with the work it negativizes, it charges it with "not" and does so along the whole breadth and depth of the "not" in question. In French, it does so with the prefixes *dés-* and *in-*, each of which has its own meaning.⁷² Whereas a word like "non-observance" can only belong to fossilized forms of speech, "inobservance" covers the totality of forms for lack, insufficiency, loss, be they active or passive, et cetera, in all the dimensions of human life. It expresses the extensivity, the intensivity, and the essence of a "not." This is why it can express an "antithesis" and meet the highest requirements of philosophical language, mystical language, poetic and literary language, and popular speech when it does create "forms." The *poeticality* of negative words is thus founded on the *uniqueness of their signifiance*.⁷³

... People debate about what burns in hell. ... I say, it is the 'not' that burns in Hell. Take a comparison! Let us suppose that someone takes a glowing coal and places it in my hand. If I were to say that the coal is burning my hand, I would be doing the coal a great injustice. If I must truly designate what is burning me: it is the 'not' that does it, because the coal has in it something that my hand doesn't have. See, it is precisely this 'not' that is burning me" (Eckhart 83). [The most recent translation of this sermon by Colledge and McGinn (1981) uses "nothing" instead of "not": "People ask, 'What is it that burns in hell?' ... But I say truly that what burns in hell is nothing. Take a comparison. Suppose that someone takes a burning coal and puts it in my hand. If I were to say that it was the coal that was burning my hand I should be doing the coal an injustice; but if I were to say properly what it is that is burning me, it is nothing, because the coal has something in it that my hand does not have. You must see that it is this nothing that is burning me" (183) but, like the Paul Petit translation into French, the other translations (C. de B. Evans's 1931 translation of Pfeiffer's edition, and Raymond Blakney's translation of 1941) all use "not" or "Not": "Observe!—it is just this 'Not' that is burning me" (127). Trans. Note]

71. [Under French law, *non-assistance à personne en danger* (failure to assist a person in danger) is considered a crime. Trans. Note]

72. Negative prefixes have different meanings in each language.

73. The reader will find in the extraordinary *Deuxième élégie XXX* by Charles Péguy many negative neologisms such as "impolitique" (14) and "inhonorable" (89). The force of negative

"Unbodied" and "uncloth'd" both express the movement of denudation that soul and body must undergo in order to "taste whole joyes" and the state of essential denudation that is the "state of joy." They express actions of the *self*. What the body and the soul leave (here momentarily) when they undress are realities that are themselves full and radiant: the body sheds the finery and clothes that adorn it and enhance it, but these are beauty; in turn, the soul sheds the radiant naked body, itself a source of great joys, itself a source of benediction.

How blest am I in this discovering thee! (l. 30)

The negative words "unbodied" and "uncloth'd" express a positive denudation, a positive stripping, leading man "from a lesser perfection to a greater one," as Spinoza says.

"To unbody," in particular, does not mean to leave behind something ugly, something negative. It is not necessary to belabor the point: Donne conceived of the body in positive terms.[74] In "Of the Progresse of the Soule (The Second Anniversarie)," he strikingly writes:

Her pure, and eloquent blood
Spoke in her cheeks, and so distinctly wrought,
That one might almost say, her body thought.[75]

Thus, the bodies of the lovers *think*.

---

words appears in this passage: "How has it been possible to arrive at, to make of this most Christian people, so deeply, so inwardly, so intimately Christian, not only in the soul, if I may say, but Christian in the heart and to the bone, this people that we know, that we see, this people of today, this people of now, this modern people, so deeply, so inwardly, so intimately unchristian [*inchrétien*], dechristianized [*déchristianisé*], dischristian [*déchrétien*], so dischristian in soul, heart, and bone. So dischristian in its blood" (244–45). We have here the antithesis of which Hopkins speaks.

74. About the soul and the body, Ellrodt says quite well that "they are in truth the two poles of speculation in Donne; his paradoxal thought moves, prompt and taut, along the axis that both opposes and links them" (*L'inspiration personnelle* 216).

75. Ellrodt's translation is as follows:

Son sang pur, éloquent
Parlait sur ses joues mêmes et si distinctement s'y mouvait, impétueux,
Que l'on aurait pu dire, ou presque: son corps pense. (*L'inspiration personnelle* 227)

Similarly in "Resurrection, imperfect" (228): "He would have justly thought his body a soule" ["Il eût non sans raison pris ce corps pour une âme"], and in the sermon to Saint Paul (234):

Donne's poem does not choose between the two nakednesses, the two worlds of joy, the two loves (women and God), and that is its deepest uniqueness: its unique *balance*. The "man of hyperboles," to use Ellrodt's words, had also praised balance. In Satyre II, he writes: "meanes blesse" as in "Going to Bed," the discovery of the female body blesses ("blest," l. 30). This poem is neither a purely profane poem—it is openly about the sacred, religion, Paradise, angels, and so forth—nor is it obviously a sacred poem; it is a poem in which human love is illuminated, from afar, by the love of God. As in Blake, Novalis, the troubadour poets and, in his own way, Hopkins, human love and divine love rest, so to speak, side by side, in equilibrium; there is no hierarchy, but a mutual presence where the love of woman is illuminated by the love of God, where the love of God is illuminated by the love of woman. It is a poem of the body-in-joy, not of the flesh.[76] It is certain that the individual Donne, caught in his complexity—of being almost simultaneously bard of all possible forms of love of women,[77] then bard of the love of God—could but rarely reach this kind of equilibrium. But the poem itself reached it and thus reaches us, at least in its original language.

We are now ready for the confrontation. It will not be linear. For such a small unit, it will be enough to take a few significant examples, among which I shall of course include the passages I have just discussed. As one would expect, the confrontation will be harsh. But since I placed this poem in such a high position, I have the right to be, while respecting the risks taken by the translators. Failure is caused by the project and is not at all linked to a resistance from the poem. If there is a resistance, it can be gotten around with another project. That is what Paz did successfully. Paz did not succeed because he is a poet, a great poet. He succeeded because he had another project. One can show that the only place in his translation that is open to criticism comes from the fact that he is *also* the poet, the great poet Paz, who (unconsciously) signs his translation at the end.

Let us begin with the beginning: the way in which Denis translated the title of the elegy[78] as "Le coucher de sa maîtresse" ["His Mistress Going

---

"Tout ce que l'âme accomplit, elle l'accomplit / Dans le corps, avec le corps et par le corps," already said in "The Extasie."

76. The word "flesh" appears only in line 24 to refer to the man's sexual organ in a state of erection.

77. Ellrodt: "Love has almost as many nuances in Donne's lyric poetry as in the theater of Shakespeare" ("Présence et permanence" 27).

78. The translation by Rothschild will only be occasionally mentioned. On the whole, it is

to Bed"] (the English editions vary between "Going to Bed" and "To His Mistris Going to Bed"). This choice shows that the translator wants to keep the poem in the category of supposedly "libertine" or "concubine" elegies. The English "going to bed" is much more direct than the Louis XIV style of *coucher de sa maîtresse*.[79] There is a dual reorientation: a *serious* poem, conjugal (and religious) in content, is granted a title that is simultaneously pompous, outdated, and inconstant; the addressee is presented, which is far from being certain, as a mistress, rather than as the poet's wife.

The rest of the translation systematically follows this transformation. For the entire beginning, that is, up to line 18, this transformation into libertine and precious poetry seems, on the whole, possible. However, several things are bothersome. I noted earlier that the undressing of the woman is punctuated, scanned by a series of four "off with's" (l. 5, 11, 15, and 17), emphasized in line 13 by a "going off." This strong and beautiful series of "off's" is twice reduced in the translation: they become "ôtez" [remove] and are reduced to three, since the "Now off with those shooes" (l. 17) becomes "Et maintenant, pieds nus" [And now bare feet], and "Your gown going off" (l. 13) becomes "Votre robe enlevée" [Your gown removed].

As these "off with's" literally structure the scene, and as two of them are lost and the three remaining ones are replaced by a verb that does not have the force of the "off," the whole movement of this part is weakened. Is it impossible to translate "off" with a preposition in French? Without submitting to the number of "off's" and through a subtle play, Paz produces the same effect—distributed in a different way—as Donne did with "off": he leaves the entire beginning without the chosen equivalent, *fuera,* and abruptly concentrates three *fuera* on the following part:

Ese feliz corpiño que yo envidio,

---

done in a curiously mannered and artificial style, and one wonders what caused it. The project is the same as in Fuzier and Denis' translation. Rothschild is familiar with the "problems" of poetry translation in English, and primarily in Elizabethan poetry. Unfortunately he is trapped by a hedonist and mannered vision of this poetry. This vision leads him to an erroneous interpretation of "Going to Bed," with the consequences that one may expect for the translation.

79. [Under the reign of kings like the Sun King, Louis XIV, the king's going to bed and getting up became official public events known as the *coucher du roi* (the setting of the king) and *lever du roi* (rising of the king), expressions that evoked the rising of the sun (*lever du soleil*). Trans. Note]

Pegado a ti come si fuese vivo:
¡*Fuera! Fuera* el vestido, surjan valles salvajes
Entre las sombras de tus montes, *fuera* el tocado,
Caiga tu pelo, tu diadema.

The impatience distributed *at regular intervals* in Donne's poem through his "off" is released *all of a sudden,* but with the same intensity, in three vertiginous lines.

Paz also renders quite well the "Unlace your self" (l. 9) as a simple and literal "Desenlaza tu *ser*," where Fuzier and Denis, who are not aware of the problematic of the self, put "Délacez-vous" [Unlace].[80]

What about the pause that follows and that evokes angels and evil spirits? Lines 19–24:

In such white robes, heaven's Angels us'd to be
Receavd by men; Thou Angel bringst with thee
A heaven like Mahomets Paradise; and though
Ill spirits walk in white, we easly know,
By this these Angels from an evil sprite,
Those set our hairs, but these our flesh upright

are translated in an incomprehensible way, in free verse and, at one point, contrary to Donne's poetics:

Le divin Paradis
Qui partout t'accompagne est celui du Prophète
[Divine Paradise
That everywhere accompanies you is that of the Prophet]

The original has its own precision that *must* be rendered with all the religious feeling and imagery that it conveys, instead of sounding like a French translation of *The Arabian Nights.* Donne does not say at all, "S'il arrive qu'un

---

80. We should also note that Paz chooses the familiar *tu* form, while the French translators use the formal *vous*. He also translates the title "Antes de acostarse" as is—actually more than as is: before (*antes*), *acostarse* (to go to bed), *acostarse con* . . . (to sleep with). This is *exactly* the situation and the moment of the poem.

Noir Esprit de blanc se vête" [If it happens that a black spirit dresses in white], but that ill spirits march in white *like* the angels of the Old Testament and *like* the loved one resembling a houri:[81] off goes the interplay at once daring, graceful, and profound between the two religious representations, between the two angels and the bad spirits.

As for the black/white opposition proposed by the translator, it is especially unfortunate and unwelcome because, as Ellrodt has pointed out, it is rarely used in Donne's poetics of colors.[82]

But it is now time to come and stay with what we have considered the center of gravity of the poem, which soars from lines 25–26 on and ends with line 35.

Only the third line of these most lyrical lines that are *also*, again, the most *precise* lines in images and vocabulary is faithfully translated:

O my America! my new-found-land,
My kingdome, safeliest when with one man man'd
My Myne of precious stones, My Emperie,
How blest am I in this discovering thee!

But what is not transferred in the translation of the lines is the *tone*—tender, grateful, and filled with wonder—that is revealed in the literalness of the statements, and to which translators unconstrained by a formalizing project could have given in: in the midst of the images that he piles up, Donne is simple, colloquial, and moved. This emotion is marked by the connection of the "O" of the beginning and the exclamation at the end:

O my America!
. . . .
How blest am I in this discovering thee!

In fact, beyond the accumulation of other images (Emperie, Myne, kingdome), "discovering" directly refers to the first line, "O my America! my

---

81. [In Islam, a virgin of perfect beauty awaiting devout Muslims in paradise. Trans. Note]
82. "It is characteristic that the ethical contrast between white and black is much less frequent and only appears in conjunction with the pre-eminent contrast of whiteness and color" (Ellrodt, *L'inspiration personnelle* 254).

new-found-land," and it is also this line that allows us to reread, to grasp the sense of the two preceding lines, which Rothschild wrongly considers to be the center of the poem:[83]

> Licence my roaving hands, and let them go,
> Before, behind, between, above, below.

Thus the translation of lines 27 and 30 is crucial—a translation focused on rendering the emotion that runs through the lines and is linguistically visible through the order of the words in line 27:

> O my America! my new-found-land,

and through the occurrence of two words that are essential (and not only in this poem) in line 30:

> How blest am I in this discovering thee!

The meaning of this lyrical passage, full of wonder, is the *discovery* of the female body (not yet of its nakedness) insofar as it is a *world,* a new world. The "roaving hands" are not so much wandering or salacious hands; they may go everywhere and even "between"—one must take Donne literally, but one must also think of these "discoverers" who follow the coasts of new lands, go *between* the shores of straits, climb *on* mountains, pass *behind* promontories, and so forth.

This discovery of the body/world of the loved one brings about a feeling of *blessedness*—"How blest . . ."—that is, a feeling that is religious at heart. Satire II said: "meanes blesse." It is possible to think that this discovery of the body/world is not experienced by Donne as something intoxicating, excessive, darkly erotic, but as something luminous and vast, like the experience of the present and of the "now" that fascinated him so much.

The translation totally misconstrues the essence of the poet's feeling by proposing

---

83. "One line only conditions the poem from start to finish, a decasyllable in five adverbs" ("Traduire 'Donne'" 78).

Dont l'exploration m'est bienheureux délire!
[Literally, "Of which the exploration is for me a happy frenzy!"]

for "How blest am I in this discovering thee!"

First this line is linked to the preceding line through "of which" and thus to "My Emperie," which is only a secondary image, whereas the last line refers to the totality of accumulated images *as far as they are dominated by the first one*. By doing so, the translators completely transform Donne's feeling of *discovery* into a simple feeling of *possession*. But here, it is the discovery that is more essential.

Dont l'exploration m'est bienheureux délire!

"Exploration" does not translate "discovering." To discover is not to explore. The man discovers this America, this "young land" constituted by his wife as she uncovers herself, as she *unlaces* her *self*; he does not explore her, even if his hands run over her body. But most importantly, "bienheureux délire" [happy frenzy] cannot correspond to "how blest." Donne is not plunged in a state of "délire" [frenzy] when seeing his wife, any more than Sappho "s'étreint follement" [embraces herself passionately] in front of the mirror while thinking she is "embrac[ing]" Philaenis. Donne knows joy, pleasure, ecstacy, but not "frenzy." Putting this word in the translation is either being merely rhetorical and using all the words interchangeably or pulling Donne toward something that he is not. It is changing the tone of the whole passage, especially of "Licence my roaving hands," which becomes—starting from "délire"—the expression of someone panting, beside himself, eager to "have his way," whereas in Donne, we find pure wonder, fervor—a fervor that right away is inverted into a reflection and into poetic thought, as if to intensify even more this feeling of fervor.

Terre-Neuve! Amérique! ô ma possession.[84]

It is hard to see why everything here has been inverted, since in the English line, the succession is meaningful and "O my America!" is the determiner:

---

84. ["New-found-land! America! O my possession." Trans. Note]

> O my America! my new-found-land,
> My kingdome.

In Denis and Fuzier's translation, the determiner is "ô ma possession," which does not even translate "kingdome."

What becomes most important in the translation are the images of possession, which plunge the possessor in a "bienheureux délire." Everything contributes to this, like putting an exclamation point after "Ma mine de pierres précieuses!"[85]

Again, there is nothing fortuitous about it: this approach forces us to pull the poem toward what for us it is not, toward a mannered eroticism, a frenzied possession, toward a "mistress" story.

The simplicity of lines 31–32, which constitute the transition toward reflection, is typical of Donne: from the heavily tonalized metaphorical lyricism ("blest") to "statements" that are almost analytical, but only for a moment:

> To enter in these bonds, is to be free;
> Then where my hand is set, my seal shall be.

The "scholarly" translation of Denis

> À qui entre en ces nœuds liberté point ne faut:
> Donc, où j'ai mis la main j'apposerai mon sceau
> [For whom enters in these bonds, freedom must not be:
> Thus, where I put my hand I shall affix my seal]

does not render this colloquial style, which a first retranslation would render as "Entrer dans ces liens, c'est être libre."[86]

Is this trivial? Donne speaks this way, in English, at this moment in the poem. We have here a micro-level, but irrefutable, example of Denis' work of *poeticizing homogenization,* which leads him in line 30 to remove the tone of wonder, and in line 31, its colloquialism. In fact, all four modes of enunciation in the poem—"contractual" lyricism, metaphorical lyricism, abstract colloquialism, and metaphysical lyricism—are translated in the *same* mode.

---

85. ["My mine of precious stones." Trans. Note]
86. ["To enter in these bonds, it is to be free." Trans. Note]

But what is crucial now is to see how Denis and Fuzier render the three metaphysical-lyrical lines, the poetic statement that has truth as a purpose: "Full nakedness!" becomes "Totale nudité," when we have seen that fundamentally nakedness cannot be "total." It can only be "full," and "full," like "whole," "all," "more," and so forth, is a word of intensity for Donne, whereas "total" first expresses something extensive or quantitative.

> As souls unbodied, bodies uncloth'd must be,
> To taste whole joyes

becomes:

> Il n'est qu'âmes sans chair et que chairs dévêtues
> Pour jouir pleinement.[87]

Everything we may have found (without even finishing the task) about the *signifiance* of negative words, of the meaning of "unbodied," "joy," "souls," "bodies," and that indicated the prodigious concentration of this line, making it a poetic enunciation with a truth purpose, all this wasn't even considered by the translators.

> Âmes sans chair . . . chairs dévêtues.
> [Souls without flesh, and undressed flesh]

Here it is not a matter of "flesh," but of "body," and Donne is a poet of the soul and the body, not of the "flesh" (unlike Baudelaire). "Unbodied" is not "without flesh" for this very reason, but also because the stripping that it expresses is not a *deprivation*. The "âmes sans chair" [souls without flesh] has something wretched about it, as any deprivation expressed by "without" does. "Chairs dévêtues" [undressed flesh] verges on the impossible in French: flesh is never either dressed or undressed; it is the body that is so. The parallelism of the two negative words "unbodied"/"uncloth'd" also disappears.

The end "To taste whole joyes" (l. 35) thoughtlessly becomes "Pour jouir

---

87. [There is only souls without flesh, and undressed flesh
To enjoy fully. Trans. Note]

pleinement."[88] There is no more joy here, joy that one would *taste,* but sexual pleasure [*jouir*]. But where in Donne is it a question of pleasure? Certainly not in this poem, which is at best the prelude to amorous pleasure. More generally, Donne does not seem to be the poet of sexual pleasure. *To taste* simply means to taste.

Thus the whole lyrical and metaphorical peak is masked, once more pulled toward the carnal, the sensual, toward everything that Donne doesn't say. We see the destructive obstinacy of the project even down to the details, made worse by unfortunate final specific choices, like "chairs dévêtues" or even "âmes sans chair," which are aesthetically (that is, from the point of view of the translators) defective.

Yet these lines are not impossible to translate. They are not easy either, if one wants to respect the letter of their verbal precision, but without naive literalism.

OCTAVIO PAZ: "ANTES DE ACOSTARSE"

Octavio Paz won his wager. He did it first by specifying what his project was:

> My translation is not literal. Rather it is an adaptation into Spanish, and in numerous cases I did not stay close to the original, although I always tried to find expressions with an equivalent value to that of English. In line 12, for instance, Donne does not speak to us about a brassiere, but about a corset; for us, the word is associated with nineteenth-century vaudeville acts so that a literal translation would have been a betrayal. Later, the poet distinguishes between good and evil spirits because "those set our hairs, but these our flesh upright." To keep the English expression

---

88. Here Rothschild's translation is completely whimsical:

> Nu! Nudité nue! À toi ta joie est due.
> Sans chair va l'âme, le corps veut chair non vêtue
> À suivre son plaisir.
>
> [Naked! Naked nakedness! To you joy is due.
> Without flesh goes the soul, the body wants flesh undressed
> To follow its pleasure. (Trans. Note)]

This is a pure word game, but where is it going?

would have been a gross error in questionable taste. All this shows that, in spite of the use and abuse of swear words with which contemporary writers want to shock us, twentieth century languages are less... down to earth, poorer and more timid than those of the sixteenth and seventeenth centuries.... Modern writers... cannot manage to get reconciled with their bodies. Language reflects this situation. Things have names, and when those names become unutterable, it is because the infection of life has also stricken words. (*Traducción* 29–30)

I wanted to quote at length these frank and modest comments to make them say everything they are saying—even between the lines. Paz does not hide his hand: it is an adaptation rather than a translation. He thus "spaced" [*espacé*],[89] but, as he says, not to the point of losing any relation with the original poem; not to the point, he also says, "of finding expressions equivalent to those of English." We shall see right away that this expression, which may seem weak or trite, reveals a *precise* truth. The lines that follow are indeed not linked to this expression, as it would seem. But they are important: unlike Fuzier and Denis, and Rothschild, it is clear that Paz has wanted to avoid at all costs anything scabrous, vaudeville-like, or coarse wherever it might stand out in the translation (which often occurs, with isolated elements, in translation). He does so because for him the essence of the poem does not lie in those things: the situation of "Going to Bed" is not that of a mistress in the nineteenth century who undresses in front of her lover. He thus replaces "corsé," which refers to "busk," with "corpiño" [brassiere].

> Ese feliz corpiño que yo envidio,
> Pegado a ti como si fuese vivo:
> ¡Fuera!

This translation is quite free but at the same time corresponds closely to:

> Off with that happy busk, which I envie,
> That still can be, and still can stand so nigh.

Placed *at the end*, the "fuera" is almost stronger than the English "off," and

---

89. [See note 48 in part I for the particular meaning of this term. Trans. Note]

most importantly the rhetoric of "That still can be, and still can stand so nigh" has been replaced by a sentence that says both something else, "clinging to you as if it were alive," and the same thing, the tenacious and silent clinging of the brassiere to the breast. A subtle re-creation that, it is true, just here, goes beyond translation (if one really insists on separating translation from re-creation—I myself insisted on it for so long, and now I wonder!—or rather on looking for the dividing line between them). But what is particularly striking is the *decidedly modernizing orientation of the translation,* which Paz does not state—except when he declares in an unexpected place that one cannot have a direct translation of "Those set our hairs, but these our flesh upright" because of the "shyness" of modern languages—thus raising a very important question.[90]

These two words of warning issued by Paz are finally something other than mere caution over details; they reveal fundamental decisions for the translation of the poem—not to orient it in a scabrous direction, not to attempt, because of our own relation to what relates to the body and because of the consequence this has on language, to transfer what is *natural* in Donne but that for us would be an "enormity." But the essential lies in the way Paz achieves his adaptation/translation. Freedom is indeed quite visible at first.

> No es enemigo el enemigo
> Hasta que no lo ciñe nuestro mortal abrazo

is quite different from:

> The foe oft-times having the foe in sight,
> Is tir'd with standing though he never fight.

Not only is it different, but it introduces in the poem a touch of *death,* of deathly embrace (*mortal abrazo*) that is not present in Donne. At the same time, what is only *aleatory rhetoric* in Donne, or a momentary mood thus

---

90. In order not to say the "unutterable word" (*bander*/to have a hard-on), Fuzier and Denis chose an unintelligible word (unless the reader consults a dictionary of Old French): "Il peut bien faire *arcer* le poil, mais pas la chair." [It can make the hair *reisen,* but not the flesh.]

We can point out all the obscure words in their translation: *busc, tortil,* and especially *affiquets,* which is only supposed to render the simple "Gems" (l. 35). This is hermetic archaism.

expressed (since we won't see any more war metaphors: the woman loved is New-found-land, not Beautiful Enemy), gains a new, almost metaphysical importance in Paz. The adaptation then appears as the rising of *a new poem* that has its *uniqueness* and, from it, enters into an extremely tight and subtle play of spacing and non-spacing with "Going to Bed."

This freedom can also be seen in the *compacting*, or *condensation*, that Paz achieves at certain times to get rid, it seems, of a certain rhetorical linearity and preciosity in Donne: there too, he is going in the opposite direction of Denis and Fuzier.

> Off with that happy busk, which I envie,
> That still can be, and still can stand so nigh.
> Your gown going off, such beauteous state reveals,
> As when from flowry meads th'hills shadow steales.
> Off with that wyerie Coronet and shew
> The haiery Diademe which on you doth grow:
> Now off with those shooes, and then safely tread
> In this loves hallow'd temple, this soft bed (l. 11–18)

become in lines 12–16 (with a sizable reduction, but the total number of lines of the two poems is the same):

> Ese feliz corpiño que yo envidio,
> Pegado a ti como si fuese vivo:
> ¡Fuera! Fuera el vestido, surjan valles salvajes
> Entre las sombras de tus montes, fuera el tocado,
> Caiga tu pelo, tu diadema.[91]

All this has been condensed, gathered (let us remember with Carey that "compacting" is a fundamental trait of Donne)—like the three *fueras,* and the shortened list of garments that are falling (busk/*corpiño*, gown/*vestido*, Coronet/*tocado*, haiery Diademe/*pelo, tu diadema*).

---

91. [That happy busk which I envy,
    Clings to you as if it were alive:
    Off! Off with the gown, arise wild valleys
    Between the shadows of your mounts, off with the coronet,
    Fall your hair, your diadem. (Trans. Note)]

> Your gown going off, such beauteous state reveals,
> As when from flowry meads th'hills shadow steales

is changed into:

> Fuera el vestido, surjan valles salvajes
> Entre las sombras de tus montes.

The change goes toward suppressing the rhetorical element in Donne and replaces it with a wonderful image that does much "spacing," in the poetic direction of the new poem.

A third liberty not very different from the previous one consists of *simplifying*. The reader will be able to notice it right away, in the two "discursive/religious" pauses of the poem. Thus lines 19–24:

> In such white robes, heaven's Angels us'd to be
> Receavd by men; Thou Angel bringst with thee
> A heaven like Mahomets Paradise; and though
> Ill spirits walk in white, we easly know,
> By this these Angels from an evil sprite,
> Those set our hairs, but these our flesh upright

become in lines 18–23:

> También de blancas ropas revestidos los ángeles
> El cielo al hombre muestran, más tú, blanca, contigo
> A un cielo mahometano me conduces.
> Verdad que los espectros van de blanco
> Pero por ti distingo al buen del mal espíritu:
> Uno hiela la sangre, tú la enciendes.

They become something more simple and more explicit than in Donne, except for the last line, which Paz has "censored":

> Those set our hairs, but these our flesh upright.
> [Uno hiela la sangre, tú la enciendes.]

Spacing, compacting, and simplification are accompanied in turn by a *total freedom* in relation to the formal architecture of the original and by completely renouncing any archaic tone—for which Paz, solidly supported by the Spanish Golden Age, would have easily found materials, as we can guess. What arises here is a *modern poem*, in "free verse," a poem like those written by Paz, among other poets. But this *modern* poem, rid of the whole *archaism* of Donne's poem—if we consider that in this poem the rhetorical/ratiocinating parts are archaic in the sense of outmoded—is all the more centered on what can be called the "essence," the "core," the "said" of the poem or its "intentionality" (and this is quite obvious *without analysis*). Solidly centered in the essence of the poem, Paz has a *dual relation* with it, which I am going to describe:

1. He keeps, with one exception, all the fundamental *linguistic and poetic traits* (which my analysis detailed).
2. He sometimes *transmutes* them in his own *universum*, which is the Hispanic *universum*, while rightly emphasizing that there is a link, recognized by Donne, between Spanish poetry and his own.

Let us look closely at the essential segments of the poem that I have analyzed and that Fuzier and Denis have systematically missed.

The series of the "off's": we have already mentioned it and evoked Paz's brilliant solution. But it is worth noticing that the lack of the first "off"

Off with that girdle (l. 5)
["Ôtez cette ceinture" (Fuzier and Denis)]

is compensated for by a skillful play with *ciñe* (l. 4), *ceñidor, desciñe* (l. 5):

Hasta que no lo ciñe nuestro mortal abrazo.
Tu ceñidor desciñe, meridiano.

Why this compensation? Because the force, the violence of the first "off," is expressed by *desciñe* and by the fact that this act, this *desciñe* [unfastens] a *ceñidor* [belt], that the violence of this first gesture of undressing is "foreshadowed," one could say, by the preceding free line where the enemy is mentioned: enemy that our "mortal embrace" *ciñe* [surrounds]. The *desciñe* reinforces the chain of Donne's privative expressions. To

> *Unpin* that spangled breastplate (l. 7)   *desprende* (l. 7)
> *Unlace* your self (l. 9)   *Desenlaza* tu ser (l. 10)

"Tu ceñidor *desciñe*" (l. 5) is added for "*Off* with that girdle" (l. 5). Paz does not miss the "self" either on line 9 ("Unlace your self") or on lines 44–45 ("shew / Thy self"), each time with a different solution:

> Desenlaza *tu ser* (l. 10)
> Descúbrete ... (l. 44)

Thus freedom does not exclude the precise relation—far from it—the specific rendering of the *essential*.

But we particularly want to know how Paz translated lines 25–35, the center of the poem.

I will leave without comments the "solutions" brought to the translation of lines 25–31, in which freedom and close correspondence alternate with ease.

Paz certainly manages to translate lines 25–26 without any problem:

> Licence my roaving hands, and let them go,
> Before, behind, between, above, below

> Deja correr mis manos vagabundas
> Atrás, arriba, enfrente, abajo y entre

where Fuzier and Denis heavily fail (heavily in the strict sense of the word):

> Laisse, laisse quêter ma main buissonnière
> Par-dessus, par-dessous, entre, devant, derrière![92]

("par-dessus" and "par-dessous" are "heavy," and so is placing "derrière" at the end of the line), and where Rothschild follows his erotic fantasies:

> Licence veut ma main rôdeuse, qu'elle erre
> En haut, en bas, entre-deux, devant, derrière.[93]

---

92. [Let, let seek my truant hand
    Above, beneath, between, in front, behind! (Trans. Note)]
93. [Licence wants my roaving hand, let it wander
    Above, below, in between, in front, behind. (Trans. Note)]

Shall we say that "Spanish allows this and that," that it is Paz, the great poet?

But from line 32 onward, a surprise awaits us. Here is how Donne's lines 33–35 are translated:

Full nakedness! All joyes are due to thee,
As souls unbodied, bodies uncloth'd must be,
To taste whole joyes.

La plena desnudez es goce entero:
Para gozar la gloria las almas desencarnan,
Los cuerpos se desvisten.[94]

We immediately realize that this version is splendid—but free, more than free. There are no longer any *joyes*. Certainly the lines correspond to Donne on other points: "Full nakedness"/"plena desnudez," Paz makes no mistake, "Unbodied"/"desencarnan," "uncloth'd"/"desvisten," the privatives are here. But the joys? The poetic joy? It has become *goce*, *goce* of what? Of *gloria*. As I said in the previous note, *goce* and *gloria* are not easily translatable into French. *Goce, jouissance,* in a strong, intense, wide, active, almost harsh sense, reminds us of the Augustinian *fruitio*. It is a multiplied echo of

To taste whole joyes.

There is something of "taste"[95]—*gustar*—in *goce*. But this *goce*, more directly than the French *jouissance* and *jouir*, may be linked to a strong, intense *joy* dwelling in the whole being. Paz, who does not forget "whole" either, also says "goce entero" (whole joy).

---

94. [Full nakedness is entire joy:
To enjoy glory souls unbody,
Bodies undress. (Trans. Note)]

But *goce* is much more that *jouissance* [enjoyment, pleasure], and *gozar* more than *jouir* [to enjoy, to come]. *Goce* and *gozar* are fundamental signifiers of Spanish. Similarly *gloria* is not simply *gloire* [glory].

95. Ellrodt rightly points out about love in Donne's poetry that "sensuality is showed to be purely tactile.... He likes to denude, to unveil, to strip, not to the gaze (there is nothing of the "voyeur" in him), but to the touch" (*L'inspiration personnelle* 141–42).

This *goce* is *goce* of something that is given in the nakedness of the soul or the body: *gloria. Gloria* is not glory, or rather our French *gloire* is no longer *gloria,* what it may have been a long time ago in the sixteenth or seventeenth century. "¡Qué Gloria!"[96] is still used in Spanish to refer to something that is wonderful. *Gloria* is the state of radiance, splendor, blossoming—what poetry in French retains when it speaks of the *gloire* of trees in bloom in the spring—but *gloria* is stronger than the French *gloire.* The difference from the French *gloire* even when it is used poetically is that from *gloria* one can *gozar,* that *gloria* is both what *goce* desires and what gives *goce.* Solidly fused to each other, *gozar gloria, goce* and *gloria* illuminate each other. In France, the "glory" of almond trees in the spring or poplar trees in the fall does not give any *jouissance,* nor does summer light.

Why did Octavio Paz choose this central signifier *goce* to "translate" *joyes* when he had at his disposal *alegirá,* and probably other Spanish words? We do not know, or rather we have the following intuition: for Paz, to the *proposal of poetic truth*

Full nakedness! All joyes are due to thee,

to the metaphysical force of this proposition (where every word counts, "nakedness" and "due" included, words that we haven't analyzed), there must correspond a proposal of truth stemming from the depths of the Hispanic metaphysical and poetic world:

La plena desnudez es goce entero.

Moreover, what Donne was not saying, that is, what the "whole joys" are "tasting," the reason why souls and bodies bare themselves, the translation could say it—the way the Hispanic tradition says it:

Para gozar la gloria.

In other words, nakedness is glory, a glory not gazed at, *mirada,* but enjoyed, tasted, *gozada.* Here "whole" means tasted, touched. What is only looked at is only partially *gozado.* Here Paz joins Donne and his taste for

---

96. [It would correspond to "How glorious!" in English. Trans. Note]

substance, for touch, for the tactile. "Essential joys." However, would Donne have thought this essence tasted by joys as glory, *gloire, gloria?* The question remains open. What is certain is that Paz's translation soars to the same poetic and metaphysical height as "Going to Bed," from its own *universum.*

Finally, I want to briefly examine the last two lines of the poem because they are the lines in which Paz makes his only mistake—if one may say so, and where Rothschild has his (almost) only success.[97]

> To teach thee, I am naked first: why than
> What needst thou have more covering then a man. (l. 47–48)

> Mírame, ven, ¿qué mejor manta
> Para tu desnudez, que yo, desnudo?

These lines are indeed quite beautiful, worthy of the troubadour poets, whom they indirectly call to mind, but Donne does not say "more covering than I," or something similar; he says, following his taste for abstraction, and for the generalization of experience: "more covering then a man."

Why "que yo, desnudo"? I argue that it is, at the end of this beautiful translation, which like the original is an *address* to the woman he loves, the "signature" of the man, and of the great poet Paz. It is he, not "a man" in general, who is the "mejor manta," the best coat. This is the reward after the long labor of the poem, which is given in "offering" (Masson, "Territoire de Babel" 158) to "Going to Bed," and the woman to whom he is speaking. It is I. Donne's poem has truly been *laid bare:* we said modernized, rejuvenated, simplified, et cetera. All this means, laid bare. Where Fuzier and Denis over-

---

97. Pour t'enseigner, le premier, nu je suis. Quoi,
   Pour te couvrir est-il mieux qu'homme sur toi?

   [To teach you, the first, naked I am. What,
   To cover you, is better than man on you. (Trans. Note)]

Apart from a few affectations, there is just more whimsy or deformations than in Fuzier and Denis:

   Regarde, je suis nu. Je ne vois pas pourquoi
   Tu te voudrais couvrir d'autre chose que moi.

   [Look, I am naked. I do not see why
   You would wish to be covered by something other than me. (Trans. Note)]

dressed it, Paz undressed it. And what became visible is its *gloria,* which we are still enjoying.

AUGUSTE MOREL: "DE SA MAISTRESSE ALLANT AU LICT"

While doing my research, I had not paid attention to this third French version of "Going to Bed," the earliest one there is: I would have had to go to the French National Library, unearth *Navire d'argent,*[98] a forgotten literary magazine—all this for a translation about which Legouis, who was usually rather fair, wondered if it was in verse or prose and observed that it was written in sixteenth-century French and that it contained serious errors. It was clear that the game was not worth the candle. Moreover, I wondered who this Auguste Morel was. Then, when Pierre Leyris told me he had Morel's version, I nonetheless seized the opportunity, and it was my third surprise, a pleasant surprise. Morel's translation could be considered like a poem of the French sixteenth century, written in the freshly vivid, still somewhat awkward language of the time. The "Ça Madame venez" [This, madam, come] and the "Ha, mon Amérique" [Ah, my America] can't fail to evoke Ronsard and the Pléiade poets. Rereadings of the translation confirmed this impression of happiness. Jean-Yves Masson's aphorism "It is not the translator who should be happy, but the translation" ("Territoire de Babel" 160) applies quite well here, for it is a translation that is undoubtedly happy.[99] It is happy because it is written not only in this freshly vivid language but also because it seems to really rise from the depth of this language. The translation does seem to be a poem of the time written with the poetic tone of the time. Its archaism is not the contrived and constrained archaism of Fuzier: it is the most natural return to a state of poetic language that is "archaic,"

98. [A literary magazine published in 1925 and 1926. The translation appears in *Navire d'argent* 1 (1925): 97–99. Trans. Note]

99. In fact, I learned from information taken about Morel that first he had been a happy translator, then that he probably had not been so happy. Morel is no other than the translator of Joyce's *Ulysses,* as the notice "Traduction intégrale par Auguste Morel" indicates. But there is also Stuart Gilbert's existence and the revision undertaken by Valery Larbaud and Joyce himself. There is good reason to think that Morel found the role he was given somewhat thankless in regard to the real labor he had had to do: the invisibility of the translator as if multiplied by the invasion of a "linguistic advisor" (Gilbert), of a forceful editor (Larbaud), and of the author himself, whose passion for translation questions probably did not make him a passive reader.

in the sense of first, originary, in the sense of the kores[100] of ancient Greece. Here *archaic* also means radiating youth, and this is what attracts us in the texts of our French sixteenth century; that is what causes our *regret*,[101] our nostalgia: as this language has definitely withdrawn in its ageless youth, as we cannot write it (Balzac did it for prose with his *Contes drôlatiques,* and Courier did it when completing Amyot's translation of *Daphnis et Chloé* in the same vein), we attempt to draw from its "treasure" to translate works of all kinds. French words from the sixteenth century seem to us livelier, newer, lighter, leading a life different from that of our words, a life that is both more ethereal and more substantial, a life to which a certain clumsiness remains associated but that nonetheless does not become a "defect," but that contributes to giving an *aura* to these words, these turns of phrase, this language. However, this sixteenth-century language does not really lend itself to the role of "treasure" that we want it to play: because a word and a turn of phrase are not easily transplanted, they keep their datedness and easily clash among *our* own words. Any translator who has tried to render Spanish or Italian diminutives with sixteenth-century French diminutives knows it. This is why the isolated archaisms can't stand on their own and always end up becoming a systematic archaism, which is the only way to avoid the disparate and the artificial.

Morel's translation is thus *entirely* archaizing, systematically archaizing, even in the spelling of the words. Although the translation abandons rhyme and an overly rigid prosody, it first appears to us as a French poem of that time, a poem that Ronsard would have *dared* to write (which he could not), even in its subtle clumsiness.[102]

A NEW TRANSLATION OF DONNE IN FRENCH

Even if the analysis of Morel's translation has been positive, the general examination of the French translations of Donne leads to a negative assessment. No existing translation is satisfactory *today.* We should not be satis-

---

100. [Statues of young maidens offered to Athena. Trans. Note]
101. [Regret evokes sixteenth-century French poet du Bellay's sonnets "Les regrets," in which he presents his conceptions of language and the role of French. Trans. Note]
102. Unfinished section.—French editor's note

fied with a translation of Donne by Morel that would render all the poet's works on this mode. It is thus necessary to illuminate the presuppositions of a new—and decisive—*transfer* of Donne in France, and those of future *retranslations* that would not repeat the previous ones.

This is the *productive* aspect of my critical work. For this work, I am not completely in a vacuum. The situation is indeed such as I have described it: the person who wants to read Donne *in French* today is left with a very small sample. Why this *absence* of Donne? Is Donne *completely* absent? He is not, first because he is neither *forgotten* nor considered as being outside our sphere of poetic interest. Then, there is the critical work of Ellrodt, a masterpiece of its kind. This does not replace translation but is part of the whole of the *transfer* of a work.

To think about a new translation of Donne in French is first to think about Donne, and especially to *rethink* him. Who is Donne? Who is this author whom we want to *transfer* into our culture and translate? Who is this man who had the following motto inscribed on his first portrait, "Antes muerto que mutado" [Rather die than change], and whose life and works seem to us both one and changing?

Was he a poet? Probably, even though we are told that he never considered himself a poet even when he "poeticized" a lot, and that he did not publish much during his lifetime.

But Donne did not always write poems. First, he stopped writing the same kinds of poems, then he progressively stopped writing poems, or almost stopped.

He stopped writing poems while remaining a writer. His various works notwithstanding, including those he had written during his period of greatest poetic activity, he was no longer the greatest poet of the times for his contemporaries; instead he had become the greatest *preacher* of England: everyone in London rushed to hear him, and these sermons were also *literary works*.

Such is Donne, as Ellrodt and Carey reveal him to us. They teach us, once and for all, that in order to know and appreciate Donne's work, we should not stop at his poetry; we must go to his prose, even if it is to come back again and again to his poetry.

All the collections of Donne's works that have existed until now are insufficient in two ways. First, they all are only collections of poems. Then, these collections all have their limits. On the whole, Legouis' choice is excellent, although it lacks too many elegies (among which is "Going to Bed"). But it contains a few epithalamions, "Of the Progress of the Soule," and so forth. The reader of Donne has never before been given such a diverse range of poetry. Gros' choice is more selective and without real coherence. Denis and Fuzier's selection is more than selective; it is restrictive. There are of course many elegies, short profane pieces, and sonnets, but no occasional pieces and, especially, a confusing division between the "profane" and "sacred" parts of the work that is supposed to order the pieces "in the sense of a spiritual ascent" (Poisson 22). In this anthology, the diversity-unity specific to Donne doesn't appear.

Thus, we must move beyond the idea of a poetic collection—if we want *transfer* to occur—in order to turn toward the idea of a volume including all of Donne's genres of writing (prose and poetry). This is so for several reasons. First, the *same network* of images, terms, representations, and figures links the "profane" and "sacred" poems, the letters, the sermons, and the books. Consequently, reading a specific poem illuminates a sermon or a letter, and vice versa: the reading of a "burning" passage from the sermons *illuminates the poetic world* of Donne. The second reason is that a volume of this kind would show us Donne as he is: a Christian poet and author. Like Milton or Hopkins, Donne is a Christian author, from the beginning to the end of his life. He is a Christian author as much in "profane" love as in prayer, letter, or sermon. He is one of the great English Christian authors of our tradition, whom we must welcome and reveal as such, whether we are Christian or not.

There is really no reason to exclude the sermons and the devotions. And this is the last reason that justifies their integration: these sermons are strong, beautiful and moving, and often terrifying. See, for instance, the *last sermon* he preached, "Death's Duell":

> But for us that die now and sleepe in the state of the dead, we must al passe this *posthume* death, this *death* after *death,* nay this death after burial, ... when these bodies that have beene the *children of royall parents,* and *the parents of royall children,* must say with *Job, Corruption thou art my father, and to the Worme thou art my mother and my sister. Miserable riddle,* when *the same worme* must bee *my mother,* and *my sister,* and *my selfe. Miserable incest,* when I must bee *maried* to my *mother* and my *sister* ... when my *mouth* shall be *filled* with *dust,* and the *worme* shall *feed,* and *feed sweetely* upon me (Ellrodt, *L'inspiration personnelle* 132)[103]

---

103. [Donne, *Complete Poetry* (748–49). Trans. Note]

or this, on faith and reason:

> But a man cannot believe that which he does not know. Conscience includes science; it is knowledge and more; but it is that first. (Donne, *Sermons* 4:34)[104]

> They are not continuall, but they are contiguous, they flow not from one another, but they touch one another, they are not both of a peece, but they enwrap one another, Faith and Reason. (Donne, *Sermons* 4:7)[105]

Or the famous passage on man, who is not an island, immortalized by Hemingway:

> No man is an *Iland*, intire of it selfe; every man is a peece of the *Continent*, a part of the *maine*; if a Clod bee washed away by the *Sea*, *Europe* is the lesse, as well as if a *Promontorie* were, as well as if a *Mannor* of thy *friends* or of *thine own* were; any mans *death* diminishes *me*, because I am involved in *Mankinde*; And therefore never send to know for whom the *bell* tolls; It tolls for *thee*. (Benoist 8)[106]

Or this, more poetic and more surprising yet: "In paradise, the fruits are ripe, the first minute, and in heaven it is always Autumne" (qtd. in Carey 274).[107]

Or this passage about the Incarnation, which fascinated him as much as what Yves Bonnefoy called the "excarnation":

> If I lacke a signe, I seeke no other but this, That God was made for me; which the Church and Church-writers, have well expressed by the word Incarnation, for that acknowledges, and denotes, that God was made my flesh: It were not strange that he who is spirit, should be made my spirit, my soule, but he was made my flesh: Therefore have the Fathers delighted themselves in the variation of that word: so far, as that Hilarie cals it a *Corporationem*, That God assumed my Body; and Damascen

---

104. ["Preached at the Spittle, Upon easter-Munday, 22 April 1622," *John Donne's Sermons*. Trans. Note]

105. ["Preached at S. Pauls, in the Evening, upon Easter-day, 28 March 1623," *John Donne's Sermons*. Trans. Note]

106. ["Meditation XVII," *Devotions upon Emergent Occasions* 102–7. Trans. Note]

107. [Donne, *Sermons* (6:172). Trans. Note]

cals it *Inhumanationem,* That God became this man, soule and body;
And Irenaeus cals it *Adunationem,* and Nysen *Contemperationem,* A
mingling, says one, an uniting, saies the other, of two, of god and man,
in one person. (*Sermons* 6:178)

Legouis cautions us against overestimating Donne's sermons (*Poèmes choisis* 20), which would be to the detriment of his great poetic works. Legouis denounces the effect produced, not by the complete sermons, but by "some well-chosen passages." But it is not a question of valorizing Donne's prose to the detriment of his poetry, nor even of wondering if this prose has "the same importance as his poetry" (*Poèmes choisis* 20). As for the issue of the "well-chosen passages" (and a Donne volume would certainly include whole sermons as well as excerpts), it must be reconsidered at the level of the *architectonics* of the new "collection": how the choice of poems, of prose pieces, the excerpts from some prose pieces, how this would be accompanied by paratextual matter, historical accounts, and iconographical elements obviously no longer falls within our scope, since now many different configurations are conceivable. Our role is only to project the idea and the contours of a new anthology that would be a *true transfer*. In *Lettres du voyageur à son retour*[108] [*Letters of the Traveler upon His Return*], Hofmannsthal's hero readily says to himself when faced with the Germans, whom he finds disconnected and fragmentary, "The whole man must move at once" [in English in the text] (*Lettre de Lord Chandos* 176).

Now, to move to our shores, *the whole Donne must move at once.*

TOWARD RETRANSLATIONS OF DONNE

To think in concrete terms about the principles of a retranslation of Donne (and primarily of his poetry), we have, it seems, two possible paths.

The first one consists of relying on the few successful translations of Donne that exist now. The second is to continue the discussion about the poetic translation of classical poets where we left it.

Let us consider the first path. To my knowledge, there are three successful

---

108. [The original essay is "Die Briefe des Zurückgekehrten" (1907). Trans. Note]

translations of Donne, that is, translations that seem to open a "translation path." This is Yves Bonnefoy's version, which I already mentioned, and Ellrodt's "Nocturne sur la sainte Lucie, le jour le plus bref," which, as he modestly says, "will only give a vague idea of the spellbinding force [of the original]" ("Présence et permanence" 3). Readers will see for themselves.

A NOCTURNALL UPON S. LUCIES DAY,

Being the shortest day
1   'Tis the yeares midnight, and it is the dayes,
2   *Lucies*, who scarce seaven houres herself unmaskes,
3   The Sunne is spent, and now his flasks
4   Send forth light squibs, no constant rayes;
5   The worlds whole sap is sunke:
6   The generall balme th'hydroptique earth hath drunk,
7   Whither, as to the beds-feet, life is shrunke,
8   Dead and enterr'd; yet all these seeme to laugh,
9   Compar'd with mee, who am their Epitaph.

10   Study me then, you who shall lovers bee
11   At the next world, that is, at the next Spring:
12   For I am every dead thing,
13   In whom love wrought new Alchimie.
14   For his art did expresse
15   A quintessence even from nothingnesse,
16   From dull privations, and leane emptinesse:
17   He ruin'd mee, and I am re-begot
18   Of absence, darknesse, death; things which are not.

19   All others, from all things, draw all that's good,
20   Life, soule, forme, spirit, whence they beeing have;
21   I, by loves limbecke, am the grave
22   Of all, that's nothing. Oft a flood
23   Have wee two wept, and so
24   Drownd the whole world, us two; oft did we grow
25   To be two Chaosses, when we did show

26 Care to ought else; and often absences
27 Withdrew our soules, and made us carcasses.

28 But I am by her death, (which word wrongs her)
29 Of the first nothing, the Elixer grown;
30   Were I a man, that I were one,
31   I needs must know; I should preferre,
32   If I were any beast,
33 Some ends, some means; Yea plants, yea stones detest,
34 And love; All, and some properties invest;
35 If I an ordinary nothing were,
36 As shadow, a light, and body must be here.

37 But I am None; nor will my Sunne renew.
38 You lovers, for whose sake, the lesser Sunne
39   At this time to the Goat is runne
40   To fetch new lust, and give it you,
41   Enjoy your summer all;
42 Since shee enjoyes her long nights festivall,
43 Let mee prepare towards her, and let mee call
44 This houre her Vigill, and her Eve, since this
45 Both the yeares, and the dayes deep midnight is.

Translation by Robert Ellrodt
NOCTURNE SUR LA SAINTE LUCIE, LE JOUR LE PLUS BREF

1 C'est le minuit du jour au minuit de l'année;
2 Sept heures seulement Lucie montre sa face;
3   Le soleil épuisé lâche en l'espace
4   Non des rayons, mais de faibles fusées;
5   Sous terre est descendue
6 Toute sève en ce monde, et la terre goulue
7 Boit l'universel baume; toute vie y reflue
8 Comme aux pieds de ce lit: pourtant ce cénotaphe
9 Semble riant auprès de moi, son épitaphe.

10 Étudiez-moi donc, vous qui devrez aimer
11 En ce monde à venir qu'est la saison prochaine:
12   Je suis toute chose défunte et vaine
13   Que l'alchimiste Amour ait transmuée.
14   Il sut, d'un art suprême,
15   Tirer des privations, de la maigreur extrême,
16   Du vide et du néant la quintessence même:
17   M'ayant détruit d'abord, il me recomposa
18   D'absence, d'ombre et de mort—choses qui ne sont pas.

19 Il n'est homme ici bas qui ne tire son bien—
20   Vie, âme, forme, esprit—de toutes créatures:
21   L'amour est l'alambic où ma nature
22   Se distille de tout ce qui n'est rien.
23   Nos pleurs ont souvent sous leurs flots
24   Noyé le monde entier, nous deux; souvent, sitôt
25   Surgi, l'émoi jaloux fit de nous deux chaos;
26   Et notre âme, souvent en extase ravie,
27   Abandonnant le corps, nous a laissés sans vie.

28 Mais la mort de l'aimée (ah! ce mot lui fait tort!)
29 Fait de moi l'élixir du Néant primordial.
30   Je le saurais, si j'étais homme encore;
31   Je pourrais bien, si j'étais animal,
32   Choisir et convoiter
33 Et, même plante ou pierre, aimer et détester;
34 Tout être, oui, tout être a quelque qualité.
35 Si j'étais comme l'ombre un néant ordinaire,
36 Encore y faudrait-il un corps, une lumière.

37 Je ne suis rien qui soit: mon seul soleil est mort.
38 Ô vous, vivants amants, pour qui ce soleil moindre,
39   Courant au Capricorne, y cherche encore
40   Nouvelle ardeur pour mieux vous poindre,
41   Jouissez de votre été brûlant!
42 De sa nuit, sombre fête, elle jouit longuement:
43 À l'y rejoindre, il faut m'apprêter à présent,

44 Car cette heure est pour elle et vigile et veillée
45 En ce minuit profond du jour et de l'année.

Here is a rhymed translation in handsome verses, which shows that it is possible to rhyme without versifying. Of course, it must be read as what it is: an attempt. But my interest here lies in the translation's tendencies and orientations. Neither archaizing nor modernizing, it indicates a middle way, a somewhat "classical" way.

This is a way that, because of the homogenizing labor of the rhymes, may not quite always restore what is colloquial, familiar, in Donne:

10 Study me then, you who shall lovers bee
11 At the next world, that is, at the next Spring:[109]

is rendered as:

10 Étudiez-moi donc, vous qui devrez aimer
11 En ce monde à venir qu'est la saison prochaine.[110]

The second line is more majestic in French. This (slight) tendency to make the lines more majestic also diminishes other prosaic elements in Donne, such as the abstract terms, in this case, the metaphysical terms:

14   For his art did expresse
15 A quintessence even from nothingnesse,
16 From dull privations, and leane emptinesse.[111]

---

109. Legouis, in *Poèmes choisis*, translates almost literally:

> Étudiez-moi donc, vous qui serez amants
> au siècle prochain, c'est-à-dire au printemps prochain. (93)
>
> [Study me then, you who shall be lovers
> Next century, that is, next spring. (Trans. Note)]

Siècle [century] is a poor translation of "world."

110. [Study me then you who shall love
in this world to come that next season is. (Trans. Note)]

111. Car son art exprima
La quintessence même du néant
Du degré des privations inertes et de la maigre vacuité. (Legouis, *Poèmes choisis* 93)

14   Il sut, d'un art suprême,
15 Tirer des privations, de la maigreur extrême,
16 Du vide et du néant la quintessence même.[112]

This is a learned and beautiful translation, but one in which the couple "nothingnesse"/"emptiness" becomes blurred (could the neologism *viduité* [from *vide*, empty] have worked here?).

Is this a mere detail? For this poem, certainly, but this kind of poetic translation, if it were to actually go into effect, that is, if it involved a more exhaustive and a broader effort, would inevitably encounter the problem of "poeticization," the problem of rendering Donne's prosaic and colloquial, not to mention rhetorical, elements.

The two translations by Yves Bonnefoy, "L'hymne au Christ, au dernier départ pour l'Allemagne" and "À Dieu, mon Dieu, dans ma maladie," evidently admirable translations, are what Etkind calls free translations. Bonnefoy abandons the rhyme scheme and all "formalities" that are too overtly traditional. This first liberty is accompanied by various liberties required by the interpretation and poetic transmutation.

Free to do as he pleases, much more so than Ellrodt was, and prepared by his experience of translating Shakespeare, Bonnefoy effortlessly solves the issue of Donne's colloquialisms in a way that we must examine. For instance, this stanza from "Hymne au Christ":

Nor thou nor thy religion dost controule,
The amourousnesse of an harmounious Soule,
But thou would'st have that love thy selfe: *As thou*
Art jealous, Lord, so I am jealous now,
Thou lov'st not, till from loving more, thou free
My soule: Who ever gives, takes libertie:
O, if thou car'st not whom I love
Alas, thou lov'st not mee.[113]

---

112. [He knew, with a supreme art,
     How to draw from deprivation, extreme leanness,
     emptiness and nothingness, the very quintessence. (Trans. Note)]
113. The italicized passage is translated by Legouis in *Poèmes choisis* as:

Comme Tu es jaloux, Seigneur, moi aussi je suis jaloux maintenant. (197)

Tu es jaloux, Seigneur. Bien, moi aussi.[114]

The colloquialism of the French version is not the same as that of the original. It is more compact, more concise; it is not *oratory* as in Donne:

As thou
 ... so ... now. ...

In its sweet harshness, the "Bien, moi aussi" seems to also render the English "now," a "now" that is so essential in Donne's poetry of the present. ("Bien, moi aussi" = "It's my turn to be jealous now.")

This correspondence in the present to the poet's answer to God leaves aside Donne's oratorical (rhetorical) turn of phrase, which is in his poem, thanks to the "now," completely wedded, united, to the colloquial expression.

To say that Bonnefoy leaves aside this oratorical aspect is to say that he *simplifies* and slightly *densifies* Donne's line. In this, as we know, he is also going along with the poet, who likes what is "compact," "dense," and "simple." But this decision to simplify and to slightly densify is a translator's decision. I mean that it is not only dictated by the desire to correspond to the love of compactness and denseness in Donne. After all, Donne also likes what is oratory, discursive, and precious. This decision is primarily dictated by the way in which the act of poetic translation appears to the translator, and indeed, at this stage, quite consciously.[115] It is not only translation à la Bonnefoy. It is a kind of translation that can be clearly discerned, first of all through the few characteristics that I have mentioned and that are not specific to Bonnefoy alone.[116] This translation produces what Goethe used

---

[As you are jealous, Lord, me too I am jealous now. (Trans. Note)]

Fuzier and Denis' translation in *Poèmes de John Donne:*

Tu es jaloux,
Seigneur, mais je le suis aussi. (243)

[You are jealous,
Lord, but I am too. (Trans. Note)]

114. ["You are jealous, Lord. Good, me too." Trans. Note.]

115. Bonnefoy has defined the tasks and the forms of English poetry translation (not only Shakespeare) in his afterword to *Hamlet*.

116. We would find them sometimes, in a more pronounced form, in Celan when he translated French or English poets.

to call the *Verjüngung* (rejuvenation) or *Verfrischung* (regeneration, freshening up). The two Donne poems seem to us as though new, young, especially after the difficult readings of their translations—difficult readings because we were only reading old stuff. This impression of rejuvenation is created by the absence of any poeticization, any rhetorization (the "qui donne liberté ce faisant la réclame" of Fuzier poeticizes and rhetorizes the colloquial and crisp "Who ever gives, takes libertie"), and by the light simplification and densification processes we have observed. The *Verjüngung* is a temporal movement: Bonnefoy's translation *presentifies* Donne, puts him in a "now" that is both his own (temporally and originarily) and ours, and takes him out of the antiquarian past in which time itself and backward-looking translations had put him. This can sometimes depend on the choice of a single word, as we can see in the first two lines of the first stanza:

In what torne ship soever I embarke,
That ship shall be my embleme of thy Arke.

Fuzier translates:

Quelle que soit la nef rompue où je m'embarque,
De ton Arche pour moi elle sera la marque.[117]

This encloses once and for all (this is the very opening of "Hymne") the poem in a majestic obsolescence [*passeité*] ("nef rompue"). Bonnefoy, on the contrary, while closely following the beginning of the first line and avoiding any inversion:

Sur quel pauvre rafiot que je m'embarque,
Il me sera le signe de ton Arche[118]

---

117. [Whatever the impaired vessel in which I may embark,
   of your ark for me it will be the mark.
The register of "nef rompue" (impaired vessel) is much higher, and so is the tone of the line. Trans. Note]
   118. [On whichever old tub I embark
   It will be for me the sign of your ark. (Trans. Note)]

places the poem in a dimension of presence that is concrete, eternal, and universal at once: who hasn't ever embarked on a "pauvre rafiot" (old tub) and, at the time of departure, hasn't felt the "pauvre rafiot" (cargo, ferry ...) to be like the emblem, the sign of something else, that here Donne calls "Arke"? On the opposite side, who has even embarked on an "impaired vessel"? It is logical to think that the ship leading from England to Germany looked more like a "pauvre rafiot" than a "nef," in any case.

The rejuvenation immediately becomes *reviviscence*. Rid of everything in it that was no longer alive, but still hardly changed (contrary to what happened with Octavio Paz), the poem lives again. This reviviscence is at the same time its emergence, its manifestation: the poem has become diaphanous.

Let me go further and add: Donne's poem has gained the freedom, the density, the diaphaneity, the youth, and the light prosaicness of a modern poem.

The light prosaicness of modern verse? What does this mean? How is a modern poem lightly prosaic? And, considering the variety of poetry in our century, is there such a thing as a modern poem? What does prosaicness mean here? What relation is there between all this and the tasks of poetic translation? These form the cluster of questions raised by my statement.

But it is a fact: modern poetry, in all the moments of its history, is "stricken" by prose. By something that we can only call *prose,* and whose definition we must leave empty, that we should definitely not attempt to define with the usual formulas, which all amount to saying that prose is what is not poetry or what, in the end, is *less* than poetry. Thus Octavio Paz, who is nonetheless a good prose writer, but perhaps too accessible, summarizes common opinions that devalue prose:

> In prose, meaning tends to be univocal, whereas ... one of the characteristics of poetry, perhaps the foremost characteristic, is to preserve the plurality of meanings. In fact this is a general property of language; poetry emphasizes it, but, softened, it is also visible in everyday language and even in prose (this circumstance confirms that prose, in the rigorous sense of the term, does not have any real existence. It is an ideal requirement of thought).... Poetry radically transforms language and does it in a direction contrary to that of prose. In one case, the tendency to fix one single signified corresponds to the mobility of signs; in the other case, the fixity of signs corresponds to the plurality of signifieds. (*Traducción* 14–15)[119]

---

119. Paz's words are but a muted echo of Mallarmé's famous lines: "Verse is everywhere in

We should not allow ourselves to be too impressed by such peremptory statements, any more than by those who claim that the distinction prose/poetry is obsolete, illusory, and relative; by those who tell us that what is essential is the notion of *writing*, rather than that of prose and poetry; and so forth.

PROSE IS THE OTHER OF POETRY

What does "prose" tell us? What does it tell readers who read what we call "great prose," who read Rabelais, Amyot, Montaigne, Pascal, Bossuet, Madame de Sévigné, Saint-Simon, La Bruyère, Montesquieu, Galland, Diderot, Chateaubriand, Joubert, Balzac, Stendhal, Nerval, Courier, Flaubert, Péguy, Proust, to name only French prose writers?

Beyond differences, immense differences, something substantive, reflexive, intricate, intertwined with itself, tied in manifold ways to the equally manifold wefts and layers of language; something protean, something that moves from the most meticulous form to the form contiguous to formlessness; something even noble, even seemingly poetic, that is always caught up by the "prosaic"; something sober even in excess; something that never soars except when it gives in—which is one of its dangers—to the pseudo flights of rhetoric; something that knots, weaves, "interweaves," as Donne would say, strings together, is well strung; something that *never ever looks like a poem [ne fait poème]* and that often wants it nonetheless, as it sometimes wants to achieve music. Here is what the masters of French prose whom we listed tell us. They are all prose writers, not poets (even if some of them were poets). None of them is ever "poetic" although they are never without ties to poetry, to this "music of tongue uttering metrified words" (Eugène Deschamps, qtd. in Davreu, *Jacques Roubaud* 46).[120]

---

language so long as there is rhythm—everywhere except on posters and on the back page of the newspaper. In the genre we call prose, there are verses—sometimes admirable verses—of all sorts of rhythms. But actually there is no such thing as prose: there is the alphabet and then there are verses that are more or less closely knit, more or less diffuse. So long as there is stylistic effort, there is versification" (qtd. in Roubaud, *La vieillesse d'Alexandre* 47). ["The Evolution of Literature," in *Selected Prose Poems* 19. Trans. Note]

120. One can be a great prose writer and a great poet. This was the case of Donne himself, of Dante, Milton, Hölderlin, Novalis, Nerval, and Mallarmé. But to be more precise, we should say: one can be a great poetry writer and a great prose writer, *in this order*. While a great poetry writer may be a great prose writer, the reverse seems less true. Goethe is here an unsettling exception: in what form was he first great? In any case, many great prose writers are only great prose writers.

In his *Système des beaux-arts,* a somewhat neglected work, the essayist Alain proposes a full reflection on prose (and, more briefly, on poetry). He attempts to define the specificity of prose in relation to poetry (and to "eloquence" by also making a distinction between poetry and eloquence):

> Prose is not poetry. In saying this, I do not mean that it is something less, with less rhythm, fewer images, and less force, but that it has no resemblance to poetry and that it affirms itself through refusing and rejecting anything that is characteristic of poetry. (307)

He evokes with great assurance the essential sobriety of prose and of *prosaic movement,* so different from poetic movement, "this controlled, sinuous movement, going around and coming back, which separates so markedly prose from any poetry and any eloquence" (314).[121] "I see a lovely modesty in its broken cadences" (309), and "the hero of a novel, even in his irrationality, is circumspect, prudent and thoughtful like prose itself" (333).

Thus, contrary to Paz and particularly contrary to Mallarmé (of whom he had to be thinking), Alain states and shows a *difference of substance* between prose and poetry (for him, the most accomplished form of prose and the most substantial one is the novel).

But as well founded as it may be, this claim is not sufficient, because in his *Système des beaux-arts,* Alain is only referring to literary prose,[122] and for me prose is also what is outside of literature, that in which and with which we speak, feel, and think every day and in the multiplicity of our *exchanges,* even if the poetic is not absent from this speaking, thinking, and multiple exchanges and communications. Prose is that in which and with which we

---

121. Similarly, Hofmannsthal says, "The purest poetry is a perfect being-within-itself, and the most accomplished prose is a perfect return upon itself. The latter quality may be even rarer that the former" (*Le livre des amis* 89). In a short inspired text titled "Un peu faute de façon," Jean-Paul Goux writes that "In prose..., syntax is what comes to confuse the limpidity of communication; it no longer disappears behind the meaning that it should transmit; it acts as a screen; it always interposes its own matter, its own consistency" (98). Goux quotes prose texts by Descartes, Racine, Claude Simon, and others where one can see this pattern. But what is expressed by a "sinuous" and "going around" movement must always, for fear of being mannered, remain sober and at the end be "returning." This is the essential difference between Proust's "returning" sentences and those that don't really "come back" such as Gracq's sentences.

122. Although he briefly mentions an "industrial prose" different from "artistic prose" (337), he rightly evokes Balzac, the author where, in an exemplary way, both types of prose are interwoven.

write letters, recipes, a user's manual, a treatise of logic, a tax return, and this critical study on translation. It may be argued that in each linguistic tradition there is an *elementary or fundamental prose*[123] that formed historically in a specific relation of differentiation with poetry, an elementary and fundamental prose supporting all the "specific" prose, even the one we speak, which has no autonomy in relation to what is written, the prose that schools normally have the task of teaching us by using *examples* from great prose texts.

Prose, *finally,* is what Mallarmé says it is with a light but deep-seated disdain:

> To narrate, teach, even describe, this is fine (even though an adequate exchange of human thoughts might well be achieved through the silent exchange of money). The elementary use of language involves that universal journalistic style which characterizes all kinds of contemporary writing, with the exception of literature. ("Crise de vers," in *Igitur* 251).[124]

It is the state of language and speech in which, being limited to pure exchange and to the empty muteness of such an exchange, we can see it infinitely *deteriorating,* proliferating in degenerated, trivial, hermetic "discourses"; Robin's "false speech"; various forms of doublespeak (not only political ones); any shore where the *linguistic in itself* [*le langagier en soi*] never ceases to agonize or to endlessly change into monstrous formations. Prose is also this: what in language we degrade and is degraded.

But this entity, up to its ultimate exhausted shores, is never without a link to poetry. In its heart, that is, in literature, this whole only stands because of and through this link. What Roubaud states here is essential:

> If the *monument* is poetry, poetry is not the only one in question: its fate also decides that of literature. It alone holds in balance, supports, in

---

123. Like the English "plain style" [in English in the text]. This fundamental prose is the prose of communicability. In 1927, Hofmannsthal regretted its absence in Germany: "We have a quite elevated poetic language and very nice and expressive popular dialects. . . . What we lack is a middle-ground language. . . . Our neighbors in the North and the South, in the East and the West have it. We alone are without it. But it is in this middle language that the face of a nation is contained at all times" (*Lettre de Lord Chandos* 423–24). For Hofmannsthal, the nation that had the most educated "middle language" was France.

124. [Modified version of the English "Crisis in Poetry" 42. Trans. Note]

language, both prose and poetry. In fact, there is no such thing as prose alone, without poetry, nothing that justifies "to narrate, teach, even describe." (*La vieillesse d'Alexandre* 197)

Without this essential link of *support* [*soutènement*], there is no prose. None, empirically, without many passages from the poetic to the prosaic, many interferences, many infiltrations, many prosifications of poetry ("proems"), many poeticizations of the prosaic.[125] But in these very interferences, the Difference of the Poetic and of the Prosaic is always finally reaffirmed, a Difference that does not exclude—to the contrary—the support of which Roubaud is speaking. Witness in France the prose writer among prose writers, Montaigne, whose *Essais* are as if innervated with poeticality (beyond the countless quotations from poetry[126]) without their ever being poetic, without it ever making sense to call them poetic.

Earlier I quoted Boris Pasternak to illustrate, at that moment, a way to think about prose that is far from the usual platitudes. It is now time to come close to his thought, because his thought *thinks* (apparently) the Difference between Prose and Poetry in another way, because it *thinks* (apparently) the support in another way, other than that of Roubaud, I mean. Pasternak's thinking does not appear as a systematic theory, but it is not a mass of isolated intuitions, either.

In "Some Statements" (1922), the poet writes:

Inseparable from each other, poetry and prose are two opposite poles.

By its inborn faculty of hearing, poetry seeks out the melody of nature amid the tumult of the dictionary and then, picking it up as one picks up a tune, improvises on this theme.

Instinctively, through its own inspiration, prose seeks and finds man in the category of speech, and, if the age does not have any, it re-creates him from memory, and evacuates him, and then, for the good of humanity,

---

125. See E. R. Curtius, *La littérature européenne et le Moyen Âge latin* vol. 1, chapter 8, part 2, "Poésie et prose," in which we find rhetoric.

126. Here we should be thinking about a new edition of the *Essais* that would, at last—and now that the quotations from Latin, Greek, and Italian poets are no longer accessible to us—translate them poetically, and not prosaically in the worse sense of the term. This would be a thorough rejuvenation of the *Essais,* and it would show support and difference.

pretends to have found him in the contemporary world. These principles do not exist in isolation. (Pasternak, *Œuvres* 1330)[127]

Here prose and poetry are posed like opposite poles, or distinct and inseparable principles, each having its own movement and its own object of research, its own quest: poetry seeks the musicality of nature, and prose seeks man as linguistic being [*être langagier*].[128] To this, let us add that poetry looks for this musicality "in the tumult of the dictionary." Prose and poetry do not exist separately, since the "element" they have in common is language. Thus Difference is exposed, rather cryptically.

In other texts, Pasternak thinks out support, in reverse, as support of poetry by *prose*. In "People and Attitudes" (1956), he writes about Blok:

> This Saint-Petersburg of Blok . . . is filled with the everyday prose that feeds poetry with its drama and its anguish; its streets resonate with the common and familiar everyday language, which refreshes the language of poetry. (*Œuvres* 658–59)[129]

But at the same time:

> For Blok, prose is the spring from which the poem arose. He does not introduce it into the range of his means of expression. For Rilke, on the other hand, descriptive and psychological devices used by the novelists of his day (Tolstoy, Flaubert, Proust, and the Scandinavians) are an inseparable part of the language and style of his poetry. (*Œuvres* 662)[130]

Here prose appears first as this familiar, *everyday* language that *refreshes* the language of poetry. The two words "everyday" and "refresh" must be taken seriously. It seems evident that prose is linked to the everyday, although this

---

127. [The English version proposes "secretly abandons him" instead of "l'écoule" (evacuates him, lets him go). See "Some Statements" 84–85. Trans. Note]

128. In the end, Bakhtin says the same thing for the novel when he speaks about dialogism during the same period. This is another thought about prose.

129. [The English translation reads: "It is full of everyday prose that feeds his poetry with drama and disquiet, and on its streets can be heard that ordinary, humdrum popular speech which enlivens the language of poetry" (*Selected Writings* 265). Trans. Note]

130. [*Selected Writings* 269. Trans. Note]

evidence could be questioned. Not all prose is "everyday prose." Not all prose is concrete. There is also a prose that is abstract, logical, and so forth. For Pasternak, and this is not valid for Blok alone, this everyday prose *nourishes* poetry—with what? With its "drama" and its "anguish," thus not with contents or objects, but with *tension(s)*. What does "refresh" mean here?

Pasternak's "Notes on Translation from Shakespeare" (1946) says about *Romeo and Juliet*:

> *Romeo and Juliet* . . . the majority of this tragedy is in blank verse. This is the medium in which the hero and heroine speak to each other. Yet no undue emphasis is placed upon the measure in this verse and it does not protrude. Here there is no declamation: form does not mask the inexhaustible yet modest content with its own self-admiration. It is an example of the ultimate in poetry, which in its finest examples is always permeated with the simplicity and freshness of prose. The language of Romeo and of Juliet is a model of guarded, staccato conversation held secretly in half-whispers. (*Œuvres* 1366)[131]

We find again *freshness,* the refreshing power of prose that here preserves poetry *at its height,* the "inexhaustible yet modest content." It protects it, but from what? From the narcissism of form, says Pasternak. But here, in Shakespeare, prose does not "refresh" poetry from the outside, as in Blok. It acts within the "blank verse" in which Romeo and Juliet speak. For Pasternak, it can only arise this way because the primary mode of expression of Shakespeare is poetry, not prose (*Œuvres* 1362),[132] and what gives shape to this "poetry, which, knowing no restraint, tosses about in powerful disarray"

---

131. [*Selected Writings* 229. Trans. Note]

132. His prose is well-rounded and polished. . . . A complete contrast to all of this is the realm of Shakespeare's blank verse. The chaotic nature of its essence and form irritated both Voltaire and Tolstoy.

Very often certain roles in a Shakespeare play pass through several stages on their way to a final solution. Some character or other first begins to speak in scenes written in verse, and then suddenly breaks into prose. In such cases the verse scenes appear as prelude, while the scenes in prose appear complete and definitive. Verse for Shakespeare was his most rapid and direct means of expression. He resorted to it as the quickest means of recording his ideas. He even went so far as to write some episodes in verse as if they were a rough draft for prose to follow. The power of Shakespeare's poetry lies in its mighty sketchiness that knows no bounds and sprawls forth in chaos. (*Selected Writings* 224)

("Notes of a Translator" 100), is prose, either as this force becomes prose, moves to prose, or is tempered, "refreshed" by prose.

But whether prose is the source, as in Blok, or the tempering, refreshing principle of poetry spurting forth as in Shakespeare, Pasternak clearly assigns it the same role of support, to which we shall soon give another name.

Simply put, for Blok, unlike Rilke, prose remains a distant source, a formless one, so to speak. According to Pasternak, Rilke's poetry has integrated the "processes" of the great novelistic prose of the period. It is quite another thing to be refreshed by the everyday prose of a city. But in both cases, prose is the *support* of poetry, and in Shakespeare as well!

In *Safe Conduct*, which was begun in 1927, Pasternak writes:

> We depict men in order to make them shoulder the weather—the weather or, which is the same thing, nature—in order to make them shoulder our passion. We fill prose with the everyday in the name of poetry. We introduce prose into poetry in the name of music. That is what I called art, in the broadest sense of the word, art keeping watch over the living species, bursting forth in the succession of generations. (*Œuvres* 545)[133]

Here we find all the terms used by Pasternak to think through the relations between prose and poetry in the first quotes I presented: "music," "man," "humanity," "nature," and "the everyday." But this time, the "logic" of the support is, if not explained, at least stated.

It is prose that, filled with the "everyday," that is, with this "familiar and everyday speech," allows poetry to be what it is, to escape its "narcissism." But this prose, which nourishes and refreshes poetry, itself needs to be nourished by the "everyday," by the (unwritten) language of the everyday, a language that is all *tension*. Enriched and sustained by this prose, which is itself enriched and supported, poetry reaches the state of music, that is, what it was seeking through a "natural gift" in "Some Statements." This does not mean that poetry

---

133. There is another, somewhat different, version of this passage. See Armand Robin, *Poésie sans passeport* (129). [The English translation of this passage is as follows: "We depict people in order to cloak them with a climate—a climate, or, which is one and the same thing, with nature—with our passion. We drag the everyday into prose for the sake of the poetry of it. We draw prose into poetry for the sake of music. That in the broadest sense of the word was what I called art, established according to the clock of the living species with all its generations" (Pasternak, *Safe Conduct* 181). Trans. Note]

becomes purely and simply musical, if only because, for Pasternak, *music* has a specific meaning. In this text, it is this sentinel art (not necessarily music in the usual sense) that, at the very least, links "prosified" poetry, through unity or opposition, to the great Time—that is, the time of the cosmos, of History, and of life. It is when reading the "Notes on Translations from Shakespeare" that we discover the status held by music (or rhythm) in *Hamlet, King Lear,* and *Romeo and Juliet*. In these three cases, music is the background that allows prosified poetry to be brought out. Music is always background music. In *King Lear*, a "tragedy sotto voce," it is the noise of unleashed nature:

> Yet in essence all that really rages in this tragedy is the night storm and, after taking shelter in the hovel, men who are frightened to death, talk in mere whispers. (*Œuvres* 1376)[134]

"In *Romeo and Juliet*," Pasternak says, "music plays ... a negative role. It embodies in this tragedy the force of society's falsehood and worldly concerns hostile to the young lovers" (*Œuvres* 1365).[135]

But it is also the "deafening rhythm" of crowd scenes and "this racket of murders and cooking pans, like peals of thunder in a percussion orchestra" (*Œuvres* 1366), that function as a music background to the tragedy of a whispered love.[136]

As for Hamlet's music, it has another function: "This music consists of a measured alternation of solemnity and trepidation. It lends the play an extreme density of atmosphere and thus projects the crucial mood still more powerfully" (*Œuvres* 1364).[137]

Pasternak speaks about the "threatening materiality" of *Hamlet*, and earlier he links this "materiality" to *rhythm*. Rhythm "brings the materiality of sound to the predominant mood that it sustains during the whole tragedy; and it ennobles and tempers the coarseness of certain scenes" (*Œuvres* 1363).[138]

---

134. [*Selected Writings* 242. Trans. Note]

135. [*Selected Writings* 228. Trans. Note]

136. [The English translation is "amidst the clatter of fighting and cooking, as if to the accompaniment of the thunderous beat of a noisy orchestra, there is played out the tragedy of calm emotions" (*Selected Writings* 230). Trans. Note]

137. [*Selected Writings* 226–27. Trans. Note]

138. [In the English version: "it imparts through sound and sustains the predominant mood of the tragedy and it ennobles and irons out certain coarse scenes of the drama" (*Selected Writings* 226).Trans. Note]

This materializing function of music may clarify the cryptic definition of this "art" that is given in *Safe Conduct*. It seems that the poem is ruled by the coexistence of the prosaic (the *prosaic* being prose "filled with the everyday") and what can be called *musaic* (to distinguish it from the "musical" in the sense of "harmonious," etc.).[139]

I must now turn to a final text, drawn from the *Discours au premier congrès des écrivains soviétiques*[140] (1934), a text that, in its opacity and extreme formulation, must have surprised more than a few people:

> What is poetry . . . ? Poetry is prose, prose not in the sense of the entirety of the prose works of such-and-such a writer, but prose itself, the voice of prose, prose in action and not in literary paraphrase. Poetry is the language of organic facts, that is, of facts that have living consequences. . . . Whatever the case may be, poetry is only this: pure prose in its original tension. (*Œuvres* 1553)[141]

Here the Difference between Poetry and Prose seems to have disappeared, but to the profit of prose. More precisely, *poetry is identified with prose*. But Pasternak is not speaking about just any identification. He underlines the fact through a series of modifiers: prose *itself,* prose *in action,* the *voice* of prose, *pure* prose, pure prose in its *original tension*.

Novalis is probably the first writer to have projected, in a letter to A. W. Schlegel, the figure of a *prosified* poetry:

> If poetry wants to expand, it can only do it by limiting itself—by contracting, by letting go of its flame,[142] so to speak, and by congealing. It

---

139. About *Romeo and Juliet*, he says that love "needs no melodious sound, its soul is filled not with sounds but truth" (*Selected Writings* 229). And in "Hommes et positions": "I have always held and still do that the music of words is not any kind of acoustical phenomenon and that it consists not in the euphony of vowels and consonants taken on their own, but in the correlation between the meaning of the sentence and its resonance" (*Œuvres* 666). [In English, the essay is "People and Attitudes," and the variant for the end of the sentence is "between the meaning and sound of words" (*Selected Writings* 275). Trans. Note]

140. [*Speech during the First Soviet Writers Congress.* The speech has not been translated into English. Trans. Note]

141. Here again, Robin proposes a variant, but this time an important one, for the end of the passage. He says, "Pure prose, in its translating tension, this is what poetry is" (qtd. in Bourdon 71).

142. [Letter to A. W. Schlegel of January 12, 1798, qtd. in Benjamin, "The Concept of Criticism"

acquires a prosaic appearance, its constituent parts join less closely[143]—its rhythmic rules thus lose some of their rigor—it adapts to the depiction of a more limited content. But it remains poetry—and consequently faithful to the essential laws of its nature; it becomes, so to speak, an organic being whose whole structure reveals its fluid origin, its originally elastic nature, its limitless character, and its aptitude for everything. The intertwining[144] of its members alone is without rule; their ordering, their relation to the Whole remains the same.... Here too, the simpler, more uniform, and more peaceful the movements of the sentences are, the more harmonious their mixture is on the whole,[145] the looser their coherence, the more transparent and colorless the expression is,—and the more perfect is this nonchalant poetry, in its seeming independence[146] of objects, in its contrast to ornate prose—Here poetry seems to renounce[147] the rigor of its requirements.... But it will quickly be revealed to whoever dares to attempt poetry in this form how difficult it is to achieve perfection in this guise.... One could call that higher poetry the poetry of the infinite. (Benjamin, *Le concept de critique* 151–52)[148]

Benjamin stresses that this romantic concept of "prosaic poetry" refers to a more radical principle, the *principle of the sobriety of art*, developed during the same period, with more depth yet, by Hölderlin:

The thesis that establishes his philosophical relation to the Romantics is

---

(174); Novalis, *Briefwechsel* (55). A closer translation of the German would be "letting go of the fuel that feeds the fire." Trans. Note]

143. [Here the German would actually read: "It will acquire a prosaic appearance, its constituent parts will no longer stand in such intimate community—or, therefore, not under such strict rhythmic laws—and it will become more capable of portraying that which is limited." Trans. Note]

144. [The German refers to "mixture." Trans. Note]

145. [The German says "inside the whole." Trans. Note]

146. [The German says "dependence" instead of "independence." Trans. Note]

147. [In German *nachlassen*, which means to "cut back, to decrease," not "to renounce" (*sich verzichten auf*). Trans. Note]

148. There is another fragment from Novalis on the same page: "Poetry is prose among the arts." Benjamin also quotes the ninety-second aphorism of Nietzsche's *The Gay Science*, in which he reflects upon the relation between prose and poetry: "It is remarkable that the great masters of prose have almost always also been poets, be it publicly or only in secret and in the 'closet'; and verily, one writes good prose only *face to face with poetry!*" [90].

the principle of sobriety in art. This principle is the essentially quite new and still incalculably influential leading idea of the Romantic philosophy of art; what is perhaps the greatest epoch in the West's philosophy of art is distinguished by this basic notion. Its connection with the methodological procedure of that philosophy—namely, reflection—is obvious. In ordinary usage, the prosaic—that in which reflection as the principle of art appears uppermost—is, to be sure, a familiar metaphorical designation of the sober. As a thoughtful and collected posture, reflection is the antithesis of ecstasy, the *mania* of Plato. Just as, for the early Romantics, light occasionally operates as a symbol of the medium of reflection, of infinite mindfulness [meditation], so Hölderlin, too, says: "Where are you, thoughtful one, who must always / Turn aside at times? Where are you, Light?"[149] In his later writings, Hölderlin sought to gain knowledge of "holy-sober" poetry. ("The Concept of Criticism" 175)[150]

The principle of sobriety, that is, what, in the form of prose, came for Pasterak to "temper," "refresh," and "terminate" (in the strongest sense of putting a term or a limit to) this poetic force, which knows "no restraint, bursting forth in powerful disarray," and so resplendent in Shakespeare? But would the "genius" Shakespeare be ruled by the principle of sobriety? That is exactly what the German romantics thought, especially A. W. Schlegel, who saw in the playwright an "abyss of marked intention, of self-awareness and of reflection" (Thalmann 9).[151]

More deeply than Schlegel, Pasternak, who also translated Shakespeare and who paid homage to the German writer, did not see in his plays a simple "reflexive play" but a *higher play between poetic eruption, musical materiality, and prosaic support,* which produces what Benjamin calls "the eternally sober consistency of the work" (*Le concept de critique* 161).[152]

Let us follow Benjamin again to see how Baudelaire, whose *Fleurs du mal,* as he tells us, "was the last lyric work that had a European repercussion" (*Un*

---

149. [Qtd. in Benjamin, "The Concept of Criticism" (175); Hölderlin, *Sämtliche Werke* (4:65). The English version reads: "Where are you, contemplative thought! That always at the set time must accompany me, where are you light?" Trans. Note]

150. [Hölderlin, *Sämtliche Werke* (4:60). Trans. Note]

151. [The German says: "ein Abgrund von Absichtlichkeit," that is, "an abyss of intention." Trans. Note]

152. [The published English translation reads: "the unassailable, sober prosaic form" ("The Concept of Criticism" 176). Trans. Note]

poète lyrique[153] 205), represents concretely and formally the entry of French poetry into this prosaicness:

> The *Fleurs du Mal* is the first book that used in poetry not only the words of ordinary [*prosaïque*] provenance but words of urban origin as well. Yet Baudelaire by no means avoided locutions which, free from poetic patina, strike one with the brilliance of their coinage. He uses *quinquet, wagon,* or *omnibus,* and does not shrink from *bilan, réverbère,* or *voirie*. This is the nature of the lyric vocabulary in which an allegory appears suddenly and without prior preparation. If Baudelaire's linguistic spirit can be apprehended anywhere, it may be captured in this brusque coincidence. Claudel gave it its definitive formulation when he said that Baudelaire combined the style of Racine with the style of a journalist of the Second Empire. (*Un poète lyrique* 143)[154]

Obviously we should not read these lines in a naive way, as if with Baudelaire poetry became prosaic through the sheer act of employing technical or urban neologisms. Benjamin is quite careful to link the deployment of this "lyrical vocabulary" or the emerging of allegory to the abrupt coincidence that their conjunction represents. Such is one of the facets of the prosaicness of the poet's own poetry; he does not mean at all to say that poetry would, from now on, go further than Hugo in the sense of a "republican" freedom and could, among other things, use all the "vile" words that had been excluded up to that point, and that are quite numerous in the French poetic tradition. It is probably true, although there are immense differences among poetic traditions, that Bonnefoy is right when he says, "All the words of a language do not lend themselves to poetic intention to the same degree" (*L'improbable* 255).[155]

That Baudelaire, with measure, I might add, has been able to "integrate" such-and-such urban or technical neologisms into his works (words that quickly became part of everyday language)—and after him, many poets—

---

153. [Titled in German *Ein Lyriker im Zeitalter des Hochkapitalismus*. In English, *A Lyric Poet* (152). Trans. Note]

154. [*A Lyric Poet* 100. Trans. Note]

155. In the same passage, in which he attempts to found this claim, he accepts the "wind, stone, fire or the "mazagrans" [coffee mugs without handles] of Rimbaud, the "wagons," and "gas" of Baudelaire.

does not mean that this is possible today or that it even makes sense: the modern technical-urban *universum* and the multispecialized "languages" that structure and invade it are not that of the poet; their poetic as well as prosaic capture is most problematic.[156] I said "as well as prosaic," for we don't even have a Zola.

Baudelaire's works are also touched by prosification in his attempts with "prose poems," and specifically those prose poems that are openly "translations" of poems from the *Fleurs du mal*. What carries this attempt is the idea of a "lyric prose."

> Who among us has not . . . dreamt the miracle of a poetic prose, musical without rhythm nor rhyme, supple and harsh enough to adapt to the lyrical movements of the soul, to the ebb and flow of reverie, to the fits and starts of consciousness? ("Le Spleen de Paris," in *Œuvres* 275)

What is new in this concept of a poetic prose is its origins:

> It is from the frequentation of enormous cities, from the junction of their countless relations, that this obsessive ideal was born. You yourself, my dear friend, did you not attempt to translate into a *song* the strident cry of the *Glazier* and express in a lyrical prose all the distressing suggestions that his cry sends all the way up to the garrets, through the highest brumes of the street? (dedication to Arsène Houssaye, "Le Spleen de Paris," in *Œuvres* 276)

Isn't this close to what Pasternak says of the "everyday prose" that "nourishes" poetry with *tension*? Isn't it striking that Baudelaire thinks that the effort to re-create the cry of the glazier in a lyrical prose is a *translation*? But it is clear that from this "dream" of a poetic prose Baudelaire expects no less than a *prose poem*—that is, he expects a poem; he is speaking of the *poeticization of prose*, the necessity of which is founded on the nature of his material or of the theme (the urban element).

But what is most remarkable in this attempt, and what differentiates it from all the subsequent attempts at poetic prose, is that, at the end of his

---

156. Robert Marteau puts it bluntly, "It is remarkable that the rise of industry has not led to the creation of any poem" (124).

dedication to Houssaye, Baudelaire recognizes that things did not happen this way, "that not only did I stay far away from my mysterious and brilliant model, but also that I was doing something . . . remarkably different" ("Le Spleen de Paris," in *Œuvres* 276).

What thing is Baudelaire speaking about? But it is enough to peruse the prose pieces "Un hémisphere dans une chevelure" and "L'invitation au voyage," as well as the corresponding poetic "original" works, to see how much the prosification of the poems and the poeticization of prose at all costs struggle with one another.[157] Far from bringing out, as Goethe thought, the "absolutely pure matter" of the poems, this prosification, especially for "L'invitation au voyage," can only be perceived, in many places, as a discursive and explicative thinning down. In both texts, the prose, as elaborate as it may be, also seems to lack consistency and continuity. The end of "Un hémisphère dans une chevelure," "When I nibble your springy and rebellious hair, it seems that I eat memories" (301), verges on triteness and vulgarity, an effect that Baudelaire certainly did not intend.

The struggle of these two movements, prosification of the poetic, poeticizing of the prosaic, makes of the prose poem, of lyrical prose, of poetic prose a *modern form of writing*, a form that bears witness both to the crisis of the poetic in general and to the attack by the prosaic on poetry. But this form is necessarily hybrid (it is based on two radically opposite postulates); *it is not ruled by the principle of sobriety, but rather, in its substance, by poetic hubris.* Baudelaire has the amazing lucidity to recognize that by writing his poems in prose, he has met prose, "somber prose" (Roubaud), the prose that will not be poeticized; "it seems that I eat memories" is not a poetic sentence.

Gifted epigones of Baudelaire, like Pierre Jean Jouve, were to rush headlong into (novelistic) poetic prose. Proust, an attentive reader of Baudelaire, was to learn the lesson in order to build an *œuvre* of pure prose freed from any poeticizing purpose.

We must conceive of this space of prosification and of sobriety (or sense of *modesty,* another fundamental word for poetry since Hölderlin) as both *one and absolutely diverse.* It is one in that it is the modern space of Western poetry. It is diverse, and diverse in three ways. There is, of course, the diversity of individual poetic trajectories, and I think that at no other period has poetry been so individuated (or is it only an appearance?)—what com-

---

157. The poeticization of prose would want to erase the first moment, so to speak.

mon ground is there between Ponge, Jouve, Michaux, Perse, and Char?—whereas there is, from afar in any case, a "family resemblance" between Scève, Ronsard, du Bartas, and even du Bellay. Then, there is the diversity of poetic traditions specific to each linguistic area or even to each national space (German, English—each with its own differences—French, Italian, Spanish, Russian, etc.). Far from receding in favor of a world poetry, these traditions persist in their being and in their fundamental features, even if, in part because of the crisis into which they have entered (which, by the way, does not affect them in the same way), they intensify their exchanges with all kinds of other traditions (hence the importance of poetic translation during the modern era[158]) and thus accede to the non-identical identity described by Jean-Christophe Bailly:

> Here the question of identity comes back again, but such that in itself friction makes it and changes it. Is an "identity" then something finished, some kind of deposit—or on the contrary an unfinishable form, a work in progress [in English in the text] that every contact heightens and strengthens? The answer is quite simple in that the most immediately verifiable identity, the identity of the individual, is an answer in itself, as experience, as experience of the other, and as experience without end. Where any a priori limitation to the possibility of the other appearing is felt as a self-limitation, what gives in to the potential of encounters is felt like the opposite of an abandonment—like the movement, the detour perhaps, which leads, in a broken line, toward itself. The capture, the time that solitude gives itself to capture, are but the equivalent of a sort of photographic developing of this potential of encounters. And the mind seizes what is most its own, what belongs to it properly speaking as task, in an incessant and passionate coming and going between the snapshot and the darkroom, between the immediacy of the capture and the slowness of the processing. The mind only isolates itself in order to develop what it has learned of itself when going out. (*Le paradis du sens* 78)[159]

---

158. See Robert Davreu's comments on tradition (26) and on poetic translation (35) in his presentation of Roubaud.
159. To assert that there still is, that there always were, poetic traditions specific to each linguistic space (be they national or not) seems obvious to me, or rather it seems to be a claim that does not dispute that these traditions, for the West, are linked by a common (in part) space, origin, or time, or closely tied times. This is not to deny that these traditions are both open

There is finally the "non-contemporaneity" of contemporary writers: to wit, beyond the differences established by individual trajectories and by traditions, there are these poetic massifs that do not quite belong to the same time frame, that are still in what for others is already, partially, the past. It may be individual works, or part of a single production that bolts toward the "before of" before the crisis, which Bailly calls "the end of the hymn" (*La fin de l'hymne*): here, Saint-John Perse may come to mind. It may also be a linguistic space that has not been affected or has been affected in a different way by the crisis.[160] We can reread Efim Etkind's book in this light and see, in his defense, in many respects naive and sometimes even obtuse, an expression of a Russian particularity (which he keeps bringing to the fore when he says, "In our country [in Russia] we translate verse with verse").

Perhaps the modern age of poetry may also be read as a return of poetry in its most particular poeticality. Thirty years ago in a text about Baudelaire, Bonnefoy was proposing to see in *Les fleurs du mal* the difficult emergence, in part aborted, of a poetic speech freed from its traditional rhetorical and anecdotal finery:

> Poetic discourse, which changed its role for Baudelaire, is no longer a theater of emotions; it is the insinuation of a voice that aims at loss; it describes and intensifies the mortal course—it also changes its nature, thanks to him. This discourse that once concealed death casts off the poor tricks it used for that

---

and deeply closed unto themselves. When we say, for instance, "Irish poetry" (in English, for those who like classifications, itself a sub-part of the Anglo-Saxon domain), aren't we thinking of a poetry that is strongly individualized? Paz claims with his usual simplifying assurance that "There is no (and there never was a) French, Italian, Spanish, English poetry; there was a poetry of the Renaissance, a baroque poetry, a romantic poetry. There is a contemporary poetry written in all the languages of the West" (qtd. in Davreu, *Jacques Roubaud* 34). If we only say this, if we freeze the truth contained in such a statement, we end up saying something stupid, especially since every major domain, as I suggested about Ireland, has its sub-domains, a number of which belong to the domain of *borderlands* (relation between French poetry and Belgian or Swiss poetry), and a number belong to the domain of (former) colonies. *Borderlands and colonies produce an abundance of poets.* The poetic destiny of colonies is quite special.

160. Aucouturier opposes "the aging of French regular verse, felt today as being archaic," to "the youth of Russian verse: it has been in existence for only two and a half centuries, but it still has, thanks to the resources specific to Russian, considerable possibilities for renewal, which all the great poets of the twentieth century, from Blok to Brodsky, through Maïakovsky, Khlebnikov, Tsvetaeva, Mandelstam, Akhmatova and, of course, Pasternak, have sought to use" (1571).

end. The picturesque, the ornamental. Affective babbling. The Romantic eagerness to say, to invoke everything in the world, to grasp everything—or, more profoundly, to say nothing at all, because the essential is silenced. (*L'improbable* 36)[161]

This poetic speech of which many modern poets, each in his own way, claim to be the heralds, seeks simultaneously (and identically) to enter into an increased poeticality and to "treat" the crisis of traditional versification forms (Roubaud, *La vieillesse d'Alexandre*). It is worth noticing that in France this movement is accompanied by a *translating work*, a *prosaic work* (writing of prose pieces), and a *reflexive work* (itself, of course, written in prose: essays, critical writings, etc.).

If we limit ourselves, for Bonnefoy, to the poetic works themselves, which strive to be the "purest," we can only say that this oeuvre, in its tone and concretion, appears full of gravity and concision, concision and gravity, always; economy of the rare "poetic words," conquered one after the other, infinitely intertwined in the space of the poem and of the collections. Furthermore, in their very abstraction (Bonnefoy, I think, speaks of poetic universals: tree, wind, fire, stone, and so forth), these poetic words link the event of a poem to some everyday empirical event, or something that belongs to the order of the everyday reverberated in and through memory:

Il y a sans doute toujours au bout d'une longue rue
Où je marchais enfant une mare d'huile. (Bonnefoy, *Poèmes* 111)

[There is probably still at the end of a long street
Where I would walk as a child a puddle of oil.]

Thus, the poetry of quintessential words (which is also that of a struggle against them) does directly evoke a dirty motor-oil puddle at the end of a dreary street in a provincial town. There are thousands of such examples in modern poetry.

But here again we have what I call the prosification of poetry, what Pasternak was alluding to when he said that "we fill prose with the everyday in

---

161. "Baudelaire's *Les fleurs du mal*" (46). Rimbaud had already told Demeny, "His form, which is so highly praised, is mean" (*Œuvres completes* 273).

the name of poetry" and that "we introduce prose into poetry in the name of music."[162]

There is thus no contradiction between, on one hand, the prosaization of poetry and, on the other, its entry into a poeticality that is free of all rhetoric and, at least in part and on the surface (Roubaud has showed us the case for the French tradition), of traditional, if not classical, forms of versification. Of course, we can guess that for modern poetry all this is not happening without struggle and suffering.

Let us go back now to one of the forms of diversity that mark the space of Western poetry, that of language and (sometimes) national traditions. As I said, it is clear that all traditions, insofar as they belong to this space and, by definition, to the same time frame of this space, are subjected to the principle of prosification, to the principle of sobriety, to the principle of modesty. This is something—all differences aside—that a North American poet shares with a French poet, a German poet, an Italian poet, a Swedish poet, and so forth. But it is equally certain that the poet shares this principle *from the vantage of his own poetic tradition, and of it alone.*

Our concern here is the English poetic tradition, the tradition of the poet, which, as productive critics, we wish to reintroduce into the space of the French poetic tradition at the point where it is now. This desire corresponds

---

162. A music that, in Rilke and Bonnefoy, appears as the "faraway song," the extreme of the poem. See R. M. Rilke, "Chant éloigné":

Ô chant éloigné, suprême lyre
. . . .
Ô chant qui naît le dernier pour conclure
L'enfance non terminée, le cœur d'antan. (*Chant éloigné* 63)

[O far away song, highest lyre
O last born song bringing to an end
Unfinished childhood, a heart of yesteryear. (Trans. Marilyn Hacker)]

And Bonnefoy, *Poèmes*:

Je célèbre la voix mêlée de couleur grise
Qui hésite aux lointains du chant qui s'est perdu
Comme si au-delà de toute forme pure
Tremblât un autre chant et le seul absolu. (137)

[I praise the voice mixed with tones of grey
Which pauses in the distances of lost song
As if beyond every pure form
Shimmered another song, the sole perfected one. (Trans. Marilyn Hacker)]

to a latent desire, a latent demand from the representatives of this tradition and from readers of poetry.

It is obvious that the translation of poetry as well (be it of old, modern, near, or distant poetry) can only be affected in this prosified space of modern poetry, and this applies whether the translation is done by poets like Celan, Bonnefoy, Roubaud, Deguy, Jaccotttet, and so forth, or by translators who are, as it is commonly said (as it is poorly said), "only" translators. Poetic translation is at the service of poetry; it is a poetic act. Robert Davreu has stated the broad lines of the nature of modern poetic translation:

> Poetry is the authentic "philology"; it is love and memory of language, and that is why it is constantly bound, in its approach, to make itself memory of poetry, in its many guises, many languages, not by copying models that would be offered, but by translating . . . in a single movement the tradition (all the traditions and, preferably those that have run dry) facing the present and the present facing the tradition. (*Jacques Roubaud* 26)

> The work of translating foreign poetry is an essential moment of poetic creation. As with the relation to tradition, it is a matter of integrating the old into the new by integrating the new to the old; similarly with tradition, there is a double movement involved, a double play, probably—one, as we know, that does not go without the betrayal of both sides where authentic faithfulness resides—of the integration of the same to the other, and of the other to the same, not without pain nor risks. (*Jacques Roubaud* 35)

To this we must add the fact that translation, and not only the translation of poetry, has been conceived of since Schleiermacher as the "result of the encounter of two personalities," as Jean-Yves Masson tells us ("Territoire de Babel" 158). This encounter takes an intense and delicate turn when poetry is involved.[163]

But this principle of sobriety, which governs the whole domain of modern poetry translation, what happens to it in concrete terms when we touch on the Anglo-Saxon tradition? This domain is unquestionably the one on which the work and the reflections of poetry translators have most focused for the

---

163. As Benjamin said, contrary to the usual platitudes uttered mainly by pretentious poets such as Kenneth White, poets are not automatically the best translators of poetry, far from it. In order to translate poetry, the poet needs an *extreme modesty*, which is rarely found. Impudence is by far the most widespread attitude.

last forty years in France. The extreme *particularity* of this relation of the French tradition (in its current state) to the English poetic tradition (along all of its trajectory) is that, among the poets of this tradition, the French tradition meets—and, it seems, in stark opposition to the nature of its own trajectory—a "concatenation" of the prosaic and the poetic that is perhaps not the equivalent of the modern principle of sobriety as I have described it, but that comes from the far reaches of the history, not only of Anglo-Saxon poetry but of the *Anglo-Saxon language and world.*

In this encounter, via translation (and all kinds of para- or non-translating *transfers*),[164] in this *unique* encounter in the modern history of French poetry translation,[165] the great founding figures are Chateaubriand, translator of Milton's *Paradise Lost,* and Baudelaire and Mallarmé, translators of Edgar Allan Poe, for the nineteenth century. In the twentieth century, in the space opened by these founders, there is Valery Larbaud, Parisot, Leyris, Bonnefoy, Masson, Mambrino, Jaujard, Malroux, Roubaud, Deguy, Déprats, Reumaux, El Etr, and so many others who should be mentioned for the translation of English or American poetry.

I shall again call on Bonnefoy to define this difference between the two poetic traditions, which he first associates with the difference between the two languages:

> Allow me—in order to show the gap it reveals between two kinds of poetry—to stop a moment and consider the English language.
> What strikes me the most about English is its great aptitude for noting

---

164. Among which there is a wonderful example given by the "translation" that Roubaud made of Shelley's "Letter to Maria Gisborne," or rather of fragments moved from the *Epipsychidion* to the "Letter to Maria Gisborne" (see Roubaud, "Lettre à Maria Gisborne").

165. I must say it again: no other poetic domain occupies, in France, the place of the English domain, even if the translations of Hölderlin, Celan, and Rilke have also marked the French poetic tradition. Translations from Italian (Dante, Leopardi, Ungaretti), from Spanish of Spain or Latin America (from Góngora to Lorca, from Paz to Vallejo, and so forth), from Russian (Mandelstam, Tsvetaeva, Pasternak, and others) are indeed important, as are the recent translations of Virgil, Sappho, Pindar, Sophocles, Euripides, and Homer. But the entirety of these translations does not have the weight of the translations from English literature. Moreover, the translations from English have a degree of self-reflection that is quite sophisticated. The magazine *Poë&sie* is a good example of the natural preponderant role of translations from English: even though it also welcomes poets, prose writers of all languages, there always seems to be a few more English texts. This reflects the priviledged position—which has nothing to do with any kind of "imperialism"— of the Anglo-Saxon domain in the field of French poetry translation.

outward aspect, be it related to human gestures or to things. A host of expressions allows one to grasp precisely and quickly the way in which the event—everything becomes event—presents itself to immediate consciousness. And as a great number of words also express "realities" that apparently differ from other realities only by the slightest nuances—for us, this would only represent various aspects of the same essence—we quickly get the feeling that English seeks to describe what consciousness perceives while avoiding any preconception about the ultimate being of these referents. It may be true that languages are structures, but this is hardly noticeable in English! Words are so numerous there, so unclassifiable, so difficult to define, and so elusive to use. Often as close in form as they already are by their meaning, without visible derivation, without any etymology that could be deemed meaningful, they push against each other in an opaque continuity, like the crystallizations of a magnificent matter—in fact, like flashes of intelligibility extracted from a reality that has deliberately been approached in an empirical way. The power to photograph, so to speak, is extreme but the capacity for hyperbole is less apparent—nonetheless, a few great essences, the sea, the bird, the spring, which belong to the universal heart of our relation to the world, are there to reveal the radiance of the epiphany, which they alone keep intact.

So, it is very probably from this tension that English poetry has drawn its remarkable energy. The consciousness of the One is alive here; this is what Blake's works prove with a violence and a clarity of purpose unmatched in our own language. And it is Coleridge who has given us the most poetic definition of the Beautiful, asserting that "the Beautiful is that in which the many still seen as many becomes one." From Marvell to Wordsworth, to Hopkins, this prescience is constant. Yeats can oppose it only with furor, overwhelmed as he is by its evident reality. But if poetic intention is the same in English as anywhere else, then, in order to develop it will have to follow paths that, as one now perceives, will be unique to it alone—even if, in doing so, a century later it were to provoke Voltaire's incomprehension. The contradictory metaphors, the images that were sketched and then abandoned, the interrupted lines, the obscurities, all this chaos of the "irregular" author of *King Lear,* what does it all mean? Simply that Shakespeare wishes at one and the same time to interiorize the real (as *The Tempest* would come so close to accomplishing) and to preserve the richness of a language that has so many words to express the aspect of things. As a result, the assertions of the exterior consciousness are simultaneously silhouetted on this stage and shown to be inadequate, like the figures of God in negative theologies. It was necessary for image to annul image so that the invisible could be felt.

Thus in fact, Shakespeare's "barbarity" constitutes his greatest seriousness. And, evidently, it is the same paradox, the same 180-degree turn of the compass that also allows John Donne, though he is very different from Shakespeare, to lift up the stone of outward aspect in order to revive the absolute. One sees him—a scandal for Racine almost as much as for Rimbaud—become attached to the anecdotal, this "exterior" vision of the human fact. But this is to show—such is the secret irony of Presence—that it is in our reaction to the inessential that our essence is revealed. It is also through existence, through being, that we must "by indirections find directions out," that is, by roundabout ways discover the way; and from this there are two consequences that ensue. First, English poetry enters the world of the relative, of meanings, of triviality (the word is untranslatable), of ordinary life, in a way that is almost unthinkable in the "most sublime" French poetry. Its gaze at the object stops, at least at first, fixes on the outside appearances that our literary tradition refuses to see; for the inattentive reader, it is sometimes hardly different from the gaze of the moralist, the humorist. But, secondly, placing itself at this common point and pursuing its own ends, poetry in English will all the more forcefully leave the mark of its difference and truth. Who has ever doubted that an English poetry exists?

But I will end here these imprudent speculations. I have offered them only to put into clearer relief the very different characteristics of French. (257–59)[166]

Further on, at the end of his essay "La poésie française et le principe d'identité" ["French Poetry and the Principle of Identity,"] when he evokes the "flaw" for him inherent in any poetry,[167] Bonnefoy returns to the differ-

---

166. [Modified translation of Yves Bonnefoy, "French Poetry" (127). Trans. Note]
167. Bonnefoy defines it thus:

And this dreaming... whether through the idea of some illusory perfection of measurable form, or the idea of the distant lady of medieval imagination, or the idea of a Faustian depletion of the possible... is the *evil* inherent in poetic intuition: the burning... form of its innermost and, perhaps, fatal flaw.

ence between the two traditions, and his comments almost take the form of a substantial critique of the French poetic trajectory:

> I will even say that, to my way of thinking, this "flaw" is more common in our language than in many others. This is because, if in the words we use there is this virtuality of presence . . . , Presence [la Présence] is no longer envisioned except as a fabulous unfolding [of this appearance], as a profusion of marble. No longer anything but a decor [from which the *I* also is absent], it is soon nothing more than a convention and the refashioning of a rhetoric. This is what Romeo unknowingly reveals when he thinks he is in love with the "beautiful" Rosalind, the symbol of outward aspect, of what one has imagined and not experienced. . . . Fortunately, he has Mercutio close by—Mercutio, that incarnation of the English language—to remind him of the obligations of "triviality."
>
> French poetry has no Mercutio. In our language it falls to the poet alone to regain self-control in this beauty of words where so often he has placed only the ghost of things. . . . Between the *exterior* identity of good sense and the *interior* identity of presence, there was for a long time—from, let's say, the poets of the Pléiade to Paul Valéry—this glorious and very alluring form of the flaw: the claim of the Idea to be its own proof and the illusory materiality of the dream's figure. (*L'improbable* 135–36)

I quote these comments at length and without hesitation because, throughout the years, they have supported Bonnefoy's whole translation oeuvre of English poetry, Shakespeare, Yeats, some Donne, and a whole body of reflections about this translation and the specific tasks it must confront. In themselves, these reflections matter more than the "solutions" that Bonnefoy

---

One should perhaps name this flaw "symbolism," because of the naive confidence one finds in the "hard lake" of the visible, in the gold and pearls one encounters there, and in the beauty of appearances, this illusory marble. These played a large part in fin-de-siècle poetry; in its shimmering surface and its ever so narcissistic and sterile essence. (123)

[The metaphor of the hard lake comes from Mallarmé's sonnet "Le vierge, le vivace et le bel aujourd'hui":

The virginal, vibrant, and beautiful dawn
Will a beat of its drunken wing not suffice
To rend this hard lake haunted beneath the ice
By the transparent glacier of flights never flown? (*Collected Poems* 67; Trans. Note)]

sometimes brings, in the name of a certain idea of freedom in translation, to what appear as problems, mainly in Yeats.¹⁶⁸

The tasks involved are numerous. As *modern* poetry translation, the translation of English poets (or writers in general) is, whether we can imagine it or not, subject to the same principles as those of poets belonging to other traditions: the principle of sobriety, or of prosification, the principle of dialogue among "personalities." These two principles presuppose both *respect* for the work to be translated and a certain *struggle* with it (and with its author).

But inasmuch as it is the *translation of this tradition*, of this *poetic universum* in which Mercutio always comes to remind Romeo of the duty of "triviality," French translation of English poetry is immediately hampered, and this is an understatement, by its own poetic essence. As Bonnefoy says in his afterword to *Hamlet*, all of Shakespeare's concreteness becomes abstract and general in the simple passage to French, as he demonstrates in the passage from *Falstaff*, even though it is translated "exactly" by François-Victor Hugo. Is that all there is to say? Certainly not, but we can understand a posteriori the fact that Chateaubriand did not dare translate Milton in verse and that Mallarmé limited himself to translating Poe's poems into prose.¹⁶⁹

When Leyris writes about his translation of Hopkins (a poet in whom the distance from the French tradition is as extreme as in Donne or Shakespeare), "If Hopkins is translated here *to a certain extent*, it is only insofar as French, after presenting itself as a smooth wall against which the battering ram of the poem struggled in vain, allowed us to suddenly glimpse a secret passageway" (*Poèmes* 16), we can wonder what this "secret passageway" is that, indeed, as translators, we always assume exists, but that we know can be "glimpsed" only after a long time, a long time during which language presents itself as that which resists,¹⁷⁰ that is at the opportune moment, the kairos. The secret

---

168. In this regard, it is enough for me that the "solutions" are openly presented as gestures of freedom, that they are neither hidden nor conceived as projections of a poetry upon another. See Bonnefoy, "French Poetry" (93–94).

169. And, we shall see, we are not dealing with just any prosification either.

170. Similarly to Claudel's "shut house" in *Cinq grandes odes*:
Cette demeure bien fermée . . .
Où the père de famille à l'importun qui frappe dans la
Nuit pour demander trois pains,
Répond qu'il repose avec ses enfants, profond et sourd. (100)

[The shut house of the parable,
Where the head of the household replies to the importunate who

passageway is not an opportunity that the French language would give through some linguistic element that, by chance or science, we would "remember." That French, in all times, has had secret passageways that allow for the translation of Shakespeare, Donne, Milton, Keats, Coleridge, Hopkins, and so forth, does not mean that these passages are accessible at all times to the French translator of poetry with a little talent. These passages were not accessible at the time of these poets. If they are becoming so, and quite slowly, it is not by virtue of some *evolution of language itself*, a language that, no one really knows how it happened, would have become more supple, richer, less normed, and less subjected to classical rules,[171] but by virtue of the entry of French poetry into the space of crisis and sobriety that I have evoked. This entry took place in the twentieth century. In 1921, when translating Moréas's poems (which the poet deemed untranslatable), Rilke discovered with wonder that French poetry, through its own evolution, *had become translatable* in German:

> What pride, what disdain in these poems, don't you think, what independence of rhythm which, at every step, seems to express ultimate decisions in its very bearing.... I spent all of yesterday afternoon in front of the house, in the sunshine, rereading a hundred times the translations I had just done, and which seemed to me to possess an equally proud and haughty decisive gait to them.... It's wonderful how, in these last years, the resources of French poetry have drawn it closer to ours; never before has it been so translatable. (*Lettres françaises* 121–22)[172]

Rarely has the kairos, the historical character of translatability, been expressed so clearly. In "Pour une poétique de la traduction" ["For a Poetic of Translation"], his preface to his collection *Les cinq rouleaux* (1970), Meschonnic similarly shows how French poetic language has changed, in his

---

knocks in the night to ask for three loaves,
That he is soundly asleep with his children, and cannot hear. (*Five Great Odes 73;* Trans. Note)]

171. I share Goethe's point of view (a depressing one) about the decadence of languages: "Words move through usage and have a tendency to decay rather than to be ennobled, to shift toward the worse rather than toward the better, to become empoverished rather than enriched" (qtd. in Simon, "Goethe sur le langage" 57). Simon adds, "The poet also must make do with a language cramped by the prejudices that it carries with itself, and that is no longer poetic."

172. [Letter of March 23, 1921, *Letters to Merline* 98–99. Trans. Note]

view with the advent of surrealism, and can thus correspond to the poetic language of the Bible:

> Every period of writing enriches the possibility of translating. Every period of writing enriches the possibility of writing. French is no longer what it was before surrealism.... Perhaps modern poetic language will be able to give to the French domain the Bible with all the poetic force of its consonantal language, with its paratactic absolutes, which are paradigms of prosody and rhythm—whereas the old poetic language was mostly subordination, and external rhythms. Thus modern French came to coincide serendipitously with biblical texts in order to steady French in rhythms where it can recognize itself through self-creation. (9–10)

The entry of French poetry into this space of crisis, which is also a space of openness, simultaneously gives to the translation of English poetry its grounding, its meaning, and its necessity inasmuch as it is an act of French poetry.

It gives it grounding because for the first time French poetry is becoming close to English poetry through the principle of prosaicness. Assuredly, this principle does not destroy the purist, the essentialist, and—whatever way one may describe it—the "fatuity" of French poetry and the concrete forms of poeticization that result from it, but it reduces this purist fatuity and frees forms of poeticization that are less "tight" and that can be open to English poetry. Here are the "secret passageways." In part. Even the contamination of French by English, in the everyday, contributes to the goals of the translator. Let us take the example of "self" in Hopkins. We saw the difficult and subtle solutions Leyris found in order to translate the verb "to self." But in many other poems, Hopkins plays with the "self," as a verb, a substantive, and so forth.

For instance, in "Binsey Poplars," we find:

> Ten or twelve, only ten or twelve
> Strokes of havoc únselve
> The sweet especial scene. (Hopkins, *Grandeur de Dieu* 60–61)

Mambrino translates:

> Dix ou douze, seulement dix ou douze

Coups détruisent, dé-réalisent
La tendre unique scène. (Hopkins, *Grandeur de Dieu* 60–61)[173]

Here no secret passage was found. But further, in "Spelt from Sibyl's Leaves," for

wáre of a wórld where bút these / twó tell, each
off the óther; of a rack
Where, selfwrung, selfstrung, sheathe-and shelterless, / thóughts
against thoughts ín groans grínd (Hopkins, *Grandeur de Dieu* 76–77)

Mambrino dares:

méfie-toi d'un monde où ces deux-là / seuls
parlent, chacun de l'autre exclu; d'un chevalet
Où self-rouées, self-nouées, sans gaine ou gîte, / pensées contre
pensées crissent et crient. (Hopkins, *Grandeur de Dieu* 76–77)

Isn't translating "selfwrung" as "self-rouées," "selfstrung" as "self-nouées," also possible because the English *self* already exists in everyday French, as in "self-made man," or "self-service," which has become a "self"? The "self," with its unique way of saying "one-self," has thus become, or has started to become, a French word, so that translating "selfwrung" as "self-rouées" is a true translation (although perhaps at the limit of the possible).

Secondly, the entry of French poetry into crisis gives the translation of English poetry its *meaning* and its *necessity,* because to open up to this poetry—this English poetry with its own prosaicness, its colloquialism, its "triviality," and everything that we mentioned about John Donne or what Bonnefoy says about Shakespeare—is not opening up to just any poetic *universum,* and Chateaubriand may have been the first to realize it. It is to embrace a *universum* that, albeit not directly in the sense that one would imitate it, can help the French poetic *universum* find the form of its prosaic modern poeticality.[174]

---

173. [Ten or twelve, only ten or twelve
Strokes destroy, un-realize
The sweet unique scene. (Trans. Note)]

174. A role that may be played currently by North American poetry, with its "international free verse," which is "infinitely translatable" (see Roubaud, *La vieillesse d'Alexandre* 204–5). The

But isn't there here a *certain circle?* If French poetry and thus the translation of French poetry "need" the English *universum* to approach their own prosaic poeticality, this presupposes that this *universum* is translatable, that is, that some secret passageways are opening in the smooth surface of the wall of the French language. But these passages can only be discovered, they can only open up if the French poetic *universum* has already been affected by the English poetic *universum,* has already been marked by *significant translations,* which, in turn, presuppose the opening of these secret passageways.

This circle is the inevitable circle of English poetry translation in France, and every translator has to go around it in his own way. What is essential is to work poetically within the circle, and this is what has been taking place in France since Chateaubriand. That the circle is not vicious but fruitful is proved by all the prestigious *œuvres* in translation previously mentioned. Not being aware of the existence, the nature, the demands of such a circle may well be the fundamental "flaw" of Denis and Fuzier.

But Donne, to finally come to him, in a way other than to Shakespeare or Hopkins, other than to Blake, Yeats, Coleridge, or Synge, other than to Eliot or Raine, represents the utmost distance for the French poetic *universum.* We can feel it in the following lines by Bonnefoy:

> One sees him—a scandal for Racine almost as much as for Rimbaud—become attached to the anecdotal, this "exterior" vision of the human fact. But this is to show—such is the secret irony of Presence—that it is in our reaction to the inessential that our essence is revealed. It is also through existence, through being, that we must "by indirections find directions out." (*L'improbable* 259)

It is a lot for one man to be a scandal for Racine and for Rimbaud. That Donne is such a scandal, and that in France he invites rejection, oblivion, misunderstanding, is what his state of current *non-transfer* displays. And

---

recent *Anthology 49+1 nouveaux poètes américains* is significant in this regard: it is conceived as a "contribution to the French literature" of today. Hocquart writes in his introductory note, "I value the idea that translation is the kind of representation I need in order to see better and understand better (in) my own language. . . . It is not an issue of influence, but an issue of reading. . . . It is only a matter of knowing if reading (here reading in French because we did not want a bilingual anthology) what Americans write can stimulate us and help us write what we write" (Hocquart and Royet-Journoud 10 and 15).

this is seen in the expressions used by translators and critics. When I read the following lines by Léon-Gabriel Gros about Legouis (who had excoriated his translations and his commentaries of Donne):

> One has the impression that the eminent scholar who knows everything there is to know about Donne and who even makes quite insightful comments about him is, in his heart of hearts, rather hostile to him, and that he does not have a "feel" for him. (209)

I was rather surprised, as the introductory work of Pierre Legouis seems most fair. Everything that can be said is that his introduction tends not to be overly impressed by Donne. Pierre Legouis quotes, in particular, another Legouis (Émile), who, on the contrary, finds Donne's *Anniversaries* "really intolerable, in spite of the sparks that illuminate them here and there" (*Poèmes choisis* 46).

My surprise grew when I read a few lines farther down the comments that Gros makes about the translation by Denis and Fuzier:

> Attempting an almost literal accuracy, pushing formal condensation to the limit, the two English specialists, steeped in Mallarmé and Valéry, achieved the impossible and transposed Donne, not only in regular verse but also in French from the end of the sixteenth century. One can only applaud such a tour de force, but the archaic bias takes away much of the relevance of Donne's poetry. (209)

How is it possible to write such a thing? And so I found myself confronted with a rather disconcerting quarrel among translators, with Legouis saying that Gros did not understand a thing about Donne and translated him carelessly, and Gros saying that Legouis knows a lot about Donne but does not have a "feel" for him. The problem did not seem so much to lie between Legouis and Gros as among Legouis and Gros and *Donne:* the first, through his slightly ironic distance toward Donne; and the second, through his careless enthusiasm, which made him say and do anything.[175]

---

175. He says about Gros' translation, which came out in 1936 in *Cahiers du Sud*, "Prose translation, peppered with many minor and major mistranslations, and preceded by a 'Presentation of John Donne,' in which the extravagance of content unites with the errors of form" (*Poèmes choisis* 52).

When I later read the review that Jean Grosjean wrote in 1962 of the Denis and Fuzier translation, I became even more surprised, not only because Grosjean praises their so-called faithfulness to Donne's "meaning and play of images" (!) but because here too a certain distance from Donne is visible, as when Grosjean uses the expression "bric-a-brac" to describe his poetry:

> John Donne's fame makes him mostly into a metaphysical poet, and, in his foreword, J.-R. Poisson is right to explain what is meant by it. We will thus be forewarned about the meaning that the bric-a-brac of fantasies and sciences, of theology and exoticism, takes on here. ("Recension de la traduction" 904).

Is it a "bric-a-brac," all this intertwining of images, concepts, and figures, that links Donne's poems in a network of "mutual translation"? A "bric-a-brac," this structural space revealed by Ellrodt and Carey? A "bric-a-brac," the whole dialectic that could "wreathe iron pokers into true-love knots," according to Coleridge?[176]

Further on, Grosjean states that "none of John Donne's successes justifies the ascendancy he holds" (906). Hence, it matters little that at the end of his review Grosjean attempts to define the "secret" and "the mystery" of Donne.

In other words, let us not take Donne too seriously, and if we translate him, we must do it so as to make him acceptable for the French poetic *universum*. This explains the "French Donne": the *English* Donne is all too scandalous.

It is therefore obvious that a retranslation of Donne must be set in motion not only in the circle described above, but also in the particular space, Donne's own, of the "poetic scandal" that he constitutes *for us*. This scandal must be recognized, held, and upheld for a true translation to see the light.

It is not a question of "feeling" Donne, of showing enthusiasm for him, like Gros or Rothschild, nor of transforming him methodically into an antiquarian form, as Denis and Fuzier did, but of translating him with sobriety, by meticulously, lovingly weaving again and again the so-called bric-a-brac of images, concepts, terms, and figures. Any retranslation of Donne will be, to use his own verbs, "interanimated," "intercharged," and "interacting"; it will have to be connecting and compacting; that is, it will have to strictly obey

---

176. [From Coleridge's poem "On Donne's Poetry." Trans. Note]

the principles of translatability internal to the work. For me, Bonnefoy's two translations do not function as models, but as sufficient indices of a retranslation that would follow the totality of modern poetry translation as we have outlined it and that extend from the most general (principle of sobriety), to the particular (English poetry translation), to the most particular (Donne).

Having reached this point, criticism must be silent. It is not its role to say how concretely Donne should be retranslated. Let us hope that criticism has fulfilled its task, sketched the global and historical space of such a retranslation, and presented the principles that this retranslation should follow. It will have exceeded its goal if, through its long digressions, it has awakened the *desire* for a retranslation.

PART III

About the Reception of the Denis and Fuzier Translation of 1962

How was the John Donne of the Gallimard edition received by the reviewers and critics of the time? Was the translators' work noticed as much as the text offered to the readers? What vision, what conception, of poetry translation is revealed when the reviews of the times are examined? What vision, or non-vision, of Donne do they reveal?

A GLOBALLY POSITIVE RECEPTION WITH "SOME RESERVATIONS"

Characteristically, out of thirteen reviews included in the Gallimard file about Donne, there is only one, that of the magazine *La Grive,* that is negative: "It is probably best when poets are translated by poets. In spite of Donne's fame, I am not enthusiastic about *Les poèmes de John Donne* translated from English by Jean Fuzier and Yves Denis. Wanting to add the difficulties of classical versification to that of a translation is an impossible task, unless a genius does it. To translate is not enough, you have to re-create."

Some articles occasionally show reservations about a specific aspect of the translated text, like, for instance, the *Figaro littéraire* article: "One can wonder whether it was really necessary to give a verse translation of these poems. Why superimpose the difficulties of French poetry on those presented by English poetry scansion and rhythm?"

But in general these criticisms of detail are accompanied by unanimous praise for the overall result.

Legouis' article in the scholarly journal *Études anglaises,* titled "Sur une traduction en vers de Donne" ["Concerning a Verse Translation of Donne"], recognizes (as one would expect) from the start the "natural" superiority of the Denis and Fuzier translation over his own because of their work with versification. "Condemned to prose," Legouis can "only admire . . . from below," especially since, for him, their prosody, the "occasional" archaism, the "free syntax" have their own necessity: "Their prosody obeys almost all the classical rules: the translators may happen to put the caesura of the alexandrine after a seventh feminine and non-elided syllable, but they can defend their choice by invoking the dislocation that Donne effected on the iambic decasyllable verse. Likewise, the free syntax is justified by the original as well as by our own French sixteenth century" (134). It is true that, as an Anglicist concerned with semantic accuracy, Legouis also wonders whether "the translation always gives the meaning of the original" and has to answer, "Alas, it does not!" (134). This is followed by three pages listing errors, major mistranslations, mistakes, and erroneous interpretations. This list, Legouis says, "seems justified because of its usefulness for French readers wanting to know the poet's thought" (137).

For me, these errors refer back to the systematic indifference of this translation to the signifying clusters and networks of Donne's works.

This academic criticism of details seems to open onto a criticism of substance when it comes to the choice of texts and to the vision of Donne that it implies. According to Legouis, this vision is dated in that it turns Donne into a precursor of Blake or D. H. Lawrence and is a "modernist preoccupation" that belongs to "the period between the two World Wars" (138). Legouis comes close to a criticism that is even more conclusive when, still referring to the analysis of Poisson's foreword, he states, "I think that it puts aside with an excessive disdain the whole middle part of the poetic works, which is excluded from the translators' selection, and offers, to say the least, a simplified view of the poet" (138).

But a few lines farther down, this criticism gives way to undiscriminating praise. The work "will be (we do not hesitate to say so) the best way to gain access to the genius of the poet" (138). Why is this so when the translation is riddled with errors and its choice of texts oversimplifies things? But Legouis does not stop here: "The foreword is right to claim 'a Franco-English metaphysical poet . . . has just been born'" (138).

After the exposure of semantic errors and the expression of reservations comes praise for the poetic "successes." In turn, Legouis praises the "alert faithfulness" of Fuzier's translation of "the message" and the "density and pressing force" of Denis's translation of Sonnet II.

In another review, the *Centre protestant d'études et de documentation* is both reserved and favorable. For the reviewer, the translation in verse has a precedent, Valéry's version of Virgil's *Bucolics*. But even if Fuzier and Denis have followed this path, they still "did not succeed. It is sometimes pleasant, sometimes unclear, sometimes successful, sometimes . . . not. But we must applaud good bilingual editions."

The *Bulletin critique du livre français* gives a rave review: "Excellent choice of poems, with very good translations. . . . We go from eroticism to mysticism . . . with the same pleasure and without a weakening of the highest poetic tension."

For Albert-Marie Schmidt, in the daily newspaper *La Réforme*, "When we read the poems of the Anglican bishop John Donne, miraculously translated in impeccable French verse by two gifted young English literature specialists . . . we feel neither surprised nor disoriented."[1]

The Belgian newspaper *Le Matin d'Anvers* expresses the general views of Francophone reviewers: "The choice of the translators Jean Fuzier and Yves Denis, who propose the original text side by side with the translation, is one of the great collections of the season. . . . These *Poèmes de John Donne* are true re-creations" (Aubusson).

Le Peuple,[2] whose knowledge of Donne seemed to be limited to what English literature history textbooks say, insists on mentioning, "from the start, their excellent translation."

The literary weekly *Lettres françaises* devotes a whole page to the translation of Donne and even reproduces the French version of "Womans Constancy"

---

1. The same critic, who is not very particular about the principles of translation, praises in the same way the version of the *Prophètes* by Grosjean (*La Réforme*, April 16, 1955) and Klossowski's translation of the *Aeneid* (*La Réforme*, Feb. 6 1965), two works that are totally opposed to the spirit of the one by Fuzier and Denis.

2. [The official organ of the French trade union CGT (the General Confederation of Labor). Trans. Note]

side by side with the original. Here, too, the appreciation is positive overall, even though it includes insightful critical comments (to which we shall return later): "For French readers, John Donne's work is . . . extremely difficult to understand; we must plunge into a world that hardly has any equivalent in our literature. . . . Under these conditions, Jean Fuzier and Yves Denis's work was an almost impossible wager. In our opinion, without avoiding any difficulty, with a desire to keep rhymes and rhythms, they have often succeeded."

Only one article, in the *Digues du temps*, makes no mention of the translation. It presents the life and works of Donne didactically to the public and totally misunderstands them, for example, in comparing Donne with the contemporary novelist Jean Reverzy.

Among all these reviews, it is clear that the ones by Legouis and Grosjean are the most serious. They act as a *guarantee* for the translation in two ways. Legouis represents academia and English specialists. Grosjean represents the community of poets; poetry translators (who, it is true, do not really constitute a "community"); and, in particular, the prestigious journal *NRF*, with its power both symbolic and real. For these reasons we should look at his review closely.

Jean Grosjean's Approval

Jean Grosjean is not just anyone. First, he is an eminent poet. Secondly, he is a translator who, throughout the years, has produced a true translation *œuvre* (*The Prophets*, the Greek tragic dramatists, Kleist, Genesis, the Gospel according to John, etc.). When it came out in 1955, his translation of *The Prophets* was saluted by critics as a literary event. In 1970, when Meschonnic published his *Cinq rouleaux,* he dedicated it to Grosjean.

Unlike the other reviewers—except for Legouis—Grosjean has read Donne. His article is a meditation on the figure of the poet as well as an examination of the translation. As I said before, Grosjean seems to harbor a secret rejection of Donne, an obvious rejection in the comments previously quoted, in spite of long paragraphs seeking to define what constitutes Donne's "exclusive feature," for instance, when he speaks of his "genius for *tutoiement*"; of the "tension of the words to their addressee," a tension that, nonetheless, does not make him a unique poet, since Grosjean finds it also in Ronsard, Corneille ("obsessed by the great glow of the vocative"), Shakespeare, and Hopkins.

Grosjean's evaluation of Denis and Fuzier's work is absolutely positive. Everything that is quoted from the translation is praised, and the praise reaches its peak in the following: "Let us note the beauty that the translators achieved. Faithful to the sense of the interplay of images, they also strove to be faithful to Donne's naturalness and its variations, to its abruptness. A light flavor of archaism reminds us that this voice is three-and-a-half centuries old. And as if these opposite difficulties were not enough, the translators felt compelled to observe the rigors of versification, for it would have been a betrayal to forget this point. To have been able to handle all this together is admirable" ("Recension de la traduction" 905).

However, it does not altogether escape Grosjean's notice that on occasion, and particularly in the "Sonnet to Death" (Sonnet X), "The tour de force is a little at the expense of the movement of the original. . . . Isn't the quatrain somewhat too dressed up in French style?" (906).[3]

But it matters little, as Grosjean, who has probably not read Alain's *Propos* or Leyris's *Reliquiae,* concedes to the translators "that it is difficult to see how to render the bareness of the English, choppy and alliterated, without ending with formlessness in our language" (906).

Is the solution then to embellish and add shape at any cost and in whatever way?

Strikingly, Grosjean speaks of the beauty of the translation everywhere in the article, as if the particularity of a poetic translation were first to be beautiful (as opposed to faithful); as if beauty were a category that characterizes Donne's poetry, but no more than that. Now, what beauty is Grosjean speaking about? Considering his examples, he is speaking of formal, rhetorical beauty, thus of the beauty that does not apply to all of Donne's poetry. No less certain is the fact that a number of the Denis and Fuzier translations, according to this criterion, are not beautiful.

We may also be surprised when Grosjean praises the translation's "light flavor of archaism," since these translations are almost entirely archaizing.

---

3. From rest and sleepe, which but thy pictures bee,
   Much pleasure, then from thee, much more must flow,
   And soonest our best men with thee doe goe,
   Rest of their bones, and soules deliverie

was rendered as:

   Le repos du Sommeil contrefait un plaisir
   Que tu nous dois donner bien plus considérable;
   Et les meillleurs s'en vont les premiers sous la table,
   Dans la paix de leurs os leurs âmes affranchir. (Fuzier and Denis 220–21).

Already Legouis approved of "the occasional archaism of the vocabulary" while seeing in it contradictorily (but accurately) a veritable "method" on the translators' part. This approval went so far that Legouis reproached Fuzier for rendering "This Extasie doth unperplex . . . us" as (once again losing the negative word) "L'extase abolit le complexe" [Ecstasy abolishes the complex], which he deems a "modernist false note" ("abolishes" inevitably reminding us of Mallarmé).

But if we go back to Grosjean, we can only be surprised by his statement that the translators were "faithful to the sense and the interplay of images . . . , to the natural and its variations, its abruptness," first, because it is a completely inaccurate statement, secondly because Grosjean has authored a translation of *The Prophets* that, his many liberties notwithstanding, strove to correspond to the very language of Amos, Ezekiel, Deborah, Osee, and Job: "Here the verb matters. It is the root of language. Nouns themselves are only acts made somewhat heavy, not objects, still less abstractions. Adjectives and adverbs—words alienable to others—are rare. Hebrew proceeds by juxtaposed clauses . . . , intonation functions as structure. . . . The originals contain an invitation: their rhythms, repetitions, alliterations, the equivalence of which the French reader should be able to find at his disposal" (qtd. in Rousselot 103). Grosjean is thus the author of a translation totally opposed to the aestheticizing and archaizing translation of Denis and Fuzier. So where does his resounding approval of this translation come from?

There is no answer, for the moment, other than Grosjean's secret repulsion for Donne and his "bric-a-brac."

This *no* to Donne revealed by the *yes* to its treacherous translation unquestionably comes from the "scandal" that, according to Bonnefoy, Donne constituted for Racine and Rimbaud. This attachment to the "anecdotal," this "exterior vision" of the human fact, this manner of approaching the essential through the trivial (the poem "The Flea" [91–92] being a typical example[4]) are probably the reasons behind the *no* of Grosjean, a poet who wants to be a poet of the essential, a translator who wants to be translator of the essential, and for whom it is probably not "in our reaction to the inessential that our essence is revealed" (Bonnefoy, "French Poetry" 126).

---

4. Already Taine had made fun of this poem.

The Illusion of Ignorance

We have to admit that almost all the critics, except for Legouis, Grosjean, and the "interim" reviewer of *Lettres françaises,* seem hardly to know Donne. This lack of familiarity ranges from total ignorance to a half-knowledge filled with lack of appreciation. It can be seen in the qualifiers applied to Donne—"baroque" (A.-M. Schmidt, who also sees in the poet a Mallarmean collection of "abolished trinkets of sonorous inanities"), "libertine," "mystical," "metaphysical"—words that are here devoid of meaning, and in the comparisons with Desportes, Sponde, La Ceppède, and so forth, taken most often from the foreword by Poisson (which serves as a reading guide). The review in *Soir* oversteps the limits of ignorance by comparing Donne to Saint John of the Cross and Pascal. This ignorance about Donne, and probably of the French authors with whom he is compared, is accompanied by an equally profound ignorance of the meaning of such terms as "mystical," "metaphysical," "libertine," and "erotic" (these last two modifiers are almost interchangeable for the reviewers, as are "religious," "mystical," "metaphysical," and "philosophical").

In this concert of ignorant voices, we must make an exception for "Mr. Intérim," of *Lettres françaises,* who rightly notices that, for a French reader, the difficulty of access to Donne is enormous, since he belongs to a world without equivalent in France, and that we must confront a "very rich language, but for this reason often obscure." Later, Mr. Intérim strongly objects to Poisson's idea "that Donne's tension can only be found in Baudelaire, Mallarmé, and Valéry." But that does not prevent him from approving of the translation.

The Illusion of Archaism

We saw that in Grosjean and Legouis the almost constant archaism of the translators is minimized ("light flavor," "occasional"), considered a "method," and praised without further comment. Gros is the only one who dares to say that this archaism removes the poet's "relevance." But the meaning of this comment is unclear. In the introduction to his translations, Gros states, "We admire Donne because he responds to our demands, to what we expect from poetry." This response to our demands may be why perhaps he would be "relevant." Quoting Bousquet and presenting this idea as if it were particularly "modern," Gros tells us that he expects poetry to "illuminate life" (104). I can't see why this idea is especially modern, or why the (alleged) fact that "Donne's poetry [is] particularly illuminating" (104) makes him a poet who is "relevant."

The other critics do not even notice this archaism. For them, it probably goes so much without saying that Donne is *like* Sponde, Desportes, and the like, that the critics find it normal for Donne to write in an "old language" as these poets do.

However, the unconditional approval (and the minimization) of this archaizing "method" does come as a surprise in Legouis and Grosjean.

Legouis' translations, which are indeed prosaic, attempt to illuminate Donne while preserving the totality of terms and images that constitute his *universum* and remind us that "this voice is three-and-a-half centuries old," better that any archaic lexicon like *arcer, affiquet,* and *tortil*.[5] It seems that Legouis is so impressed by the translators' prowess in versification that he looks down upon his own work and loses a good part of his critical sense. The sentence "Condemned to prose as we are, we can only admire them from below" is appalling. It reveals a lack of understanding of the value and the dignity of what can be called *scholarly translation,* which is a specific form of translation as introduction, and of *philological translation,* which is indispensable to any literary transfer of a foreign work.

We then understand (up to a point) how Legouis would end up backing a translation that, unlike his own, makes Donne unreadable because of its archaism and its aesthetic formalism.

As for Grosjean, we already explained his position.

But if archaism is so *fascinating,* it is because another powerful mirage emerges on the horizon.

The Illusion of Pure Poetry

As I said, the illusion first becomes visible through continual praise (started by Poisson) for the *beauty* of the translations. One should not forget, as Jean-Yves Masson has pointed out, that what is primarily asked of a translation is that it be "good," that is, faithful, trustworthy, and so forth. But for Poisson, as for Grosjean, *beauty* seems almost synonymous with fidelity. This erroneous assumption is still prevalent among the literary reviewers of prestigious periodicals ("Let's mention the beautiful translation by . . .").

---

5. When Gros writes, in opposition to Legouis, that "the more accurate a translation is, the more hermetic Donne's poetry is" (84), he is saying something untrue. Legouis' translation is accurate and transparent. It is the one by Fuzier and Denis that is hermetic. What reader will understand what is meant by "alleu d'un autre maître" [*alleu* of another master] in Sonnet XIV, where Donne only says "to'another due," and Legouis "alors qu'elle a un souverain légitime" [when it has a legitimate master]?

For Grosjean, the beauty of the translation results from the happy union of fidelity to the meaning, to the interplay of images, to the "abrupt" naturalness of Donne—in short, fidelity to everything! The work of versification comes to give to this happy union the appropriate form, the stamp of "true poetry." It is as if it were all so evident! Grosjean realizes the problem when he mentions "opposite difficulties." But fortunately, the translators "have been able to handle all this"; the contradictions have thus been solved ("How?" one wonders), and the result is "beautiful."

But all this, the happy union of fidelity to meaning, to the interplay of images, to the rhythmic idiosyncrasies of Donne with versification work, is but rhetoric. For Grosjean, as for the others, beautiful means having a *captivating and attractive form*. The French tradition has long believed that a beautiful translation should be seductive. And it can hope to be seductive only through *form*, that is, through the excellence of the versification work. Mr. Intérim states that it is by committing to keep "rhymes and rhythms" that the translators have "often succeeded."

In turn, this fascination with formal perfection is one of the (central) forms of the fascination with pure poetry. The names of Mallarmé and Valéry turn up in all the reviews, for the poets have the reputation of having dealt in pure poetry and having been impeccable "magicians of verse." For Gros, our "young English specialists" are "keen on Mallarmé and Valéry" (how does he know?). They have thus translated Donne within the horizon of these poets' poetics, as Poisson implicitly invited them to do when he claimed that Donne's "tension" can be found in Valéry and Mallarmé ("Donne's spoken style is jaw-breaking and tense, precisely like Mallarmé's style" [22]).

The reviewer of *Lettres françaises,* Mr. Intérim, challenges these statements: "We should ... ask whether the correspondence [with Mallarmé and Valéry] is not essentially due to an optical effect. The resurrection of Donne was achieved in relation to modern metaphysical poetry, precisely because he has been perceived as the ancestor of so-called pure poetry. This is to put Donne on a Procrustean bed" (15).

Mr. Intérim knows of course that, under the impetus of T. S. Eliot, there was a reevaluation and a reinterpretation of Donne in the twentieth century.

But (and we'll come back to this) it is Valéry's shadow in particular that haunts the critics, even when he is not mentioned. Thus Denis and Fuzier are said to have translated "like Valéry." As they are not the poet, they must have done so somewhat artificially (Legouis says with a touch of irony, "They used a rhyme dictionary. And why not?" Valéry himself used a thesaurus [see

Valéry 207–22]). They have been skillful, brilliant, sometimes inspired, where the Master was working in the Extraordinary and produced—certainly with unrelenting efforts—"beautiful and faithful" translations of Virgil. As they are not poets, but just "young English specialists" (here "young" means likable inexperience, passion, energy, and complete faith in what one is doing, faith that the old English specialists—i.e., Legouis—no longer have), they translated like the poet. Hence their success. Thus criticism operates with the following implicit premise: the translator of poetry who is not a poet must imitate the poetry and the translation work of poets. And the man to imitate here is Valéry because he translated Virgil in verse. Thus the poet of "pure poetry," of strict versification constraint, does become (almost unconsciously) the model for the translation of an English poet characterized by, among other things, his "colloquial style," his notorious prosodic incorrectness,[6] and his systematic mix of images, themes, and concepts, in short, by his "intercharged" character.

Such is the mirage of pure poetry.

The Absence of Criticism of the Project

None of the reviewers, *none,* seeks to examine the project of Fuzier and Denis, even in appealing, obviously, to another concept. Certainly, the reviewer of *La Grive* rejects the idea of a translation "in classical verse," but he does not so much reject it as a project but because this task requires some "genius," and the power to "re-create" things is reserved for poets only.

None of these reviewers examines the project and its various aspects. This failure is not due to the fact that these are necessarily short reviews, but to the fact that the *very idea* of such an examination does not cross their minds. And why should they examine the project, since the result seems excellent to almost all the reviewers? All of them (except the critic from *La Grive*) are impressed by the hard work of the "young English specialists" and the "beauty" of their version.

But how can one be so blind?

From which horizons can this disastrous translation (a few passages in the *Sacred Sonnets* excepted perhaps) be *perceived* as beautiful and faithful?

This question takes us back, necessarily, to the horizon of the 1960s, or

---

6. Ben Jonson said to Drummond of Hawthornden that Donne, "for not keeping of accent, deserved hanging" (462, qtd. in Legouis, *Poèmes choisis* 31).

rather to the period that seems to go roughly from 1955 (the publication date of Grosjean's *Prophètes,* of Jaccottet's *Odyssée,* and of Mounin's *Belles infidèles*) to 1974 (publication date of the issue on translation in *Change* and the exchange of letters between Michel Deguy and Léon Robel, which synthesizes a number of previous discussions and works).

The horizon of the 1960s is articulated into two sub-horizons: the translation horizon and the poetic horizon. As we shall see, these are horizons that both connect and do not connect; they don't have a *Zusammenhang,* a connection. Morever, each horizon is not homogeneous. However, we must postulate both a certain *density* of each horizon, and the existence of a single horizon that includes them both: that of the "period" in question (which covers twenty to thirty years).

THE TRANSLATION HORIZON OF THE 1960S

Even if we do not rely on systematic "surveys" (which are not as necessary as one may think, and which presuppose, in any case, a conceptual and hermeneutic framework, without which we are reduced to the level of pure empirical recollection), it is obvious that these years saw the emergence of a movement of translation and of reflection about translation (and not only poetic translation) that differed from that of the previous period, which was dominated, it seems to me, by the translations of Armand Robin, by Valery Larbaud's *Sous l'invocation de saint Jérôme* (1946), and by the translation of a fragment of *Finnegan's Wake* by Philippe Soupault.

This movement did not affect all the domains of the translation of literary works. It coexisted with non-movements characteristic of the field of translation, which itself does not constitute a "world" unlike the "world of letters," at least in France and for the period under consideration.

The list of translations in the table is not exhaustive, but representative. Almost all the works listed constitute "translation events" (except for the Donne translations by Legouis and Gros, added in order to better situate them in the framework of the period). Their status as translation events is supported by the analysis of the reviews for each translation. Musil's *Man without Qualities,* translated by Philippe Jaccottet (1956), is a literary, not a translation, event but was not without repercussions on the image of translation in France. Heidegger's *Essais et conférences,* translated by Préau

Year	Translation(s)	Translators	Translation Works/Journals	Authors
1955	Poèmes choisis by Donne	P. Legouis	Les belles infidèles	G. Mounin
	Les prophètes	J. Grosjean		
	La mort de Virgile by Broch	G. Kahn		
	L'Odyssée	Ph. Jaccottet		
1956	L'homme sans qualités by Musil	Ph. Jaccottet		
1957	Reliquiae by Hopkins	P. Leyris		
	Hamlet by Shakespeare	Y. Bonnefoy		
1958	Essais et conférences by Heidegger	A. Préau	La stylistique comparée du français et de l'anglais	J.-P. Vinay and J. Darbelnet
	Poésie non traduite II	A. Robin		
1959	Poèmes by Shakespeare (Pléiade-Gallimard)	J. Fuzier		
1960	Jules César by Shakespeare	Y. Bonnefoy		
	Les solitudes by Góngora	Ph. Jaccottet		
1961				
1962	Poèmes by John Donne	J. Fuzier and Y. Denis		
1963			Les problèmes théoriques de la traduction	G. Mounin
1964	Le naufrage du Deutschland by Hopkins	P. Leyris		
	L'Enéide by Virgil	P. Klossowski		
	John Donne	L.-G. Gros		
1965	Le roi Lear by Shakespeare	Y. Bonnefoy		
	Œuvres complètes by Dante	A. Pézard		
1966				
1967	Œuvres by Hölderlin	Ph. Jaccottet et al.		
1968	Roméo et Juliette by Shakespeare	Y. Bonnefoy		
1969				
1970	Les cinq rouleaux	H. Meschonnic		
1971	Les troubadours	J. Roubaud	"La tâche du traducteur"	W. Benjamin (trans. M. de Gandillac)
1972				
1973			"Poétique de la traduction," in Pour la poétique II	H. Meschonnic
			"Joyce traduit par Joyce," Tel quel 55	J. Risset
			"La traduction en jeu," Change 19	
1974				

(1958), opens the era of the translation of Heidegger, which will be marked by constant, difficult reflection, which is still open, about the translation of his works. Last, I have not been able to include in the table the translations of Dante, Góngora, Hölderlin, Pindar, and Kleist, which were published with commentaries in Michel Deguy's *La revue de poésie* during the 1960s, as none of the back issues was available.

This translating activity is accompanied by a reflection on translation unprecedented in France since the nineteenth century (Courier, Chateaubriand, Littré, Mallarmé, etc.). It particularly affects the translation of poetry, philosophy (see Gérard Granel's introduction to the translation of *Was hießt denken?* [*Qu'appelle-t-on penser?*]), and the Bible (Grosjean, Meschonnic) but does not include the translation of novels, essays, and theater.[7] This reflection is associated with the names of Bonnefoy, Leyris, Deguy, Robel (and his group), Roubaud, Meschonnic, Klossowski, Grosjean, Granel, and Walter Benjamin, more precisely his essay "The Task of the Translator," translated into French as "La tâche du traducteur" by Maurice de Gandillac in 1971.

I must put in a different category publications like Vinay and Darbelnet's *La stylistique comparée du français et de l'anglais* [*Comparative Stylistics of French and English*] (1958), a book that created a considerable stir in academic circles even though it had no validity with regard to the translation of literary works,[8] and, especially, the publications of Georges Mounin. Mounin first published in 1955 *Les belles infidèles,* a solid book on literary translation that demonstrates a thorough knowledge of the French tradition of translation. In spite of unduly overestimating Leconte de Lisle's translations of Homer (presented as a model and a French literary masterpiece in itself), *Les belles infidèles* remains a book that can be read and reread with sustained interest. But later Mounin progressively moved from a reflection on poetry and the translation of poetry in essayistic form to research oriented toward linguistics and, with regard to translation, to a positivist approach increasingly aimed at being "scientific." Thus, in 1963, he published *Les problèmes théoriques de la traduction* with a foreword by Dominique Aury.[9] The book seems to have been an immediate success.

7. It will only appear in the 1980s.
8. Duneton has shown how the methods advocated by these authors for literary translation, in particular for the translation of Lawrence, produce regrettable arrhythmic results and can *only* produce such results [151–57].
9. This foreword is excessively humble, not to say painfully servile toward the one who

This success was totally undeserved, as the book is nothing but a compilation of linguists' opinions about the differences between languages and the various "problems" that these differences may pose to translators, as well as the (so-called) visions of the world that they embody or produce. Many of the "problems" evoked are only problems for linguists who don't know anything, it seems, about the fact that translators deal with *œuvres*, with texts, and not with isolated linguistic units. In short, this book, which is often interesting, if naive, in no way deserves the importance and, in particular, the symbolic role given to it. When Sherry Simon, a translation scholar from Quebec, speaks "of the symbolic 'father' of translation theory, George Mounin" (157), I tell myself that it is time, high time, to try to put an end to this misconception. Mounin is not the "symbolic father" of anything whatsoever. He is not the father of later "translation theories," nor of reflection on translation in France. It is time, high time, that *Les problèmes théoriques de la traduction* stop being considered, especially abroad, as the ne plus ultra of French thought on translation. For, if there is a "symbolic father" of French reflection on translation, it is Valery Larbaud, with his *Sous l'invocation de saint Jérôme*.[10] It takes all the confused and ignorant pretentiousness of Georges Steiner to call this work "lacking in rigor" (*Après Babel* 225).[11] With its disparate, sometimes offhanded, and discontinuous appearance, with its slightly aestheticizing language, *Sous l'invocation de saint Jérôme* is a great nurturing, seminal book that we should read and reread.[12]

"knows": "For the first time in France a linguist does translators the honor of taking their activity seriously" (Mounin, *Les problèmes* viii); "we did not know anything about the foundations of our profession. With *Les problèmes théoriques de la traduction*, our familiar universe becomes a new world" (xii). There is so much deference for Mounin, who, at the end of his book, comes to the exciting conclusion that "Contemporary linguistics succeeds in defining translation like an operation that is relative in its success, variable in the levels of communication it reaches" (278). And this is the deep knowledge that Aury has drawn from the "scholar's" book! Whom are we fooling? Moreover, Mounin grossly underestimates all the classical works on translation, that is, all the works previous to the key works that those by Fédorov and Vinay and Darbelnet supposedly are, and with which "scientific" theories of translation *at last* supposedly begin. We have indeed sunk right back into the most obtuse positivism, into a scientism at which true science now laughs.

10. [Translated by Jean-Paul de Chezet as *An Homage to Jerome: Patron Saint of Translators*. Trans. Note]

11. [Steiner's original English version mentions "Valery Larbaud's inspired but unsystematic *Sous l'invocation de Saint Jérôme* [sic] of 1946" (*After Babel* 249). Trans. Note]

12. Meschonnic was able to pay it homage, mentioning its "language that has its value of experience, in spite of its aesthetic approximations from another time" (*Pour la poétique* 352).

Larbaud is at once a remarkable prose writer, a captivating poet, and a highly skilled critic (*Domaine anglais* and *Domaine français*[13] are excellent openings to the literature of both countries), an important translator (Whitman, Joyce, and Butler), and during his lifetime a major mediator of the national and international world of letters. We could not dream of a better "symbolic father" for French translation. Moreover, his knowledge of the history of French translation, and of French and foreign translation theorists, has remained unrivaled. Indeed, who knew who Tytler was in 1946?

With regard to poetry translation, reflection has progressively risen to the level of a *fundamental debate,* the stakes of which Deguy and Robel articulated in letters published in 1974 in the review *Change*. In his letter to Robel, Deguy evoked the translating work of *La revue de poésie* (the former version of *Po&sie*), its meaning, and its practices:

> "Translation," in the sense of "regulated transformation of a language by another" in the case of poetry, is less a question of cancelling the distance between a source text and a target text, of making it disappear following the criterion of the *belle infidèle* according to which the characteristic of a successful translation was that it hid its *title,* and thus could go unnoticed, and could have been taken for an "original text" by the reader unaware of the traffic—more than of making manifest this distance as difference in our language.... The target text, shaped by the effort to translate, presents itself for what it is: displaced and hybrid. The receiving language winces and squeaks under the effort, at the resistance point of its "maternity." That it is capable as a poem of many more discrepancies than the consensus of users and grammarians tolerates, needs to be proven every time.... I am finally coming back to practice: two requirements, correlative in their difference of scale, seem to provide maxims for the translation transaction: ... work of interpretation through thought, the difficulty of which, as always in such cases, lies in that one must have found while searching in order to keep on searching while finding. The other requirement is that of literality: "literally and in all directions" out of fear of not letting any bias of elegance "dispense with" a virtuality; of turning toward the inexhaustible vein of significance of the text to translate without prematurely blocking

---

13. [The complete titles are *Ce vice impuni, la lecture. Domaine anglais* and *Ce vice impuni, la lecture. Domaine français*. Trans. Note]

the reading on a "universal signifier." This constraint then sends us into two opposite directions: that of the "word by word" (this is why I found it necessary to support Klossowski's translation of the *Aeneid*, against all the destroyers, as you remember, of the hypallage:[14] *Ibant obscuri* as "ils allaient obscurs" [they went obscure]) . . . ; and that of the "as many words as will be required for one word," in the way Pascal Quignard translated *Lycophron*. ("La traduction en jeu" 49–50, 52–53)

In his response, Robel evoked a "precursor" of Klossowski, Briusov, who is claimed to have given a "prodigiously literal" version of Virgil. According to Robel, this translation from 1920 had been recently "unearthed" by the Russian poetician Gasparov and was giving rise—as did Klossowski's *Énéide*—to heated discussions in the USSR.[15] Robel added:

Gasparov, whose work is a rather brilliant defense and illustration of literalism in poetic translation, claims that in translating literature, there are only two valid positions: "free" translation and "literal" translation. The first would be suitable for periods of extensive culture and the second one for periods of intensive culture (to summarize very quickly).

But if I am granted the proposition that a text is the whole formed by all its significantly different translations, then we must admit that there is a certain legitimacy in all these translations, but also a typology and a hierarchy of translations, as there is a hierarchy of texts depending on the possibilities of translations they offer. I keep thinking that we must place at the top of the hierarchy of translations that which, in its turn, acts most as a text and thus offers in turn the greatest number of possibilities of translations. *But to this end, it is necessary to restore the deep structure, the phono-semantic network* of the original poem which, when read, offers the means of successive transmutations.

---

14. [Rhetorical figure through which something that belongs to one thing is attributed to another word. Trans. Note]

15. As I think I showed in "La traduction et la lettre ou L'auberge du lointain," Klossowski's French *Aeneid* is not literal in the common sense of the word. If by "literal" we mean the reproduction of the factual distribution of words and sentences of the original, it is clear that Klossowski's work is not literal in this sense, which is absurd: "What is 'translated' is the global system of the inversions, end positioning, and displacements, rather than their factual distribution along the lines of the *Aeneid*" (140).

Any translation thus implies a transformation.... I am happy to see that we can bring our positions closer for and through the translating effort. ("La traduction en jeu" 54–55)

Robel accompanied his letter with a fragment of Briusov's literal translation translated into French. In a certain way, his answer was not an answer to Deguy's statement. It was a simple presentation of his group's positions. In themselves, these positions were neither the same as nor the opposite of those presented in *La revue de poésie*. It is quite certain that at the top of the "hierarchy" of translations, there is the one that "acts most as a text." The translation that acts most as a text is the one based on the analysis of the "deep structure" and of the "phono-semantic" network of the original poem. Hence Robel concluded that the translation that acts most as a text, that is, that has the most textual density, is in turn translatable. Here the practice of the Polivanov circle[16] becomes a pure game or pure experiment, for what *sense* can the translation of its translation have for the original? But this is not the place to discuss this concern: the essential for Robel was that at the top of his hierarchy there is the translation that "acts as a text" because it is based on an analysis of the original's structures. This approach has obviously nothing to do with Deguy's position, which is founded on the dialectic of literality and of the "use of as many words as needed to translate one word."[17]

Thus were drawn two extreme positions with regard to poetry translation, two positions based on different premises and principles, but that are not necessarily opposite. These positions, and the debate to which they gave

---

16. [This interdisciplinary group, named after the Soviet linguist Evgeny Polivanov and founded in Paris in 1969 by poet Jacques Roubaud and musicologist and mathematician Pierre Lusson, was interested in questions of formal language and poetry. Trans. Note]

17. This last principle seems to be found in Bayen's translation of *Oedipus at Colonus*: "He recalls us home, obsessively; to translate amounts to multiplying variations. Sometimes I left the variation around a word, an expression or a line, and gave a double translation" (21–22). See also Georges Mailhos, who analyzes seven translations of the Heraclitus fragment "physis krupterkai philei": "If... Heraclitus was called the 'obscure one' it is because he became incomprehensible through being repeatedly translated clearly. To let an *original* text *work through* in order to open it to its possibilities, to let it *wait*, is to give oneself all the guaranties of a worthy faithfulness, conquered by will, not philologically imposed. Between an original always kept in its Greek writing—but, in this case, *reported* as a quotation in a text written much later...—and an honest translation, which is thus unclear because of lexical simplicity (*physis*: 'nature'; *philô*: 'to love'; *kryptomai*: 'to hide') and syntactic simplicity (subject, verb, etc.) comes a translation that attempts to make the aphorism *readable*" (*Les tours de Babel* 234).

rise, were themselves directly linked to a fundamental event of the 1960s, which totally *determined* Deguy's and Robel's statements, that is, *the arrival in the French translating space of two foreign reflections on translation:* first, German reflections (Heidegger and Walter Benjamin); second, the Russian reflections. The first influenced Deguy (and Meschonnic for Benjamin); the second influenced Robel.

It was the second time that German thinking on translation exerted a massive influence on the fields of translation and on reflections upon it in France. The first time was with Madame de Staël, who introduced the "ideas" of the German romantics, in particular those of A. W. Schlegel, who summarized and popularized all the ideas of Schleiermacher, von Humboldt, and Goethe on the subject. Considering the fame of Madame de Staël, it is absolutely impossible that the French translators I have mentioned did not read Staël's *De l'Allemagne* [*Of Germany*] and "De l'esprit des traductions" ["The Spirit of Translations"],[18] even if neither of these texts nor the name of the author is ever cited (this veiling of sources is typically French).

It was probably at that time that the powerful tradition of Russian thought, from Pushkin to Pasternak and beyond, to the authors mentioned by Robel and later by Etkind, penetrated into France and had an influence.

Thus the so very vital epistolary debate between Deguy and Robel was determined by two foreign horizons of reflection on translation, and, for those years, these horizons were the only ones; the English and Italian horizons were not taken into account.[19] The English horizon (to which Steiner briefly alludes) was, in particular, strangely absent.

In this debate about poetry translation, *two new forms of translation surged forward,* two forms that affirmed their specificity, while at the same time meeting in the reflection and the practice of Jacques Roubaud, a friend of the two "opponents," both a contributor to *La revue de poésie* and a member of the Polivanov circle led by Robel, Lusson, and others.

---

18. An excerpt from another text published in Italy, "De la manière de traduire et de l'utilité des traductions," can be found in *Cent ans de théorie française de la traduction:* "A. W. Schlegel wrote a translation of Shakespeare which, being both exact and inspired, is quite national in Germany" (Staël 89).

19. It is now, and quite slowly at that, that they are coming near. For the Italian horizon, see "Foscolo, Leopardi et la traduction de l'Antique" in Michel Orcel, *Langue mortelle* (144), and Giovanni Gentile, "Du tort et du droit des traductions." Now we must add Latin American (Borges, Paz, Haroldo de Campos), North American, Canadian, and Quebecois reflections.

One form finds its origin in the experience of French translation, language, and poetry based on German thinking on translation;[20] the other originates in a "formal" reflection on poetic translation, rhythm, and versification work (in the broad sense of the term).

In terms of their respective projects, the various translations mentioned for this period may be situated *between* these two positions, which can be termed extreme positions in that they belong to the movement or current just mentioned, whose main point can be summarized in Jaccottet's words: "If we persist in thinking that it is possible to read Homer without knowing Greek and to draw from it something else besides facts, to hear in it only a much muted echo of the wonderful music of the original, we must then translate, as far as it is possible and without falling into absurdity, *according to the very letter of the text*" (postface 408–9).

This is a statement broad enough to include the positions of both Deguy and Robel—the differences come later.

But besides this movement, which, although it may not be quantitatively dominant, nonetheless produces the overwhelming majority of translations influential at the time and influential now, there are other currents, the most important being the one embodied by Pézard's Dante. Pézard's Dante, a completely archaizing translation, realizes an old dream dating from the philology of the nineteenth century, and of Littré in particular. Here I must make a digression that is not without interest: the tendency of Gallimard's Pléiade collection to use, for old foreign works, translations of the period that also seem archaic. Amyot's Plutarch, the *Romans picaresques espagnols* [*Spanish Picaresque Novels*], and Cervantes's *Don Quixote* are published in versions from the period, sometimes mixed together. The reason given is that modern versions (from the nineteenth and twentieth centuries) would have no "flavor." When there are no versions of the same time period available, the editors attempt to produce translations that are the equivalent of old texts, as in Fuzier's translation of Shakespeare's poems, and especially in the monumental Dante by Pézard.

20. And on the research on Hölderlin, which arrived decisively in France with the translation of Heidegger's book *Erlaüterungen zu Hölderlins Dichtung*, published in French as *Approche de Hölderlin*, by H. Corbin, Michel Deguy, F. Fédier, and J. Launay [in English, *Elucidations of Hölderlin's Poetry*. Trans. Note]. As Lacoue-Labarthe has observed, "In fact, in France, Hölderlin was transmitted to us by Heidegger" (Hölderlin, *Hymnes, elégies* 11). Before that, there indeed were the translations by Jouve, Bianquis, Roud, Guerne, and Faye.

Beyond the Pléiade collection, this valorization of the archaic can spill over to the translation of contemporary works, at the level of the translation of foreign words whose meaning has, according to the translators, no equivalent in modern French. Hence the use of Old French, for instance in the translation of Heidegger's *Holzwege*[21] by Brokmeier, in which *weise* [way, manner] is translated as *guise*.[22] The translation of Heidegger's *Einführung in die Metaphysik*[23] by Gilbert Kahn follows similar choices, the choice of old words or the creation of neologisms that look like old words: *parence* pour *Vorschein* [appearance], *patence* for *Erschlossenheit* [disclosedness, disclosure (of being)], *déclusion déterminée* for *Entschlossenheit* [resolve, resoluteness].

. . .

Denis and Fuzier's translation fits in this archaizing trend, which emphasizes meter and versification (thus "formal" in a certain sense, which is, however, not the sense of Robel and his group). As we have seen, it is according to these principles that Fuzier introduced Shakespeare's poetry for the Pléiade edition in 1959. But whereas this position (archaization and formalism) is roughly *contemporary and homologous* with that of Pézard, *it is not so for the English domain,* in which Bonnefoy's and Leyris's positions predominate, and by far; their positions belong to the translation movement of the 1960s (even if each of them has a specific stance and does not necessarily recognize the positions of other translators of this movement: Leyris acknowledges Klossowski's *Énéide*, but with reservations, unlike Deguy). This means that this position does not operate in the same *time frame*. It does not operate in the same time frame as someone like Robel or Roubaud. As I have already said, this position stems from nineteenth-century archaism, the archaism that tempted a "philologist" like Littré (see Mounin, *Les belles infidèles* 105–7, 123) as well as a poet like Leconte de Lisle (see Mounin, *Les belles infidèles* 133 and following),[24] and that is linked to the "historicism" specific to that

---

21. Published as *Chemins qui ne mènent nulle part* [*Paths That Lead Nowhere*] by W. Brokmeier. [In English, published as *Off the Beaten Track*. Trans. Note]

22. [In French, *guise* is never used alone but in the collocation *à ma guise;* the other examples are neologisms. Trans. Note]

23. [In English, *An Introduction to Metaphysics*. Trans. Note]

24. About his translation of the *Iliad,* Mounin mentions the "fundamental model made of glass through which you can at least see the authentic color of Homeric times" (148), a "masterpiece of French language in itself" (*Les belles infidèles* 157). Jaccottet's translation of the *Odyssey* also came out the same year as *Les belles infidèles* in unacknowledged contemporaneities. In his book,

century, a historicism that marked philology, poetry, and literature. These valiantly *archaizing* translations are also *erudite* translations, which put into play, in their project and in their implementation, an enormous amount of knowledge and skill—more so than the other translations, and which, of course, require a certain amount of knowledge from the readers—more so than the other translations.

What is clear, in any case, is that the choice of this type of translation, which Fuzier made for Shakespeare and Donne, constitutes a departure from the dominant trend (qualitatively and chronologically) of English poetry translation, which no "specificity" of Shakespeare's and Donne's poetry justifies in itself. The anthology of Elizabethan poets by Philippe de Rothschild (1969) belongs to the same category, but with an excessive naïveté.

There is one last thing to mention about the translation horizon of the 1960s: it is not unified, and if it is torn between trends that are both antagonistic and intertwined, between contemporary and non-contemporary trends, it is *also* because the translation field of literary works *does not constitute a world;* rather it is composed of a scattered multiplicity of translating islands, of translating *monads* that communicate. This insular and monadic (sometimes autistic) structure of the translation field of literary works does not date back to the 1960s. It still exists today, but to a lesser degree. In the 1960s and 1970s, the dialogue between Deguy and Robel, a fruitful dialogue, was exceptional in a "world of letters" where it had nonetheless been common practice since the beginning of time.

MALLARMÉ, VALÉRY, AND THE POETIC HORIZON OF THE 1960S

This horizon will only be mentioned in order to illuminate the horizon of poetry translation, which it found in its necessity.

First, it is clear that, during this period, a number of poets, quite different from each other, and sometimes belonging to overlapping generations, enter into an *experience of poetry that is that of a long crisis,* and not only the crisis of

---

Mounin advocates a historico-archaeologizing translation model that dates from the nineteenth century, and that harkens back to what we consider the most dated things in the nineteenth century. This is a surprising anachronism coming from a specialist on the poet René Char.

verse. Hölderlin's *Wozu Dichter?* [*What Are Poets For?*] belongs here. Within this experience of the long crisis, these poets (Bonnefoy, Deguy, Jaccottet, Roubaud, Marteau, and Réda come to mind) rethink their relation to their modern founding fathers, Baudelaire, Rimbaud, Mallarmé, and, closer to our times, the surrealists and Valéry. They reflect critically on poetry. The poetic horizon of the 1960s is that of a "critical poetry." This reflection is identical to or, rather, is carried by the same movement as the reflection on its history and on its own tradition. There is among these poets, during all these years, a (re)reading of the poetic tradition, and not only of the national tradition. And the way in which this tradition is read is not, for example, that of the nineteenth century. The crisis of the "formality of essence" leads a number of poets to rediscover the poetic *massifs* where this "formality" shone most brilliantly: the baroque poets, the Spanish Golden Age, the Elizabethan poets (hence the revival of mannerism, and aestheticism where there is no current of this kind), Dante, Pindar, Sappho, and so forth. The massifs of French medieval poetry and the troubadours are rediscovered (in a different way from that of the period when Bédier wrote). We can see how the poetic horizon of the 1960s projects the boundary lines of "another" history of Western poetry on the translating horizon, with names that until now have been more or less unknown, names like Góngora, Donne, Hölderlin, and names now otherwise illuminated like Homer, Sappho, Pindar, Virgil, Dante, Shakespeare, and Milton.

It is in this constellation that we must situate the possibility and the necessity of a (re)translation of Donne. The necessity of translating Donne was there during those years when Góngora was being translated (by Jaccottet). The "French Donne" came at a favorable moment. Its failure is not caused by a lack of *kairos*.

But we must see that this return to baroque writers, to Góngora, to Dante, and so forth, also occurs in a very intense and very close relationship with Mallarmé and Valéry, that the relayed comments we find about Donne, Valéry, and Mallarmé in Poisson and the reviewers refer back to the unquestionable fact that poetic translation is dominated by the figures of Mallarmé and Valéry. Such is the case that one might ask: Should we translate Mallarmé's way or Valéry's way—*that is the question* [in English in the text]. Does this question make sense? If so, what kind of sense? In truth, it has several meanings; no one at the time posed the question this way, but it was on everyone's mind. It had even been Benjamin's question in "The Task of the Translator."

To translate "Mallarmé's way" does not mean to translate as Mallarmé translated Poe, in "prose" (as tightly as one may wish, but prose all the same), nor does it mean to translate poetry in verse, following the "defense" of verse advocated by Mallarmé; it means to translate in such a way that poetic translation "remunerates the flaw of languages."[25]

It is even in this that poetry turns into translation, enters into *a necessary translating destiny*—one that has been unfailing ever since. To translate Mallarmé's way is to translate following Alain's recommendation (after reading Mallarmé), as Mallarmé had poeticized under the imprint, under the massive impetus of English, or the other language (or "language other," to use Genette's words [*Mimologiques* 273][26]) now necessary to any "national" poetry. Thus the convergence of Alain and Benjamin bears witness to the significance of Mallarmé for poetic translation. But we could also call on Artaud and his "translation" of Lewis Carroll ("Ye Carpette Knyghte," translated as "Le chevalier mate-tapis") and Armand Robin: it is the same constellation.

Clearly it is in such a horizon that we can consider translating Donne's "massy diamonds," to use Quincey's expression, and the "fixed stars and fugitive heavenly bodies" of Góngora. And we probably need to look back toward the French baroque or pre-classical massif (at the time when Ponge wrote his *Pour Malherbe* [*For Malherbe*]). It is clear that it is also in such a horizon that Leyris could translate Hopkins, that Klossowski could retranslate the *Aeneid,* Mallarmé's way or, if you prefer, Heraclitus's way.

What about Valéry? Is he the alternative to Mallarmé? In what sense?

During this period, Valéry is (except for those who have always considered

---

25. ["Crise de vers" in Mallarmé, *Igitur* (245). Mallarmé's statement applies to verse. Trans. Note]

26. "English somewhat plays the role in the Mallarmean system [held in the *Cratylus* by the 'language of the Gods,' borrowed from Homer] of a nostalgic or consolatory myth into which are projected from afar all the virtues in which one's own language is lacking as a *real* natural language—the one that I write in and speak in. A linguistic paradise lost or, if you prefer, a *linguistic utopia* almost recognized and accepted as such. For Mallarmé, therefore, English (as he dreams of it) is the site and the object, not of true *jouissance,* but of regret: the specular image of a lack.... All this ... has little to do with real English, as it exists and is spoken. And all the other natural languages, or rather any other language, would have done just as well—that is, served as the 'supreme' language: the very one that 'is lacking,' and whose lack and *default* [*défaut*] (in the strong sense of 'to default') are embodied, if I may say so, in real language. Moreover, the English-French relationship could as well be reversed, as the supreme language is almost always, for every natural language, the one facing or opposite it." [Modified version of the published translation (*Mimologics* 214). Trans. Note]

him a dinosaur) first the man who defended a certain form of the formality of essence, a classical form, a form summarized by the perfect correspondence of sound and sense. Then, more than Mallarmé, he is the poet who committed the "poetic sin," who (re)directed French poetry on the path of "pure poetry." He has, so to speak, lost Baudelaire and Rimbaud and given a false image of Mallarmé: that of Valéry himself.

But Valéry is also the secret reader of Nietzsche, the admirer of Descartes and Leonardo da Vinci; he is, and this is important, the founder of *Poetics*. That Poetics was born, reborn, with Valéry is not only a restitutional event. With Valéry, the reflective aspect of poetry, the fact that any poetry must also be a poetics, is given ratification and a foundation. Not only is Valéry a great poetician, but he has also *founded,* in the strict sense of the term, modern poetics.

Finally, Valéry is a translator or, rather, he is the (commissioned) translator of Virgil—and we must never forget that in France, since the sixteenth century, Virgil has been the supreme ambition of poetic translation ("La traduction et la lettre" 128–30). Valéry is Virgil's translator and the writer who reflects on translation by translating; the fact that he is all the other figures of Valéry previously mentioned makes him a significant translation figure.

The double study of horizons that we have just done shows that Fuzier's archaizing and "Valérian" translation is indeed an anomaly in relation to the contemporary translation of English poetry, but that it is perfectly linked to certain currents of the poetic horizon and of the translating horizon. It is thus normal that most of the critics have perceived it in this way and, like Poisson, have found it "beautiful and faithful." That some found it "exact" and "literal," in complete disregard for any comparison—even hasty—with the original, shows that, for them too, it had to be so, as it came from "specialists" who "knew." Legouis alone ventured to note, in the benign form of errors of interpretation, of mistranslations, and the like, the non-exact, the non-literal aspect of this translation (which, however, goes well beyond that), but, as we saw, he did so without questioning its project.

And yet there was *also* a rejection. This rejection is expressed by the silence of all those critics of poetic translation and of English translations who did not write anything, that is, who did not report on this translation. This silence is rather heavy, if we consider that the only three critics who have a "name" are, in order of decreasing fame, Jean Grosjean, Pierre Legouis, and Albert-Marie Schmidt.

The translation of Fuzier and Denis was read; it progressively sold until it was out of stock. It reappeared in 1980 and then was the basis of the special issue on Donne in the L'Âge d'Homme series (although there was no evaluation of the translator's work either by the editor or by the other contributors).

Then, it disappeared.[27]

We spoke of a translation that is not dead, but that has lived and that no one today can read, and this is so in a double way: the translation is impossible to find and it is unreadable. And now, at the end of our course, we know somewhat better why.

27. [It became available again in the paperback series Poésie/Gallimard in 1992 under the title *Poèmes de John Donne*. Trans. Note]

Works Cited

Alain. *Propos de littérature.* Paris: Gonthier, 1964.
———. *Système des beaux-arts.* Paris: Gallimard, 1953.
Amyot, Jacques, trans. *Les vies des hommes illustres.* Vols. 1 and 2. By Plutarch. Ed. G. Walter. Paris: Bibliothèque de la Pléiade-Gallimard, 1951.
Arendt, Hannah. *Condition de l'homme moderne.* Trans. G. Fradier. Paris: Calmann-Lévy, 1983.
———. *Essai sur la révolution.* Trans. Michel Chrestien. Paris: Gallimard, 1967.
———. *The Human Condition.* Chicago: University of Chicago Press, 1958.
Arlt, Robert. *Les sept fous.* Trans. Antoine Berman and Isabelle Berman. Paris: Belfond, 1981.
Aubusson, Brice. Rev. of *Poèmes de John Donne,* trans. Fuzier and Denis. *Le Matin d'Anvers,* April 24, 1962.
Aucouturier, Michel. "Avertissement." *Œuvres.* By Boris Pasternak. Paris: Bibliothèque de la Pléiade-Gallimard, 1990. 1569–72.
Aulotte, Robert. *Amyot et Plutarque.* Geneva: Droz, 1965.
———. "Jacques Amyot, traducteur courtois." *Revue des sciences humaines* 94 (1959): 131–39.
Bailly, J.-C. *La fin de l'hymne.* Paris: Bourgois, 1991.
———. *Le paradis du sens.* Paris: Bourgois, 1988.
Bakhtin, Mikhail. *Le principe dialogique, suivi de Écrits du Cercle de Bakhtin.* Paris: Le Seuil, 1992.
Balibar, Renée. *L'institution du français.* Paris: PUF, 1985.
Bandia, Paul. "Le concept bermanien de 'l'Etranger' dans le prisme de la traduction postcoloniale." *TTR* 14.2 (2001): 123–39.

Baudelaire, Charles. *Œuvres*. Paris: Bibliothèque de la Pléiade-Gallimard, 1951.
Bayen, Bruno, trans. *Œdipe à Colone*. By Sophocles. Paris: Bourgois, 1987.
Belmont, G. "Table ronde: Traduction prosaïque ou traduction prosodique?" *Encrages* 4-5 (1980): 176-88.
Benjamin, Walter. *Charles Baudelaire: A Lyric Poet in the Era of High Capitalism*. Trans. Harry Zohn. London: NLB, 1973.
———. *Charles Baudelaire, un poète lyrique à l'apogée du capitalisme*. Paris: Payot, 1982.
———. *Le concept de critique esthétique dans le romantisme allemand*. Trans. Philippe Lacoue-Labarthe and Anne-Marie Lang. Paris: Flammarion, 1986.
———. "The Concept of Criticism in German Romanticism." *Selected Writings, 1913-1926*. Ed. Marcus Bullock and Michael W. Jennings. Cambridge, Mass.: Belknap Press of Harvard University Press, 1996. 116-200.
———. *Mythe et violence*. Trans. Maurice de Gandillac. Paris: Denoël, 1971.
———. "The Task of the Translator." Trans. Harry Zohn. *Theories of Translation: An Anthology of Essays from Dryden to Derrida*. Ed. Rainer Schulte and John Biguenet. Chicago: University of Chicago Press, 1992. 71-82.
Benoist, Jean-Marie, ed. *John Donne*. Lausanne: L'Âge d'Homme, 1983.
Berman, Antoine. "L'âge de la traduction: 'La tâche du traducteur' de Walter Benjamin, un commentaire." *La traduction-poésie. À Antoine Berman*. Ed. Martine Broda. Strasbourg: Presses Universitaires de Strasbourg, 1999. 11-37.
———. "Critique, commentaire et traduction (Quelques réflexions à partir de Benjamin et Blanchot)." *Poésie* 37.2 (1986): 88-106.
———. "Critique des traductions: John Donne." *Poésie* 59 (1992): 3-20.
———. "De la translation à la traduction." *TTR* 1.1 (1988): 23-40.
———, trans. *Des différentes méthodes du traduire*. By Friedrich Schleiermacher. Paris: Seuil, 1999.
———. *L'épreuve de l'étranger*. Paris: Gallimard, 1984.
———. *The Experience of the Foreign: Culture and Translation in Romantic Germany*. Trans. S. Heyvaert. Albany: SUNY Press, 1992.
———. "Observations sur la traduction des œuvres complètes de Freud aux PUF." *Cinquièmes assises de la traduction littéraire. Traduire Freud : La langue, le style, la pensée*. Arles: ATLAS/Actes Sud, 1989. 106-56.
———. "Recension de la traduction de *Macounaíma*, de M. de Andrade, par J. Thiériot." *NRF* 326 (1980): 133-35.
———. "Les systèmes d'aide publique à la traduction en Europe." *Encrages* 17 (1987): 12-22.
———. "Tradition-translation-traduction." *Po&sie* 47 (1988): 85-98.
———. "La traduction et la lettre ou L'auberge du lointain." *Les tours de Babel*. Antoine Berman et al. Mauvezin: Trans-Europ-Repress, 1985. 35-150.
———. "La traduction et ses discours." *Meta* 34.4 (1989): 672-79.
Blake, William. *Marriage of Heaven and Hell*. In *Complete Writings*. Ed. Geoffrey Keynes. London: Oxford University Press, 1966. 148-58.

———. *Œuvres*. Vol. 3. Trans. Pierre Leyris. Paris: Aubier/Flammarion, 1980.
Blanchot, Maurice. *De Kafka à Kafka*. Paris: Gallimard, 1994.
Bonnefoy, Yves. "Baudelaire's *Les fleurs du mal*." *The Act and the Place of Poetry*. Ed. John Naughton. Trans. Richard Pevear. Chicago: University of Chicago Press, 1989.
———. *Entretiens sur la poésie*. Paris: Mercure de France, 1990.
———. "French Poetry and the Principle of Identity." Trans. Richard Stamelman. *The Act and the Place of Poetry*. Ed. John T. Naughton. Chicago: University of Chicago Press, 1989. 118–36.
———, trans. *Hamlet*. By William Shakespeare. Paris: Mercure de France, 1962.
———, trans. "A Hymne to Christ, at the Authors Last Going into Germany." By John Donne. *Palimpsestes* 2 (1990): 2–3.
———, trans. "Hymne to God My God in My Sicknesse." By John Donne. *Palimpsestes* 2 (1990): 4–5.
———. *L'improbable et autres essais*. Paris: Gallimard, 1980.
———, trans. *Jules César*. *Œuvres complètes de Shakespeare*. Vol. 4. Paris: Club Français du Livre, 1960.
———. *Poèmes*. Paris: Mercure de France, 1986.
———, trans. *Quarante-cinq poèmes de Yeats, suivi de La Résurrection*. Paris: Hermann, 1989.
———, trans. *Le roi Lear*. By William Shakespeare. Paris: Mercure de France, 1965.
———, trans. *Roméo et Juliette*. By William Shakespeare. Paris: Mercure de France, 1968.
———. "Translating Poetry." Trans. John Alexander and Clive Wilmer. *Theories of Translation: An Anthology of Essays from Dryden to Derrida*. Ed. Rainer Schulte and John Biguenet. Chicago: University of Chicago Press, 1992. 186–92.
———, trans. *Trois des derniers poèmes*. By John Donne. Losne: Éd. Thierry Bouchard/Yves Prié, 1994.
Bourdon, Alain. *Armand Robin ou La passion du verbe*. Paris: Seghers, 1981.
Bourguignon, André, Pierre Cotet, Jean Laplanche, and F. Robert. *Traduire Freud*. Paris: PUF, 1989.
Brisset, Annie. "Poésie: Le sens en effet, étude d'un translème." *META* 29.3 (1984): 259–66.
———. *Sociocritique de la traduction*. Quebec: Éd. du Préambule, 1990.
Brisson, Luc, trans. *Phaedrus*. By Plato. Paris: Flammarion, 1988.
Broch, Hermann. *The Guiltless*. Trans. Ralph Manheim. Boston: Little, Brown, 1974.
———. *Les irresponsables*. Trans. A. R. Picard. Paris: Gallimard, 1961.
———. *La mort de Virgile*. Trans. A. Kohn. Paris: Gallimard, 1955.
Broda, Martine, trans. "La tâche du traducteur." By Walter Benjamin. *Po&sie* 55 (1991): 150–58.
———, ed. *La traduction-poésie. À Antoine Berman*. Strasbourg: Presses Universitaires de Strasbourg, 1999.
Brunet, Philippe, trans. *Poèmes et fragments*. By Sappho. Paris: L'Âge d'Homme, 1991.

Carey, John. *John Donne: Life, Mind and Art*. London: Faber and Faber, 1981.
Carroll, Lewis. "Ye carpette knyghte. (Le chevalier mate-tapis)." Trans. A. Artaud. *Cahiers du Sud* 287 (1948): 2.
Casanova, Pascale. *La république mondiale des lettres*. Paris: Le Seuil, 1999.
———. *The World Republic of Letters*. Trans. M. B. DeBevoise. Cambridge, Mass.: Harvard University Press, 2004
Cayron, Claire. *Sésame, pour la traduction*. Bordeaux: Le Mascaret, 1987.
Chateaubriand, François-René de. "Remarques." *Po&sie* 23 (1982): 112–20.
Cinquièmes assises de la traduction littéraire. Traduire Freud : La langue, le style, la pensée. Arles: ATLAS/Actes Sud, 1989.
Claudel, Paul. *Cinq grandes odes*. Paris: Gallimard, 1957.
———. *Five Great Odes*. Trans. Edward Lucie-Smith. London: Rapp & Carroll, 1967.
Colledge, Edmund, and Bernard McGinn, trans. *The Essential Sermons, Commentaries, Treatises, and Defense*. By Meister Eckhart. New York: Paulist Press, 1981.
Cordonnier, Jean-Louis. "L'homme décentré. Culture et traduction, traduction et culture." Diss. Université de Franche-Comté, 1989.
Curtius, Ernst Robert. *La littérature européenne et le Moyen Âge latin*. Paris: PUF, 1956.
Dante. *De l'éloquence vulgaire*. Trans. F. Magne. Paris: La Délirante, 1985.
———. *De vulgari eloquentia*. Trans. Steven Botterill. Cambridge: Cambridge University Press, 1996.
Davreu, Robert. "Antoine Berman, penseur de la traduction." *Poétique de l'étranger* 3 (2002): 20–25.
———. *Jacques Roubaud*. Paris: Seghers, 1985.
Dayre, Éric. "Thomas de Quincey: La mer n'est pourtant pas si sublime qu'on pourrait d'abord se l'imaginer... (Sur le vacancier romantique: Théorie de la digression)." *Po&sie* 54.4 (1990): 14–36.
Deguy, Michel. *Actes*. Paris: Gallimard, 1966.
Déprats, Jean-Michel. "La traduction: Le tissu des mots." *Le marchand de Venise*. By William Shakespeare. Trans. Déprats. Paris: Comédie-Française/Sand, 1987. 140–44.
De Quincey, Thomas. "Rhetoric." *Selected Essays on Rhetoric by Thomas De Quincey*. Ed. Frederick Burwick. Carbondale: Southern Illinois University Press, 1967. 81–133.
Derrida, Jacques. *Schibboleth pour Paul Celan*. Paris: Galilée, 1986.
Dolet, Étienne. "Manière de bien traduire d'une langue en aultre." *Anthologie de la manière de traduire. Domaine français*. Ed. Paul A. Horguelin. Montreal: Linguatech, 1981. 53–54.
Donne, John. *Complete Poetry and Selected Prose*. Ed. John Hayward. Bloomsbury: Nonesuch Press, 1929.
———. *Devotions upon Emergent Occasions and Death's Duel*. New York: Vintage, 1999.

———. *John Donne's Sermons*. Ed. Kimberly Johnson. February 23, 2007. Brigham Young University, Harold B. Lee Library. www.lib.byu.edu/dlib/donne/ (accessed Oct. 10, 2008).
———. *The Sermons of John Donne*. Ed. George R. Potter and Evelyn M. Simpson. 10 vols. Berkeley: University of California Press, 1953–1962.
Du Bellay, Joachim. *Les regrets, précédé de Les antiquités, et suivi de La défense et illustration de la langue française*. Paris: Gallimard, 1967.
Duneton, Claude. *Parler croquant*. Paris: Stock, 1973.
Eckhart, Maître. *Œuvres de Maître Eckhart, sermons-traités*. 1942. Trans. Paul Petit. Paris: Gallimard, 1987.
Ellrodt, Robert. *L'inspiration personnelle et l'esprit du temps chez les poètes métaphysiques anglais*. Vol. 1. Paris: José Corti, 1960.
———, trans. *Poésie*. By John Donne. Paris: Imprimerie Nationale, 1993.
———. "Présence et permanence de John Donne." *John Donne*. Ed. Jean Marie Benoist. Lausanne: L'Âge d'Homme, 1983. 17–29.
Etkind, Efim. *Un art en crise. Essai de poétique de la traduction poétique*. Lausanne: L'Âge d'Homme, 1982.
Even-Zohar, Itamar. *Papers in Historical Poetics*. Tel Aviv: Porter Institute for Poetics and Semiotics, Tel Aviv University, 1978.
Foucault, Michel. *Histoire de la folie à l'âge classique*. Paris: Gallimard, 1972.
———. *Les mots et les choses*. Paris: Gallimard, 1966.
———. *The Order of Things*. Trans. Alan Sheridan. New York: Vintage Books, 1973.
Freud, Sigmund. *Œuvres complètes*. Vol. 13. Paris: PUF, 1989.
———. *The Standard Edition of the Complete Psychological Works of Sigmund Freud*. Trans. and ed. James Strachey. London: Hogarth Press and the Institute of Psychoanalysis, 1966.
Friedrich, Hugo. "On the Art of Translation." Trans. Rainer Schulte and John Biguenet. *Theories of Translation: An Anthology of Essays from Dryden to Derrida*. Ed. Rainer Schulte and John Biguenet. Chicago: University of Chicago Press, 1992. 11–16.
Fuzier, J. "John Donne et la formalité de l'essence—essai d'interprétation prosodique et rhétorique du Sonnet sacré XIV." *John Donne*. Ed. Jean-Marie Benoist. Lausanne: L'Âge d'Homme, 1983. 39–49.
———, trans. *Poèmes*. By William Shakespeare. Vol. 1 of *Œuvres complètes*. Paris: Bibliothèque de la Pléiade-Gallimard, 1959.
Fuzier, J., and Y. Denis, trans. *Poèmes de John Donne*. 1962. Paris: Gallimard, 1991.
Gadamer, Hans-Georg. *Truth and Method*. Trans. Joel Weinsheimer and Donald G. Marshall. New York: Continuum, 1991.
Genette, Gérard. *Mimologics*. Trans. Thaïs E. Morgan. Foreword by Gerald Prince. Lincoln: University of Nebraska Press, 1995.
———. *Mimologiques, voyage en Cratylie*. Paris: Le Seuil, 1976.
———. *Palimpsestes*. Paris: Le Seuil, 1982.

———. *Palimpsests: Literature in the Second Degree*. Trans. Channa Newman and Claude Doubinsky. Lincoln: University of Nebraska Press, 1997.

Gentile, Giovanni. "Du tort et du droit des traductions." Trans. Charles Alunni. *Cahiers du Collège international de philosophie* 6 (1988): 7–10.

Goethe, J. W. von. *The Autobiography of Goethe: Truth and Poetry from My Own Life*. Trans. John Oxenford. London: Bell & Sons, 1903.

———. *Poésie et vérité*. Trans. Pierre du Colombier. Paris: Aubier, 1941.

Goldschmidt, Georges-Arthur. *Quand Freud voit la mer*. Paris: Buchet-Chastel, 1988.

Goux, Jean-Paul. "Un peu faute de façon." *Recueil* 1 (1984): 95–100.

Granel, Gérard. *L'équivoque ontologique de la pensée kantienne*. Paris: Gallimard, 1970.

———, trans. *Qu'appelle-t-on penser?* By Martin Heidegger. Paris: PUF, 1959.

Gresset, Michel. "De la traduction de la métaphore littéraire à la traduction comme métaphore de l'écriture." *Revue française d'études américaines* 18 (1983): 502–18.

———. "Le 'parce que' chez Faulkner et le 'donc' chez Beckett." *Les lettres nouvelles* 19 (1961): 124–38.

Gros, Léon-Gabriel. *John Donne*. Paris: Seghers, 1964.

Grosjean, Jean. "Note du traducteur." *Genèse*. Trans. Grosjean. Paris: Gallimard, 1987. 15–16.

———, trans. *Les prophètes*. Paris: Gallimard, 1955.

———. "Rescension de la traduction des *Poèmes de John Donne* par J. Fuzier et Y. Denis." *NRF* 19 (1962): 904–6.

Guerne, Armel. "Introduction: Novalis ou la vocation d'éternité." *Œuvres complètes*. By Novalis. Trans. Guerne. Paris: Gallimard, 1975. 1:7–31.

———, trans. *Les romantiques allemands*. Paris: Desclée de Brouwer, 1963.

Harland, Richard. *Superstructuralism: The Philosophy of Structuralism and Poststructuralism*. New York: Methuen, 1987.

Heidegger, Martin. *Approche de Hölderlin*. Trans. H. Corbin, Michel Deguy, F. Fédier, and J. Launay. Paris: Gallimard, 1962.

———. *Chemins qui ne mènent nulle part*. Trans. W. Brokmeier. Paris: Gallimard, 1962.

———. *Elucidations of Hölderlin's Poetry*. Trans. Keith Hoeller. New York: Humanity Books, 2000.

———. *Essais et conférences*. Trans. André Préau. 1958. Paris: Gallimard, 1980.

———. *Introduction à la métaphysique*. Trans. Gilbert Kahn. Paris: Gallimard, 1967.

———. *An Introduction to Metaphysics*. Trans. Ralph Manheim. New Haven, Conn.: Yale University Press, 1959.

———. *Off the Beaten Track*. Trans. Julian Young and Kenneth Haynes. Cambridge: Cambridge University Press, 2002.

Hocquard, Emmanuel, and Claude Royet-Journoud, eds. *49+1 nouveaux poètes américains*. Royaumont: Action Poétique/Un Bureau sur l'Atlantique, 1991.

Hofmannsthal, Hugo von. *Lettre de Lord Chandos et autres essais.* Trans. J. C. Schneider and A. Kohn. Paris: Gallimard, 1980.
———. *Le livre des amis.* Trans. Jean-Yves Masson. Paris: Maren Sell, 1990.
Hölderlin, Friedrich. *Essays and Letters on Theory.* Trans. and ed. Thomas Pfau. Albany: SUNY Press, 1988.
———. *Hymnes, élégies et autres poèmes.* Trans. Armel Guerne. Paris: Flammarion, 1983.
———. *Œuvres.* Ed. Philippe Jaccottet. Paris: Bibliothèque de la Pléiade-Gallimard, 1967.
———. *Sämtliche Werke.* Vol. 6. Ed. Friedrich Beissner. Stuttgart: Kohlhammer, 1945.
Hopkins, Gerard Manley. *De l'origine de la beauté, suivi de poèmes et écrits.* Trans. J. P. Audigier and R. Gallet. Paris: Éd. Comp'act, 1989.
———. *En rythme bondissant (Lettres choisies).* Trans. R. Callet. Paris: Obsidiane, 1989.
———. "Epithalamion." *Poems of Gerard Manley Hopkins.* Ed. Robert Bridges and W. H. Gardner. New York: Oxford University Press, 1948. 171–73.
———. *Grandeur de Dieu.* Trans. J. Mambrino. Paris: Granit, 1980.
———. *The Letters of Gerard Manley Hopkins to Robert Bridges.* Ed. Claude Colleer Abbott. London: Oxford University Press, 1955.
———. *Le naufrage du Deutschland.* Trans. Pierre Leyris. Paris: Le Seuil, 1964.
Horguelin, Paul A., ed. *Anthologie de la manière de traduire. Domaine français.* Montreal: Linguatech, 1981.
Humphrey, Lawrence. *Interpretatio Linguarum Seu de Ratione Convertendi et Explicandi Autores Tam Sacros Quam Prophanos.* Basel: Frobenius, 1559.
Intérim. Rev. of *Poèmes de John Donne,* trans. Fuzier and Denis. *Lettres françaises,* March 21, 1962: 2.
Jaccottet, Philippe, trans. *L'homme sans qualités.* By R. Musil. Paris: Le Seuil, 1956.
———. Postface. *L'Odyssée.* By Homer. Trans. Jaccottet. Paris: FM/La Découverte, 2004. 401–10.
———, trans. *Les solitudes.* By Luis de Góngora y Argote. Geneva: La Dogana, 1984.
Jauss, Hans Robert. *Ästhetische Erfahrung und literarische Hermeneutik.* Vol. 1. Munich: Fink, 1977.
———. *Pour une herméneutique littéraire.* Trans. Maurice Jacob. Paris: Gallimard, 1988.
Jonson, Ben. *The Complete Poems.* Ed. George Parfitt. London: Penguin Books, 1988.
Joyce, James. *Dubliners.* New York: Modern Library, 1954.
Khatibi, Abdelkebir. "De la bi-langue." *Écritures, publication des Actes du Colloque de l'Université Paris 7 (UER de Textes & Documents).* Ed. A.-M. Christin. Paris: Le Sycomore, 1980. 196–204.
Klossowski, Pierre, trans. *L'Enéide.* Paris: André Dimanche, 1993.
Ladmiral, J.-R. "Pour une théologie de la traduction." *TTR* 3.2 (1990): 121–38.

Larbaud, Valery. *An Homage to Jerome: Patron Saint of Translators*. Trans. Jean-Paul de Chezet. Marlboro, Vt.: Marlboro Press, 1984.

———. *Sous l'invocation de saint Jérôme*. Paris: Gallimard, 1946.

Legouis, P., trans. *Poèmes choisis*. By John Donne. Paris: Aubier, 1955.

———. "Sur une traduction en vers de Donne." *Études anglaises* 16.2 (1963) : 134–39.

Leyris, Pierre. "Confessions de traducteurs." *L'âne* 4 (1982): 41.

———. Introduction. *Macbeth*. By William Shakespeare. Trans. Leyris. Paris: Aubier Montaigne, 1977.

———. "Notes sur un poème de Hardy traduit par Valéry." *Palimpsestes* 2 (1990): 7–18.

———, trans. and ed. *Poèmes accompagnés de proses et de dessins*. By Gerard Manley Hopkins. Paris: Le Seuil, 1957.

———. "Une posture." *L'âne* 4 (1982): 41.

———. "Pourquoi retraduire Shakespeare." *Œuvres complètes de Shakespeare*. Trans. Leyris. Paris: Club Français du Livre, 1954.

———, trans. *Reliquiae, vers, proses, dessins*. By Gerard Manley Hopkins. Paris: Seuil, 1957.

Lohmann, J. *Philosophie und Sprachwissenschaft*. Berlin: Duncker und Humblot, 1965.

Lusignan, Serge. *Parler vulgairement*. Montreal: Presses de l'Université de Montréal, 1986.

Luther, Martin. *Œuvres*. Geneva: Labor et Fides, 1964.

———. *An Open Letter on Translating*. Trans. Gary Mann. Guttenberg, 1995.

Mailhos, Georges. "Traduire, un avant-dire." *Les tours de Babel*. Antoine Berman et al. Mauvezin: Trans-Europ-Repress, 1985. 231–248.

Mallarmé, Stéphane. *Collected Poems*. Trans. Henry Weinfield. Berkeley: University of California Press, 1994.

———. "Crisis in Poetry." *Selected Prose Poems, Essays, and Letters*. Trans. and ed. Bradford Cook. Baltimore: Johns Hopkins Press. 34–43.

———. *Igitur, Divagations, Un coup de dés*. Paris: Gallimard, 1976.

———. *Poems*. Trans. Roger Fry. New York: New Directions, 1951.

Malroux, Claire, trans. *Poèmes*. By Emily Dickinson. Paris: Belin, 1989.

Marcel, Jean. *Jérôme ou de la traduction*. Ottawa: Léméac, 1990.

Marteau, Robert. *Recueil*. 2. Mareuil-sur-Mauldre: Éd. Qui Vive, 1985.

Masson, Jean-Yves, trans. *Les cygnes sauvages à Coole*. By William Butler Yeats. Lagrasse: Verdier, 1990.

———. "Territoire de Babel. Aphorismes." *Corps écrit* 36 (1990): 157–60.

Meschonnic, Henri. "Poétique d'un texte de philosophie et des traductions: Humboldt, sur la tâche de l'écrivain de l'histoire." *Les tours de Babel*. Antoine Berman et al. Mauvezin: Trans-Europ-Repress, 1985. 183–229.

———. *Pour la poétique*. Vol. 2. Paris: Gallimard, 1973.

———. "Pour une poétique de la traduction." *Les cinq rouleaux*. Trans. Meschonnic. Paris: Gallimard, 1970. 9–18.

---. *La rime et la vie*. Lagrasse: Verdier, 1989.
Minière, Claude, trans. "Au sujet de John Donne." By John Carey. *Po&sie* 45 (1988): 103–17.
Momigliano, Arnaldo. *Sagesses barbares*. Paris: Gallimard, 1991.
Morel, A., trans. "Elegy XIX: Going to Bed." By John Donne. *Le navire d'argent* 1 (1925): 97–99.
Mounin, Georges. *Les belles infidèles*. Paris: Cahiers du Sud, 1955.
---. *Les problèmes théoriques de la traduction*. Paris: Gallimard, 1963.
Naïs, Hélène. "Traduction et imitation chez quelques poètes du XVIème siècle." *Revue des sciences humaines* 180 (1980): 33–49.
Nietzche. "Die fröhliche Wissenschaft." Trans. Peter Mollenhauer. *Theories of Translation: An Anthology of Essays from Dryden to Derrida*. Ed. Rainer Schulte and John Biguenet. Chicago: University of Chicago Press, 1992. 68–70.
---. *Le gai savoir*. Paris: Gallimard, 1985.
---. *The Gay Science*. Trans. Josephine Nauckhoff. Cambridge: Cambridge University Press, 2001.
Nouss, Alexis, ed. "Antoine Berman aujourd'hui." *TTR* 14.2 (2001).
Novalis. *Briefe und Dokumente*. Vol. 4. of *Werke Briefe Dokumente*. Ed. Ewald Wasmuth. Heidelberg: Lambert Schneider, 1954.
---. *Briefwechsel mit Friedrich und August Wilhelm, Charlotte und Caroline Schlegel*. Mainz: Verlag von Franz Kirchheim, 1880.
---. "Sophie, Oder über die Frauen." *Critical and Miscellaneous Essays*. Vol. 2. Trans. and ed. Thomas Carlyle. London: Chapman and Hall, 1869. 249–310.
Orcel, Michel. *Langue mortelle*. Paris: L'Alphée, 1987.
Paepcke, Fritz. "Textverstehen-Textübersetzen-Übersetzungskritik." *Übersetzungswissenschaft—eine Neuorientierung (Zur Integrierung von Theorie und Praxis)*. Ed. Mary Snell-Hornby. Tübingen: Francke Verlag, 1986. 106–17.
"Paideia." *Oxford English Dictionary*. New York: Oxford University Press, 2008.
Pasternak, Boris. "Notes of a Translator." *Modern Russian Poets on Poetry*. Ed. Carl R. Proffer. Ann Arbor, Mich.: Ardis, 1974. 96–101.
---. *Œuvres*. Trans. Catherine Perrel. Ed. M. Aucouturier. Paris: Bibliothèque de la Pléiade-Gallimard, 1990.
---. *Safe Conduct*. Trans. Alec Brown. London: Elek, 1959.
---. *Selected Writings and Letters*. Trans. Catherine Judelson. Moscow: Progress Publishers, 1990.
---. "Some Statements." *Modern Russian Poets on Poetry*. Ed. Carl R. Proffer. Ann Arbor, Mich.: Ardis, 1974. 81–86.
Paz, Octavio. *Lecture et contemplation*. Trans. Jean-Claude Masson. Paris: La Délirante, 1982.
---. *Traducción: Literatura y literalidad*. Barcelona: Tusquets Editores, 1971.
Péguy, Charles. *Deuxième élégie XXX*. Paris: Gallimard, 1955.
Pergnier, M. "Existe-t-il une science de la traduction?" *Traduction et traducteurs au Moyen Âge*. Ed. Geneviève Contamine. Paris: Éd. du CNRS, 1989. xiii–xxiii.

Pézard, A., trans. *Œuvres complètes*. By Dante. Paris: Bibliothèque de la Pléiade-Gallimard, 1965.

Poisson, Jean-Roger. Foreword. *Poèmes de John Donne*. Trans. J. Fuzier and Y. Denis. 1962. Paris: Gallimard, 1991. 7–22.

Raine, Kathleen. *Isis errante*. Trans. François-Xavier Jaujard. Paris: Granit, 1978.

———. *Le premier jour*. Trans. François-Xavier Jaujard. Paris: Granit, 1980.

———. *Sur un rivage désert*. Trans. Marie-Béatrice Mesnet and Jean Mambrino. Paris: Granit, 1978.

Räkel, H.-H. S. "'Die sache selbs, der sprachen art, ein christlich hertz.' Les principes d'une théorie de la traduction selon Martin Luther." *TTR* 3 (1990): 81–95.

Rener, F. M. *Interpretatio: Language and Translation from Cicero to Tytler*. Amsterdam: Rodopi, 1989.

Rev. of *Poèmes de John Donne*, trans. Fuzier and Denis. *Bulletin critique du livre français*, May 1962.

Rev. of *Poèmes de John Donne*, trans. Fuzier and Denis. *Centre protestant d'études et de documentation*, 1962.

Rev. of *Poèmes de John Donne*, trans. Fuzier and Denis. *Digues du temps*, March 1962.

Rev. of *Poèmes de John Donne*, trans. Fuzier and Denis. *Le Figaro littéraire*, February 24, 1962.

Rev. of *Poèmes de John Donne*, trans. Fuzier and Denis. *La Grive*, June 1962.

Ricœur, Paul. *Du texte à l'action. Essais d'herméneutique II*. Paris: Le Seuil, 1986.

———. *From Text to Action: Essays in Hermeneutics II*. Trans. Kathleen Blamey and John B. Thompson. Evanston, Ill.: Northwestern University Press, 1991.

———. *On Translation: Thinking in Action*. London: Routledge, 2006.

———. *Sur la traduction*. Paris: Bayard, 2004.

———. *Le temps raconté*. Vol. 3 of *Temps et récit*. Paris: Le Seuil, 1985.

Rilke, Rainer Maria. *Chant éloigné*. Trans. Jean-Yves Masson. Lagrasse: Verdier, 1990.

———. *Letters to Merline*. Trans. Jessie Browner. New York: Paragon House, 1989.

———. *Lettres françaises à Merline*. Trans. Philippe Jaccottet. Paris: Le Seuil, 1984.

Rimbaud, Arthur. *Œuvres complètes* Paris: Gallimard, 1954.

Risset, Jacqueline. "Joyce traduit par Joyce." *Tel quel* 53 (1973): 47–58.

Rivière, J. J., trans. *Le poème*. By Parmenides. Paris: PUF, 1957.

Robin, Armand. *Écrits oubliés*. Vol. 2. Rennes: Éd. Ubacs, 1986.

———. *Poésie sans passeport*. Rennes: Éd. Ubacs, 1990.

Rothschild, Philippe de, trans. *Poèmes élisabéthains (1525–1650)*. Paris: Seghers, 1969.

———. "Traduire 'Donne.'" *John Donne*. Ed. Jean Marie Benoist. Lausanne: L'Âge d'Homme, 1983. 75–79.

Roubaud, Jacques, trans. "Lettre à Maria Gisborne." By Percy Bysshe Shelley. *Po&sie* 16 (1981): 74–80.

———. "Le silence de la mathématique jusqu'au fond de la langue, poésie." Po&sie 10.3 (1979): 110–24.
———, trans. *Les troubadours, anthologie bilingue.* Paris: Seghers, 1971.
———. *La vieillesse d'Alexandre. Essais sur quelques états récents du vers français.* Paris: Ramsay, 1988.
Rousselot, J. *Poésie et prophétie.* Paris: Âge Nouveau, 1955.
Savignac, J. P., trans. *Œuvres complètes.* By Pindare. Paris: La Différence, 1990.
Schlegel, Friedrich. *Kritische Schriften.* Ed. Wolfdietrich Rasch. Munich: Hanser, 1971.
Schleiermacher, Friedrich. "On the Different Methods of Translation." Trans. André Lefevere. *German Romantic Criticism.* Ed. A. Leslie Willson. New York: Continuum, 1982. 1–30.
Simon, Joseph. "Goethe sur le langage." Trans. Helena Schulz-Keil. *Po&sie* 57 (1991): 87–103.
Simon, Sherry. Rev. of *La traduction.* Ed. Jean-René Ladmiral. *TTR* 2.2 (1989): 157–58.
Soupault, Philippe. *Souvenirs de James Joyce.* Paris: Charlot, 1945.
Spinoza, Benedictus de. *The Collected Works of Spinoza.* Vol 1. Trans. Edwin Curley. Princeton, N.J.: Princeton University Press, 1985.
———. *Éthique.* Trans. B. Pautrat. Paris: Le Seuil, 1988.
Spitzer, Leo. *Études de style. Précédé de Léo Spitzer et la lecture stylistique, par Jean Starobinski.* Trans. E. Kaufholz, A. Coulon, and Michel Foucault. Paris: Gallimard, 1970.
Staël, Germaine de. "De la manière de traduire et de l'utilité des traductions." *Cent ans de théorie française de la traduction.* Ed. Lieven d'Hulst. Villeneuve-d'Ascq: Presses Universitaires de Lille, 1989. 86–89.
Steiner, George. *After Babel: Aspects of Language and Translation.* London: Oxford University Press, 1992.
———. *Après Babel.* Paris: Albin Michel, 1978.
Stevens, Wallace. *Opus Posthumous.* New York: Alfred A. Knopf, 1989.
Thalmann, Marianne. "A. W. Schlegel." *A. W. Schlegel, 1767–1967.* Bad Godesberg: Inter Nationes, 1967. 5–30.
Thiériot, Jacques, trans. *Macounaíma.* By Mário de Andrade. Paris: Flammarion, 1979.
Toury, Gideon. *In Search of a Theory of Translation.* Tel Aviv: Porter Institute for Poetics and Semiotics, Tel Aviv University, 1980.
———. "The Translator as a Nonconformist-to-be, or: How to Train Translators so as to Violate Transnational Norms." *Angewandte Übersetzungswissenschaft: Internationales Übersetzungswissenschaftliches Kolloquium an der Wirtschaftsuniversität.* Ed. Sven-Olaf Poulsed and Wolfram Wilss. Denmark: Århus, 1980. 180–94.
"La traduction en jeu." *Change* 19 (1974): 47–55.
Valéry, Paul. *Œuvres.* Paris: Bibliothèque de la Pléiade-Gallimard, 1959.
Venturini, Joseph. "Traité de la poésie, extraits." *Po&sie* 40 (1987): 109–22.
Venuti, Lawrence, trans. "Translation and the Trials of the Foreign." *The Translation Studies Reader.* Ed. Lawrence Venuti. London: Routledge, 2000. 284–97.

Vinay, J.-P., and J. Darbelnet. *Stylistique comparée du français et de l'anglais.* 1958. Paris: Éd. Marcel Didier, 1977.

Yourcenar, Marguerite. *La couronne et la lyre.* Paris: Gallimard, 1979.

Zuber, Roger. *Les "belles infidèles" et la formation du goût classique.* Paris: Armand Colin, 1968.

Index

"À Dieu, mon Dieu, dans ma maladie," 165
Actes (Deguy), 94
Adaptations, *vs.* translations, 41–44, 145–55
Ademar, Guillem, 129–30
Aeneid (Virgil), 9; Klossowski's translation of, 2, 23–25, 78, 94, 95n10, 203n1, 216, 220
Alain, 110–11, 170, 223
Amyot, Jacques, 1, 24–25, 31–32, 219
Antigone, Hölderin's translation of, 2, 23–25
Approche de Hölderlin (Heidegger), 219n20
Archaism, 99–101, 106–8; linked to historicism, 220–21; in *Poèmes de John Donne*, 205–8, 220; of translations, 12, 15, 219; in translations of "Going to Bed," 150, 155–56
Archaization, *vs.* rejuvenation, 19
Arendt, Hannah, 50n33
Aristotle, translation of *Nicomachean*, 23–25
Arlt, Roberto, 49, 68
Art. *See* Principle of the sobriety of art
Artaud, 223
"Au sujet de John Donne" [About John Donne], Minière's translation as, 89
Aubier publisher, 89, 95

Aucouturier, Michel, 184n160
Aulotte, Robert, 31–32
Aury, Dominique, 213

Bailly, Jean-Christophe, 64n63, 183
Balzac, 170n122
Barthes, Roland, 3, 27n9
Bastos, Roa, 68
Baudelaire, Charles, 67, 178–82, 184–85, 188, 222
Bayen, Bruno, 64n63, 217n17
Beaufret, Jean, 94
Being and Time (Heidegger), 5
Being-in-languages, 59
Belmont, George, 62n60
Benjamin, Walter, 25, 178; "The Concept of Criticism in German Romanticism" by, 4n1, 178–79; literary criticism and, 4–5; "The Task of the Translator" by, 2, 23–24, 213, 222–23; translation and, 27n12, 187n163, 218; on translation criticism, 3, 26
Benoist, Jean-Marie, 113–14, 124
Benveniste, Meschonnic and, 5, 35
Berman, Isabelle, 34n20, 49
Bianquis, Geneviève, 23–25
Biases, of translators, 33

Bible, translations of, 4, 9–10, 19n26, 25, 33
"Binsey Poplars" (Hopkins), 194–95
Blake, William, 89, 189
Blanchot, Maurice, 3
Blok, A. A., 173–75
Bollack, Jean, 64n63
Bonnefoy, Yves, 111, 186n162, 192; on Baudelaire, 184–85; characteristics of translations by, 19–20, 165; on Donne, 159–60, 206; on English poetry, 166n115, 188–92; on translation, 20, 96, 220; translations of Donne by, 11, 89, 126–27, 134n69, 161, 165–68, 199; translations of Shakespeare by, 60, 94, 165; translations of Yeats by, 56–57, 76, 78–79
Borges, Jorge Luis, 3
Brisset, Annie, 5, 47; in Tel Aviv school of translation criticism, 4, 36; on translations, 45, 53n43, 70
Brisson, Luc, 25
Briusov, 216–17
Broch, Hermann, 131–32
Brunet, Philippe, 47n30, 63
Bruni, Leonardo, 10
Bucolics (Virgil), 9, 203
Bulletin critique du livre français, on *Poèmes de John Donne*, 203

Campos, Haroldo de, 16n22
Carey, John, 11, 89, 113n29, 114n31, 115, 148
Carpentier, Alejo, 33n18
Carroll, Lewis, 223
Catullus, Markowicz's translation of, 47n30
Cayron, Claire, 58
Celan, Paul, 166n116; du Bouchet's translations of, 25, 34n20; Meschonnic on translations of, 4, 33
Centre protestant d'études et de documentation, on *Poèmes de John Donne*, 203
Cervantes, Miguel de, 219
Change ("La traduction en jeu"), 94, 211, 215–18
Chant des chants [Song of Songs], translated by Meschonnic, 94
Chateaubriand, François-René de, 32, 52, 188; translations of Milton by, 2, 23–25, 192
Cicero, 8

Cinq grandes odes (Claudel), 192n170
Clarity of exposition, in translation criticism, 5–6
Clason, Meyer, 62
Claudel, 192n170
Coleridge, Samuel, 189
Colledge, Edmund, 134n70
Colloquialism, Donne's, 111–12, 117–18, 164–66
Commentativity, in translation criticism, 5–6
Comparatists, translations by, 41
"The Concept of Criticism in German Romanticism" (Benjamin), 4n1
Conquest, translation as, 8n6
Corbin, H., 219n20
Cordonnier, Jean-Louis, 33n18
Critical poetry, of 1960s, 222
Criticism, 3–5, 28n15. *See also* Translation criticism; need for, 26–27, 30; translation's relation to, 27–28
Cultures. *See also* Literary transfers: norms of, 37–39; polysystems of, 36, 39; receptor, 43–44

D'Ablancourt, Perrot, 31–32, 45, 76
Dacier, Madame, 41–42
Daniel, Arnaut, 130
Dante, Pézard's translations of, 94, 100, 219
Darbelnet, J., 213
Davreau, Robert, 187
De Gandillac, Maurice, 213
De l'Allemagne [Of Germany] (Staël), 218
"De l'espirit des traductions" ["The Spirit of Translations"] (Staël), 218
De Quincey, Thomas, 109
"De Sa Maitresse Allant Au Lict." *See* "Going to Bed" (Donne), translations of
Death, 147, 158
"Death's Duell" (sermon by Donne), 158
Defectivity, of translations, 29–30
Deguy, Michel, 3, 94, 213; correspondence with Robel, 211, 215–19, 221; on meaning of translation, 215–16; translation of Sappho by, 23, 25
Denis, Yves, 92–94, 220. *See also under* "Going to Bed"; Poèmes de John Donne
Déprats, Jean-Michel, 60, 111, 134n69

Der goldene Schlüssel [The Golden Key] (Grimm), 23–25
Derrida, Jacques, 36, 67
Deuxième élégie XXX (Péguy), 135n73
Dialectic, rhetorical *vs.* poetic, 116
Dickinson, Emily, 56–57
Dignification, of translation criticism, 30
Digressivity, in translation criticism, 5–6, 71–72
Digues du temps, on Donne, 204
Dolet, Étienne, 75n77
Don Quixote (Cervantes), Amyot's translation of, 219
Donne, John, 90n3. *See also* "Going to Bed"; *Poèmes de John Donne;* collections of works by, 157–58; colloquialism of, 111–12, 117–18, 143, 164–66; criticisms of translations of, 25, 111–13, 197, 202; distinctiveness of, 14, 111–13, 204; Englishness of, 111; "French," 12–13, 98–100, 106–8, 119; French translations of, 2, 11–12, 71–72, 88–90, 94–95, 156–57, 166–68; Grosjean and, 204–6; hard for French readers to understand, 204, 207; influence of, 18–19; key words for, 129n52, 132; body as, 136, 136n74; joy as, 127–30, 132; nakedness, 130–32, 137, 152–54; self as, 116–18, 133–34; touch as, 118–19, 124; on love, 137n77, 152n95; metaphysical thinking of, 14; poetics of, 112, 140; poetry of, 96–97, 166–67; precise use of words by, 132, 139–40; prose of, 18; prose *vs.* poetry of, 96, 157–58, 160, 169n120; reception in France, 21, 196–98; relations among poems of, 12–14, 112–14, 127; religion of, 18, 122n45; resurrection of, 209; retranslations of, 160–69, 198–99, 222; reviewers' lack of familiarity with, 204, 207; sermons by, 158–60; study by L'Âge d'Homme, 11, 225; style of, 112, 115n33, 124, 210n6; compactness of, 148, 166–67; content and, 108, 113; experiential/reflexive dimension of, 113, 127n48; spoken, 101–2; use of contraries, 113n29, 114n31; use of privative constructions, 133–36, 144, 151–52; use of the present tense, 120, 166; tactility of, 124, 152n95, 153; translators' characterizations of, 18, 197; unavailability of works, 11, 88–90; uniqueness of poems, 14, 118, 120–22, 127
Dossier John Donne, 89
Dostoyevsky, Fyodor, 41–42
"Doux bruits et cris" ["Sweet Cries and Noises"] (Daniel), 130
"The Dream" (Donne), 99
Du Bellay, Joachim, 45–46, 57, 99
Du Bouchet, 25, 33, 34n20
Duneton, Claude, 213n8
Durand, René L. F., 33n18

Eckhart, Meister, 134–35
Éditions Charlot, 88–89
Einführung in die Metaphysik (Heidegger), 220
El arpa y la sombra (Carpentier), 33n18
Elegy X, "The Dream" (Donne), 99
Elegy XIX, "Going to Bed" (Donne). *See* "Going to Bed" (Donne)
Elegy XVII "Variety" (Donne), 129
Eliot, T. S., 25, 209
Ellrodt, Robert, 11, 122n45; on distinctiveness of Donne, 111–13; on Donne's style, 102n14, 108, 120n44, 127n48, 129n52, 132, 136n74, 140; on "Going to Bed," 122; on love in Donne's poetry, 137n77, 152n95; translations by, 19, 164; translations of Donne by, 89, 123n46, 157; translations of Donne's "A Nocturnall upon S. Lucies Day" by, 11, 161, 164–65
Engagé analyses, Meschonnic's, 32–36
England, poetry of, 108–9, 113
English as regret, for Mallarmé, 223n26
"Epithalamion" (Hopkins), 130
Eroticization, of Donne, 14
Essais (Montaigne), 172
Essais et conférences (Heidegger), 211
Ethics, of translations, 74–76
Ethnology, relation to translation, 65
Etkind, Efim, 12n14, 47n31, 71, 103, 165, 184, 218
Études anglaises, on *Poèmes de John Donne,* 203
Euripidis (directed by Bayen), 64n63
Even-Zohar, Itamar, 4, 36, 40
The Experience of the Foreign (Berman). *See L'épreuve de l'éstranger*
"The Extasie" (Donne), 92, 124

Faulkner, William, 61
Fédier, François, 75n77, 219n20
Figaro littéraire, on *Poèmes de John Donne,* 201-2
Finnegan's Wake, Soupault's translation of, 211
Fleurs du mal (Baudelaire), 178-81
Formality of essence, 104, 108, 222, 224
49+1 nouveaux poètes américains (edited by Hocquart), 50n34
Foucault, Michel, 5, 64n64
Fragments (Novalis), Guerne translating, 76
France: interest in translations in, 103, 188n165, 213, 218-19; poetry of, 12, 98-100, 107; reception of Donne in, 196-98; scarcity of translations of Donne in, 88-90; two schools of poetry translation in, 218-19
Freedom, of translators, 34-35, 41, 44, 75n77, 76-77, 165, 206; "law of translation" and, 45-46; Paz taking, 147-51
French, translations into: of Donne poems, 11-12, 155-57, 198-99, 204, 207; opening up to English *universum,* 195-96; "secret passageways" for, 192-94, 196
"French Poetry and the Principle of Identity" (Bonnefoy), 188-91
Freud, Sigmund, translations of, 24-25, 62
Functionalism, *vs.* reflection on translating subject, 45
Functionalist school, contributions of, 47, 49
Fuzier, Jean. *See also* "Going to Bed"; Poèmes de John Donne: background of, 92-94; translation style of, 167, 221; translations of Shakespeare, 96, 98-99, 220-21

Gadamer, H. G., 63, 65
Galland, Antoine, 43
Gallimard: Pléiade collection of, 219-20; *Poèmes de John Donne* published by, 92, 95, 201
Gandillac, Maurice de, 2, 23-25
García Yebra, V., 68
Garneau, 75-76
Garnerone, Sylviane, 52n38
Gasparov, 216
Genette, Gérard, 3, 55-56
Georgics (Virgil), 9
German romanticism, 4n1, 10, 218

Germany, influence on French translation, 218-19
Gilbert, Stuart, 155n99
Goethe, J. W. von, 166-67, 193n171, 218; on goals of translation, 19, 27n11; on prose vs. poetry, 102, 169n120
"Going to Bed" (Donne), 81-82; criticisms of translations of, 90-91, 137-45, 151; Denis' translation of, 12, 14-16, 23-25, 82-84; failings of, 90-91, 137-45, 151; intensifying Donne, 117, 119, 144-45; key words in: body, 141-44; joy, 127-30, 132, 144-45, 152; nakedness, 130-32, 144, 152-54; offs, 150; self, 139, 151; love in, 137; modes of enunciation in, 143-44; Morel's translation of, 15-16, 85-87, 94, 155-56; Paz's translation of, 16-18, 87-88, 90, 109, 145-55; poems related to, 88, 124, 127; privative constructions in, 133-34, 144, 151-52; religion and, 18, 137, 139-40; Rothschild's translation of, 84-85, 120-21, 137n78, 141, 145n88, 151, 154; sexuality of, 144-45, 151; structure of, 121-23; title of, 137-38; tone of, 15, 140, 143; translations of, 2, 12, 23-25; translations simplifying, 148-50; uniqueness of, 13-14, 120-22, 127; writing of, 120
Goldschmidt, G.-A., 39, 68
Góngora, Luis, 96, 222-23
Goux, Jean-Paul, 170n121
Grande sertão: Veredes (Rosa), 62
"Great Other," 35n21
Greece/Greek, 9, 63
Gresset, Michel, 52n38
Grimm's tale, translations of, 2, 23-25
Gros, Léon-Gabriel, 88-89, 207; Donne and, 18, 158; on translations of Donne poems, 15, 197
Grosjean, Jean, 19n26; on beauty of translation, 208-9; on *Poèmes de John Donne,* 21, 198, 204-6, 208; translation of *The Prophets* by, 94, 203n1, 204, 206, 211
Guerne, Armel, 2, 23-25, 76
Guillén, Jorge, 90
The Guiltless (Broch), 131-32

Hamlet (Shakespeare), 94, 176
Hardy, Thomas, 25
Hebrew, translations into, 38

Heidegger, Martin, 54n44; on horizon, 62–63; influence of, 5, 218; works by, 211–13, 219n20, 220
"Heimkunft" ["Return"] (Hölderin), 130
Heraclitus, translation of, 217n17
Hermeneutics, 5, 52n39, 63–65
"Heroicall Epistle" (Donne), 133
Hesiod, 9
History, influence on translations, 46
Hocquart, Emmanuel, 50n34, 196n174
Hofmannsthal, Hugo von, 3, 170n121, 171n123
Hölderlin, Friedrich, 61, 219n20, 222; on the principle of the sobriety of art, 178–79; on translation, 31, 32, 71; translation *of Antigone* by, 2, 23–25
Hölderlinstudien, 31
Holzwege (Heidegger), 220
Homer, translations of, 9, 29, 41–42, 52
Hopkins, Gerard Manley, 19, 20n28, 89; Leyris's translation of, 43, 94, 192, 194; works by, 51, 134
Horace, on translations, 29
Horizon. *See* Translation horizon
Humboldt: Meschonnic and, 5, 33, 35; translations by, 33, 71; on translations' relation to original, 37–38
Humphrey, Lawrence, 9
Husserl, Edmund, 62–63
"A Hymne to Christ, at the Authors Last Going into Germany" (Donne), 11
"Hymne to God, my God, in my Sicknesse" (Donne), 124–27; Bonnefoy's translation of, 11, 126–27; joy in, 128–29

Identity of aspiration, Donne's, 122n45
Iliad, Mounin's translation of, 220n24
Immanent consistency, of translations, 50
Immanent life, of translations, 50
In Search of a Theory of Translation (Toury), 36
Incarnation, Donne's fascination with, 159–60
Incontournable, 54n44
Interpretatio: Language and Translation from Cicero to Tytler (Rener), 9
Intuitivity, of translators, 48, 62

Jaccottet, Philippe, 96, 219, 222; translation of *Man without Qualities* by, 94, 211;

translation of the *Odyssey* by, 52, 211, 220n24
Jakobson, Roman, 3, 5
Jauss, Hans Robert, 3, 5, 63
Jerome, Saint, 8n6, 57
Jews, and Septuagint Bible, 9–10
John Donne: Life, Mind and Art (Carey), 11, 89
"John Donne et la formalité de l'essence" ["John Donne and the Formality of Essence"] (Fuzier), 93
Jonson, Ben, 210n6
Jouve, Pierre Jean, 23–25, 34n20, 182
Joy, in Donne's key words, 127–30, 152
Joyce, James, 155n99
Judgment, in analysis of translation, 6

Kafka, Franz, 33, 39, 68
Kahn, Gilbert, 220
Kierkegaard, Søren, 18
Klossowski, Pierre, 32; *Aeneid* translated by, 2, 23–25, 78, 94, 95n10, 203n1, 216, 220
Kristeva, Julia, 27n9

"La dormeuse" (Valéry), 90
La Réforme, on *Poèmes de John Donne*, 201, 203, 210
La revue de poésie (Po&sie), 89, 94, 188n165, 213
La stylistique comparée du français et de l'anglais [Comparative Stylistics of French and English] (Vinay and Darbelnet), 213
"La tâche du traducteur" ["The Task of the Translator"], translated de Gandillac, 213
"La traduction et la lettre," about Milton, 14n15
La viellesse d'Alexandre (Roubaud), 12–13
L'Âge d'Homme, 89–90; Fuzier published in, 92, 96; issue on Donne, 11, 225
Lambert, 4, 36
Language, 27n9, 65, 109, 223n26; decadence of, 193n171; English compared to French, 188–89; evolution of, 193–94; in French translations of Donne, 71–72; original and translations', 51–52, 70–71; untranslatable terms in, 71, 147
Laplanche, Jean, 24–25

Larbaud, Valery, 3, 46n29, 155n99, 211, 214–15
Latin, as first language, 8
Launay, J., 219n20
"Le coucher de sa maîtresse." *See* "Going to Bed" (Donne), Denis' translation of
Le Peuple, on *Poèmes de John Donne*, 203
Legouis, Pierre, 89, 128n49, 165n113, 197; on Donne, 18, 160; on Morel's translation of "Going to Bed," 15, 155; on *Poèmes de John Donne*, 21, 202–4, 206, 208; translations of Donne by, 94–95, 97n11, 102, 133n66, 157–58, 164n109
L'épreuve de l'éstranger (Berman), 1–2, 24, 52
Les "belles infidèles" (d'Ablancourt), 31–32, 211, 213
Les cinq rouleaux (Meschonnic), 193–94, 204
Les fleurs du mal (Baudelaire), 67, 184–85
Les problèmes théoriques de la traduction (Mounin), 65n67, 213–14
"Letter to Maria Gisborne" (Shelley), 188n164
Lettres françaises, on *Poèmes de John Donne*, 203–4, 207, 209
Leyris, Pierre, 60; on other translators' work, 25, 155, 220; translating Hopkins's poems, 19, 43, 51, 94, 192, 194; translation project of, 52, 96, 220
"L'homme décentré. Culture et traduction, traduction et culture" (Cordonnier), 33n18
L'homme sans qualités. *See* The Man without Qualities
"L'hymne au Christ, au dernier départ pour l'Allemagne" (Donne), 165–68
"Lincolnes Inne" (Donne), 123–24
Linguistics, 65, 213–14
L'inspiration personelle et l'esprit du temps (Ellrodt), 11
"L'invitation au voyage" (Baudelaire), 182
Lisle, Leconte de, 220
Literality, 75n77
Literary criticism. *See* Criticism; Translation criticism
Literary transfers, 7, 107; among language cultures, 42–43; of Donne, 89, 96, 101, 157–58, 160; in translation projects, 60–61, 96, 101
Literature, translated *vs.* native, 39–41, 43

L'Matin d'Anvers, on *Poèmes de John Donne*, 203
Lohmann, J., 8
Lortholary, 39
Los siete locos (Arlt), translation of, 49
Love: in Donne's poems, 113; in "Going to Bed," 120, 137, 141–43
"Loves Progresse" (Donne), 124
Lucian, translation *vs.* original of, 45
Lusson, Pierre, 217n16, 218
Luther, Martin, 9, 43–44

Macbeth (Shakespeare), 75–76
Mailhos, Georges, 217n17
Mallarmé, Stéphane, 12; influence of, 209, 222; on prose *vs.* poetry, 168n119, 170–71, 223; translating Poe, 188, 192, 223; translation horizon of 1960s and, 221–25; Valéry compared to, 110, 223–24
Malroux, Claire, 56–57
Mambrino, 194–95
The Man without Qualities (Musil), 94, 211
Markowicz, André, 47n30
Marteau, Robert, 181n156
Masson, Jean-Yves: translating Yeats, 56–57, 78–79; on translation, 34n20, 47, 74–75, 187
Max und Moritz (Busch), translations of, 38
Mayotte, 64n63
McGinn, Bernard, 134n70
Meschonnic, Henri, 25, 94, 204, 214n12; on evolution of French poetic language, 193–94; forms of translation analysis and, 32–36, 48–49; influences on, 5, 218; on original *vs.* translation, 71, 75; rejection of, 36, 47; on rereading, 71–72; translation criticism and, 4, 6–7, 70
Metaphorical networks, 52n38
Metaphysical thinking, Donne's, 14, 112–13, 164
"Methoden des Übersetzens" (Schleiermacher), 68
Migration, in transfers among cultures, 7
Mille et une nuits [Arabian Nights], 43
Milton, John, 2, 14n15, 188, 192
Minière, Claude, 89
Modesty, 187n163. *See also* Principle of the sobriety of art

Montaigne, Michel, 172
Mora, Edith, 23, 25
More, Anne, 120
Morel, Auguste, translation of "Going to Bed" by, 12, 15–16, 85–87, 94, 155–56
Mounin, Georges, 29n17, 65n67, 220n24; *Les problèmes théoriques de la traduction* by, 213–14; translation of *Belles infidèles* by, 211, 213
Music, 176–77, 186n162
Musil, *The Man without Qualities* by, 94, 211

Nakedness, in Donne's key words, 130–32, 137, 152–54
Naufrage du Deutschland (Hopkins), 51
Neutrality: as goal of translation criticism, 4; of readers of translations, 47–48
Nicomachean (Aristotle), 23–25
Nietzsche, 8n6
"A nocturnall upon S. Lucies day" (Donne), 11, 133, 161–65
Norms, and translations, 37–39, 41–43, 45
"Notes of a Translator" (Pasternak), English *vs.* French translations of, 17
"Notes on Translation from Shakespeare" (Pasternak), 174, 176
Novalis, 58n51, 76, 177–78
NRF, *Poèmes de John Donne* announced in, 95

Ocampo, Victoria, 90
Odyssey, Jaccottet's translation of, 52, 96, 211, 220n24
Oedipus in Colonus (Bayen's translation of), 64n63, 217n17
Oeuvre, translators', 24n5, 30
"Of the Progresse of the Soule" (Donne), 124, 158; key words in, 119, 129, 136
"On appelle cela traduire Celan," Meschonnic on translations of, 33
On Revolution (Arendt), 50n33
"On the Lady Elizabeth" (Donne), 123n46
"On the Origin of Beauty" (Hopkins), 134
Oresme, Nicole, 1, 7, 23–25
Originals: language irrupting into translation, 70–71; the necessary *vs.* the aleatory in, 54–56; reading translations without comparison with, 49–51; readings of, 51–57; readings parallel to, 54; respect for, 74–76; translations compared to, 5–6, 66–73, 100, 203–4
Œuvres (Freud), 24–25

Palimpsestes, "Hymne to God, my God, in my Sicknesse" in, 11
Paradise Lost (Milton), Chateaubriand's translation of, 2, 23–25, 188
Paratexts, 60–61, 93
Parmenides, edited by Beaufret and translated by Rivière, 94
Pasternak, Boris, 3, 178; "Notes of a Translator" by, 17; on prose and poetry, 102, 172–77, 185–86
Paz, Octavio, 3; criticisms of translation of "Going to Bed," 137–39, 154; "Going to Bed"' adapted rather than translated by, 16–18, 145–55; on prose and poetry, 168–69, 170, 183n159; translation of "Going to Bed" by, 2, 12, 23–25, 87–88, 90, 109; use of *gloria*, 153, 155; on writing of "Going to Bed," 120
Péguy, Charles, 135n73
Peletier, Jacques, 45
"People and Attitudes" (Pasternak), 173, 177n139
Periphery/center schema, 40
Perse, Saint-John, 25
Pézard, A., 94, 100, 107, 219
Phaedrus (Plato), 23–24
Philological translation, 208
Philosophy, relation to translation, 65
Pindar, 129
Plato, 23–24, 25
Pléiade collection, Gallimard's, 219–20
Plutarch, Amyot's translation of, 24–25, 31–32, 219
Poe, Edgar Allan, translations of, 188, 192, 223
Poèmes choisis (Legouis), 128n49, 133n66
Poèmes de John Donne (trans. by Fuzier and Denis), 11–12, 14, 18, 88, 92–93, 147n90, 165n113. *See also under* "Going to Bed"; archaism in, 107, 207–8, 220; expectations of, 95; flaws in, 108, 111–13, 196, 202–3, 205; goals of, 94–95; losing distinctiveness of Donne, 111–13; "Loves Progresse" in, 124; Poisson's foreword to, 202–3, 207, 209; published by Gallimard, 95; reception of, 21, 95, 201–6,

Poèmes de John Donne (cont.)
210–11, 224–25; reviewers on, 197–98, 201–2, 204–10; "Sappho to Philaenis" in, 13, 117–18, 132–33; selection of poems for, 12, 96–97, 101, 158; translation horizon of, 94–96; translation project of, 96–101, 108, 210–11; versification in, 117, 201–2

Poèmes élisabéthains (trans. by Rothschild), 89, 94

Poèmes et fragments (Sappho), 47n30

Poetic field, English *vs.* French, 13

Poeticality: Donne's, 112; of translations, 74, 76, 95

Poetics, Valéry as founder of, 224

Poetics of color, Donne's, 140

Poetry: beauty of, 208–10; diversity in Western modern, 182–83, 186; Donne's, 112–14, 157–58, 160; English, 108–9, 113, 166n115, 195–96; English *vs.* French, 107, 186–92, 194; French, 15, 179–81, 193–95, 222, 224; negative words in, 133–36; North American, 196n174; poetic speech and, 184–85; prosaicness of, 168, 178, 179–81, 194; prose and, 20, 101–2, 169–86, 169n120; prosification of, 177–78, 182, 185–86, 192; of quintessential words, 185; reflective aspect of, 224; Roubard on, 171–72; traditions of, 183–84; translations as poetic act, 187, 210; translations "in verse" of, 97–98, 101–3; translations of, 20, 110, 166n115, 192, 213, 218–19, 221–25

Poisson, Jean-Roger, 12, 208; on Donne, 18, 101; *Poèmes de John Donne* and, 93–94, 96–98, 100, 202–3, 207, 209

Politics, and translation, 65n65

Polivanov, Evgeny, 217n16, 218

Polysystem, translations in, 36, 39–41

Poësie (La revue de poésie), 89, 94, 188n165, 213

Pound, Ezra, 3

"Pour une poétique de la traduction" ["For a Poetic of Translation"] (Meschonnic), 193–94

Préau, André, 54n44, 211–13

Principle of the sobriety of art, 178–79, 182, 186–88, 192

The Prophets, Grosjean's translation of, 94, 203n1, 204, 206, 211

Prose: devalued, 168–69, 171; Donne's, 101–2, 157, 160; Mallarmé and, 171, 223; poeticization of, 181–82; poetry translations and, 20, 101, 164–65, 192; poetry's relation to, 20, 168–86

Proust, Marcel, 26–27, 182

Psychoanalysis, relation to translation, 65

Raines, Kathleen, 60

Räkel, H.-H. S., 9n8

Readability, of translations, 70–71, 90–91

Readers, of translations, 47–48

Reading: of originals, 51–57; of other translations, 64, 67–69; parallel, 51n36, 52–54; rereading and, 71–72; of translations, 49–51

Reflection, in the principle of the sobriety of art, 178–79

Reflexivity, in translation criticism, 5–6, 62, 71

Rejuvenation, as goal of translations, 19

Religion, 10n11; Donne's Christianity, 18, 122n45, 158–60; in Donne's poems, 113, 137, 139–40; Donne's sermons, 158–60

Renaissance, translation form of, 10

Rener, Frederick M., 9, 9n8

Respect, of translation for original, 74–76

Retranslations: differences among, 94; of Donne, 160–69, 222; need for sense of history in, 46–47; translations and, 42, 78

Revelation, as goal of translation, 43

Reverzy, Jean, 204

Rhetoric, crisis of, 105–6

Rhyme, 164. *See also* Versification

Rhythm, in poetry and prose, 176–77

Ricoeur, Paul, 5, 51n37, 63, 71n70

Rilke, Rainier Maria, 10n11, 104, 104n19, 175, 186n162, 193

Rimbaud, Arthur, 185n161, 206, 222

Rivière, J. J., 94

Robel, Léon: Deguy's correspondence with, 211, 215–19, 221; on two positions of translation, 216–17

Robert, Marthe, 2, 23–25

Robin, Armand, 57, 175n133, 177n141, 211, 223

Romans picaresques espagnols, Amyot's translation of, 219

Romanticism, 178–79. *See also* German Romanticism

Rome, 8–11
Romeo and Juliet (Shakespeare), 177n139
Rosa, Guimarães, 62
Rothschild, Philippe de, 15; anthology of Elizabethan poets by, 94, 221; translation of "Going to Bed" by, 2, 12, 15–16, 23–25, 84–85, 90–91, 120–21, 137n78, 141, 145n88, 151, 154; translations of other Donne poems by, 11, 89–90, 117n38
Roubaud, Jacques, 12–13, 130, 188n164, 217n16; on poetry, 171–72; on poetry translations, 103–6, 218
Roud, 23–25
Russia, 103, 218

Safe Conduct (Pasternak), 175, 177
"Sailing to Byzantium" (Yeats), Bonnefoy's translation of, 76
Saint Jerome, Bible translation starting with, 10n11
Sappho, translations of, 23, 25, 47n30, 63–64
"Sappho to Philaenis" (Donne): reflection/reciprocity in, 115–16; self in, 116–18; touch in, 124; translations of, 13, 117–18, 132–33
Savignac, J. P., 52, 129
Schlegel, A. W., 43–44, 178, 218
Schlegel, Friedrich, 3, 6, 26–27, 78
Schleiermacher, Friedrich, 68, 218
Schmidt, Albert-Marie, 203
Scholarly translation, 208
Science of translation, 48
Self, 71, 136, 194; in "Going to Bed," 123, 139, 151; in "Sappho to Philaenis," 116–18
Semiotics, as influence on Brisset, 5
Sept fous (Arlt), 68
Septuagint Bible, 9–10
Sermons, Donne's, 158–60
Sexuality: in "Going to Bed," 144–45, 151; in "Sappho to Philaenis," 115–16
Shakespeare, William, 189–90; Bonnefoy's translations of, 165, 192; Fuzier's translations of, 92, 96, 98–99, 220; mix of prose and verse in, 34n20, 174n132; principle of the sobriety of art and, 178; Schlegel's translation of, 43–44, 218; translations of, 34n20, 60–61, 68
Shelley, Percy Bysshe, 188n164

Simon, Sherry, 193n171, 214
Sobriety. *See* Principle of the sobriety of art
Socio-critical analyses, 36–41
Sociology, as influence on Brisset, 5
"Some Statements" (Pasternak), 172–73, 175–76
"Sonnet to Death" (Donne), 205
Sonnets (Shakespeare), 68, 92, 96, 98–99
Souls, nakedness of, 132
Soupault, Philippe, 211
Sous l'invocation de saint Jérôme, Larbaud's translation of, 211, 214–15
"Spelt from Sibyl's Leaves" (Hopkins), 195
Spitzer, Leo, 3, 35
Staël, Madame de, 218
Starobinski, Jean, 3
Steiner, Georges, 28n13, 47n31, 214
Strette (Celan), 33
Structuralism, as influence on Brisset, 5
Style, analyzing originals', 51–52
Subjectivity: of translation analysis, 72; of translators, 69
Sur, poetry translations in, 90
"Sur une traduction en vers de Donne" ["Concerning a Verse Translation of Donne"] (Legouis), 203
Surrealists, influence of, 222
Système des beaux-arts (Alain), 170

"The Task of the Translator" (Benjamin), 2, 23–24, 213, 222
Tel Aviv school, of translation criticism, 4, 32, 36, 43–44
Textual zones, 50–51, 69
Theater, and retranslations, 64n63
Theocritus, Virgil's works considered translations from, 9
Toury, Gideon, 43, 47; on analysis of translations, 38, 70; schemata of, 39–41; in Tel Aviv school, 4, 36–37; on translation norms, 38–39, 44–45; on translations as secondary, 39–41
Traductology, 4, 53–54
Trakl, Georg, 4, 33, 61
Transfer. *See* Literary transfers
Transformation systems, 31
Translating position, 58–60, 62–66
Translating subject, 5, 45, 57
Translatio studii, Oresme in, 7

Translation (process), 36, 65; between English poetry tradition and French, 186–88; as field, 38n24; field of, 41, 53, 224; French tradition of, 213, 218; intuitivity and reflexivity in, 48, 62; meaning of, 30, 76–77, 187, 215–16; parallel readings in, 52–54; positions of, 216–17; systems of, 53–54, 56–57; types of, 208; in verse, 201–3

Translation analysis, 2, 23–25, 31, 47n31. *See also* Translation criticism; evaluation of translator's work in, 74; forms of, 32–41, 48–49; procedures in, 4, 48–49, 71; readability of, 70–71; writing of, 5–6

Translation criticism, 28n15, 54, 203n1; development of, 3–4, 28; as a genre, 2–4, 30; goals of, 4, 31, 70–71; of "Going to Bed," 137–45; lack of, 210–11; methodology in, 31–32; need for, 30; as negative *vs.* positive, 25–26, 28–29, 32, 35, 114; original's confrontation with translation in, 66–73; productivity of, 6–7, 78–79, 157; readability of, 5–6; by reviewers, 78, 211, 224

Translation events, 211

Translation hermeneutics, 65

Translation horizon, 224; of Mallarmé and Valéry, 221–25; of *Poèmes de John Donne*, 94–96; of 1960s, 210–20; translating position and translation project in, 62–66

The Translation of Languages (Humphrey), 9

Translation projects, 61, 96, 137; definition of, 59–60; different for same original, 78–79; discordances in, 69–70; of Fuzier and Denis, 96–101, 108, 210–11; Paz's "Going to Bed," 145–46; translating position and, 62–66

Translation systems, 91

Translational spaces, 42n26

Translations (products), 4, 10, 14n15, 46n28, 221; adaptations *vs.*, 17, 41–44; bilingual or monolingual, 60, 100; characterizations of Donne through, 18; comparisons of, 67–69, 78–79, 217; context for, 4, 24n6, 31; ethics of, 74–76; failings of, 14n15, 15, 29–30, 33–34; French *vs.* English meanings of word, 7n5; goals of, 7, 19, 70–71; influences on, 46, 51n36; interest in, 94, 95n10; key terms in, 61–62; learning how to read, 49–51; as literary transfers, 42–43; meaning of, 8n6; native literature and, 39–41, 43; need for, 27, 30, 35; norms and, 36–39, 41n25, 42; original language irrupting into, 70–71; originality or lack of, 29–30; originals and, 45, 74–75; originals compared to, 5–6, 31, 36–38, 66–73, 100, 203–4; poeticality of, 12–13, 74, 76, 103; of poetry, 97–98, 101–3, 110, 208–10; purposes of, 24, 27n11, 30, 74n76; reading and readers of, 47–51, 70–71; reception of, 6, 77–78; relation to criticism, 27–28; Renaissance form of, 10; retranslations and, 42, 64, 67–68, 71, 78; in Rome and Latin culture, 8–9; rules for, 61–62; source oriented *vs.* target oriented, 36, 38, 40–41, 44–45; translators' position on, 58–59; truth of, 43–44; by Valéry, 209–10

"The Translator as a Nonconformist-to-be" (Toury), 44–45

Translators, 204; background of, 46–47, 57–58, 92–94; biases of, 33; bodies of work by, 24n5, 67; characteristics of, 9, 46–47, 52–53, 62, 75–76, 187n163; evaluation of work of, 74; freedom of, 34–35, 41, 44–46, 72, 75n77, 76–77, 206; goals of, 74; positions of, 58–59; processes of, 67–68, 92–94; subjectivity of, 59, 69

Translemes, 53n43

Trial (Kafka), 68

Troubadours, 103–4, 129–30, 222

Truth, 43–44, 144, 153

Übersetzungskritik, 32

Ulysses (Joyce), 155n99

"Un hémisphere dans une chevelure" (Baudelaire), 182

"Un peu faute de façon" (Goux), 170n121

Ungaretti, Giuseppe, 3

Valéry, Paul, 209–10; "La dormeuse" by, 90; Mallarmé compared to, 110, 223–24; translation horizon of, 221–25; translations by, 25, 203, 224

"Variety" (Donne), 129

Venturini, Joseph, 105n20

Versification, 164, 186; by Fuzier and Denis, 101–3, 117, 220; in *Poèmes de John Donne*, 201–2, 208–9; Roubaud on, 103–6

Vialatte, Alexandre, 68
Vinay, J.-P., 213
Violence, Paz adding, 150–51
Virgil, 9, 203, 216, 224
Von Humboldt, 218

"Wenn aus der Ferne" ["If from a Distance"] (Hölderin), 23–25

"Womans Constancy" (Donne), 203–4
Wozu Dichter? (Hölderin), 222

Yeats, William Butler, 56–57, 76, 78–79
Yo el supremo (Bastos), 68

Zuber, Roger, 31–32

LaVergne, TN USA
06 October 2009
159939LV00002B/1/P